Venomous Tongues

THE MIDDLE AGES SERIES

A complete list of books in the series is available from the publisher.

Venomous Tongues

Speech and Gender in Late Medieval England

SANDY BARDSLEY

PENN

University of Pennsylvania Press

Philadelphia

Printed in the United States of America on acid-free paper

10 9 8 7 6 5 4 3 2 1

Published by
University of Pennsylvania Press
Philadelphia, Pennsylvania 19104-4112

Library of Congress Cataloging-in-Publication Data

Bardsley, Sandy.
Venomous tongues : speech and gender in late medieval England / Sandy Bardsley.
p. cm. — (The Middle Ages series)
Includes bibliographical references and index.
ISBN-13: 978-0-8122-3936-2 (cloth : alk. paper)
ISBN-10: 0-8122-3936-9 (cloth : alk. paper)
1. English language—Middle English, 1100–1500—Sex differences. 2. Language and culture—England—History—To 1500. 3. Women—History—Middle Ages, 500–1500. 4. Sex differences (Psychology)—Great Britain—History—Medieval period, 1066–1485. I. Title. II. Series.

PE525.B37 2006
306.44'09420902—dc22 2005058588

Contents

Introduction
Speech, Gender, and Power in Late Medieval England

Go forth, and let the whores cackle!
Where women are, are many words:
Let them go hopping with their hackle [finery]!
Where geese sit, are many turds.[1]

To the author of the fifteenth-century morality play quoted above, speech was a waste product, something as odious and polluting as goose dung. He was not alone in his disgust: throughout late medieval England, the "sins of the tongue" attracted acute concern. Clerics railed against blasphemers, liars, and slanderers, while village and town elites prosecuted those who abused officials, gossiped in court or church, or committed the newly devised offense of scolding. Poets illustrated the varieties and the consequences of dangerous speech, while artists depicted the gaping mouth of hell and the demons who recorded illicit words. Nor was the playwright alone in connecting problematic and excessive speech with women. Indeed, he was tapping into an association that has perhaps existed as far back as records stretch. Yet during the late Middle Ages, this association grew both more intense and more tangible in its consequences, affecting the lives of both women and men in new and important ways. This book examines the complex relationship between speech and gender in late medieval England, focusing both on the ways in which the discourse about speech was constructed and on the consequences of this discourse for ordinary, nonelite people.

In the historiographical debates about the status of late medieval and early modern women, little attention has been paid to perceptions of their voices, and yet a woman's ability to speak and be heard constituted a key component of her status. Certainly it was not the only measure of women's status: as historians have pointed out, we must also examine women's wages, the occupations available to them, their participation (or lack thereof) in guilds and local courts, their age at marriage and frequency of marriage, and their patterns of migration. Yet attitudes toward women's voices also reflected and helped constitute their status, and the late Middle Ages were a period in which perceptions of women's speech underwent a sea change. Views of female speech mattered because those whose speech was disparaged lost social and cultural power as a result. An assertive woman who was deemed to be a scold, for instance, found herself ridiculed for speaking her mind. Her words were received with the cultural caveat that she occupied a problematic category, that she was out of control and a threat to propriety and good governance. As poems, plays, ballads, and court prosecutions showed, a woman who scolded was associated with other crimes against social order too: sexual disorder, assault, and eavesdropping. In the home she was a menace to her husband; in the community she represented a threat to the more generalized (and increasingly popular) notion of good governance. Condemnations of women's speech played an important role in determining women's status, for even if an individual woman escaped such charges, her voice was surely restrained, her words tempered, by the ever-present fear of falling into the category of the scolding woman.

Late medieval England was primarily an oral culture. As Chris Wickham has pointed out, even modern academics inhabit a world shaped by oral communication above all else. Despite the existence of faculty handbooks, meeting minutes, and email, for instance, faculty rely heavily on conversations, face-to-face interactions, and even gossip to negotiate their way through the decision-making processes of university politics.[2] In medieval English villages and towns, where most people had few or no skills of literacy, this dependence on orality must have been even more profound.[3] This is not to suggest that villagers and townspeople never came into contact with written documents or were never affected by their contents. Indeed, many were well aware of the power that the written word could have over their lives. Those who wanted proof that they were freeborn, for instance, sought verification of their status in the eleventh-century Domesday Book, in which ancient rights of manorial tenants were recorded alongside lists of land and stock.[4] Parishioners knew that their priests, in theory if not always in practice, were literate enough to read from the Bible and other religious texts. And they knew that systems of justice and administration—from the bureaucracy of the royal court to that of their own local communities—relied on the written word for recording and communicating decisions. Yet while they were aware of the power of the written word, most medieval English peasants and townspeople depended almost exclusively on speech as a means of communication. When they made short-term loans or contracts, the agreements were almost always oral. When they exchanged news and gossip about crops, goods for sale, weather, and local happenings, they did so with spoken words. And when they received instructions from local landowners, juries, priests, and representatives of the king, they listened to the speech of someone else. While documents were present at the margins of village and town communities—primarily the places in which they intersected with structures of higher authority—speech was at the center of information, culture, and power.

The centrality of speech to medieval life inevitably prompted concern about how it might be used. Because the power of speech was not dependent on formal education, it was unlimited by the social constraints that literacy reinscribed. Accents, vocabulary, and modes of address varied according to status, but anyone who could speak—peasants, servants, women, children—had the capacity to wield the power of the spoken word. The metaphorical "tongue that is your sword" thus sliced through the very social boundaries that written documents reinforced.[5] Orality was not only the topic of the discourse on illicit speech but also the primary medium by which the discourse was perpetuated.

"Discourse" is a term that scholars have used in a variety of ways: in using it here, I mean a set of habits of thought and speech familiar to much of the population. These associations were not merely functional (such as the association between fish and water, for instance), but rather helped constitute the power relations of late medieval England. This book focuses on a discourse that specifically associated speech with evil, with social disorder, and with women. As Pierre Bourdieu has pointed out, all successful discourse has the effect of awakening experiences among those who participate in it.[6] The discourse on the evils of women's speech succeeded, was perpetuated, and left its mark in surviving texts and artwork precisely because it felt meaningful and awakened experiences for a sizable group of people (both men and women). This discourse was more than just a conversation among a small group of friends or among members of one family: it was a set of associations understood (if not necessarily endorsed) by much of the late medieval English population. The meanings it evoked were likely variant: while some may have been invested in promoting the discourse, others may have resisted it or have attempted to contest it. The association between women and illicit speech might perhaps be compared with modern discourses about, say, the association between feminism and man-hating or between Christianity and "family values." While many of us might hasten to complicate and critique such associations, and others of us may approve them, they nonetheless resonate as successful (and powerful) discourses.

Who or what drove this discourse on the associations between women and illicit speech, ensuring its circulation and perpetuation? While some theorists have argued that discourse, ever slippery, takes on a life and an agency of its own, I am skeptical.[7] Certainly any discourse is indeed slippery and readily moves beyond the intentions of its originators. But I would argue that it does so only because those who repeat it have a stake in its perpetuation and adaptation. In order to identify the major perpetuators of the discourse on women's illicit speech, we need to examine briefly the political and social context of late medieval English towns and villages.

Manors—as well as many towns—were owned by members of the nobility who served as landlords and drew profits from rents, peasant labor on the demesne (land controlled directly by the lord and not rented out to peasants), and various other perquisites. Among these perquisites were fees and fines from the manorial or borough courts. Yet lords typically meddled little in the day-to-day affairs of the village or town: as long as they received what seemed an appropriate sum from the courts, they largely left villagers and townspeople to regulate themselves. Manorial and borough courts were instead dominated by members of a local elite, a group drawn from the wealthier members of the peasantry, craftspeople, or townsfolk. As Christopher Dyer has pointed out in examining power relationships within villages, this local "oligarchy" was by no means a small or closed circle and it was not sufficiently powerful to run village affairs entirely for its own benefit. The boundaries between more "respectable" and prosperous families, on the one hand, and poorer families, on the other, were highly permeable, but there were also tensions between the two groups. Belonging to the local elite brought some very real benefits. Members of more prosperous peasant families were far more likely to hold such positions as bailiff, juror, or churchwarden and were thus more able to participate in defining local legal and social norms.[8] Anne DeWindt's work on the jury of Ramsey (Huntingdonshire) has highlighted the very real authority of such local elites in the small town setting, too. Although townspeople did try to circumscribe the power of the jury in various ways, it nonetheless wielded considerable local clout.[9] These jurors and other local officials, then, were best poised to promulgate the discourse on speech, its evils, and its association with women. This is not to imply that they were always completely successful in doing so: jurors' presentments could be challenged successfully, and people outside the local elite could resist the message that officials sought to send. Nonetheless, the cultural and legal power of local elites was considerably more real and immediate in the lives of ordinary villagers and townspeople than that of landlords.

The demographic disaster of the Black Death, which hit England particularly hard in the years 1348–49, complicated further the relationship between local elites and their communities. The death of one-third to one-half of the population left behind a society that was disrupted, confused, and sometimes in spiritual crisis. From an economic standpoint, the plague would ultimately benefit the peasantry and townspeople, including both local elites and those less fortunate. Fewer people meant more resources were available for each family. In the longer term, fewer people meant higher wages and lower food prices for those who remained. Tensions between landlords and peasants thus increased sharply as landlords tried to prevent wage rises and keep their tenants from moving away in search of better conditions. Newly empowered by the changing ratio of resources to people, however, peasants and townsfolk increasingly questioned established systems of authority. Rebels marching on London in 1381 uttered a catch cry that echoed throughout Europe: "When Adam delved and Eve span, Who was then a gentleman?"[10] In other words, they pointed out that there was nothing natural or God-given about social class, that no nobles existed in the Garden of Eden. Such a concept, invoking the idea of a "state of nature" several centuries before the Enlightenment, horrified their social superiors. In the wake of plague and rebellions, these same peasants and townspeople found themselves disparaged not only for their insubordinate and unruly deeds, but also for their disruptive and defiant voices. Drawing on a preplague discourse on the "sins of the tongue," the nobility vented their frustration at the increased social and economic power enjoyed by their social inferiors after the demographic crisis. Peasant voices, articulating as they did a dangerous social message, were condemned by chroniclers and poets as resembling both the pathetic bleating of sheep and the dangerous roaring of thunder.

For the local elite, however, this condemnation of peasant voices proved uncomfortable. In the century after the plague, the Black Death helped members of this wealthier group of peasants disproportionately, enabling them to buy lands abandoned by their neighbors, take over positions of local authority left vacant by high mortality rates, and hoist further their social and economic status in the local arena. During the fifteenth century, many would manage to rise into the yeomanry; a few, like the well-documented Pastons of Norfolk, would even aspire to the ranks of the lower gentry. For such individuals, a discourse that condemned all peasant voices conflicted with efforts to distinguish themselves from the rabble at large. In their efforts to distance themselves from the evils of insubordinate and disruptive speech, jurors, bailiffs, chamberlains, and officers of the peace adopted and adapted the discourse of deviant speech by prosecuting illicit speakers, along with a multiplicity of other petty criminals, in local and ecclesiastical courts. As

Marjorie McIntosh has shown, these local leaders—jurors, bailiffs, and heads of established families—found "language for misconduct" in the "broader textual environment" that surrounded them.[11] Even those who could not read participated in discourses about appropriate behavior and "good governance" through sermons, plays, wall paintings, works of lay piety read aloud in socially aspirant households, and discussions that took place in the context of jury presentments. As I will argue, however, this local-level concern with "good governance" was heavily gendered: whereas disruptive speech by men was typically labeled "rebelliousness" or "contempt," disruptive speech by women in the postplague context was more likely to garner the label of "scolding" or "defamation." Attitudes toward problematic speech were thus a result of class tensions as much as they were a result of gender tensions, and this slippage between class and gender tells us a great deal about late medieval English society.

As well as mapping changes between speech, sin, and gender in general, this book focuses closely on the crime of scolding, which was prosecuted widely from the second half of the fourteenth century. Scolding was a highly adaptable label, flexible enough to encompass the behavior of those who gossiped maliciously about their neighbors as well as those who had loud, public arguments. Although similar to defamation insofar as it involved malicious spoken words, scolding was nonetheless treated by the courts as a separate offense. Between 80 and 95 percent of those prosecuted as scolds were women. Not every jurisdiction prosecuted scolding but those that did seemed to find it a useful category: in the small town of Middlewich (Cheshire) in the early fifteenth century, at least one-third of the population appeared in court connected to scolding in some way, whether as alleged scold, pledge (guarantor) for an alleged scold, or target of an alleged scolding. In nearby Macclesfield, one case in every forty-five heard by the borough court in the late fourteenth century involved a scolding allegation.[12] Scolds continued to be prosecuted throughout England as late as the nineteenth century. During these five hundred years, the character of the scold was defined, condemned, celebrated, and satirized. The scold morphed into the shrew and the fishwife. She lent elements of her character to the early modern witch, to the Shakespearean-era merry widow, and to the modern bitch. She also bequeathed something to the gossipy man conventionally described as an "old woman," the man whose masculinity is undermined by his participation in an activity still associated with women. From the earliest emergence of scolding as a social and legal category in the fourteenth century, however, the scold served as an archetype and a focus for the more generalized cultural concern about illicit and dangerous speech. Literary and artistic constructions of troublesome female speech reinforced prosecutions of scolds; prosecutions of scolds underscored messages about women's garrulity in popular literature and art. Together they sent an important message: women's voices were potentially problematic and should not be trusted.

The Status of Late Medieval English Women: "Golden Age" vs. "Patriarchal Equilibrium"

Indeed, women's association with disorderly and disruptive speech helps explain why their status did not improve after the Black Death of the mid-fourteenth century. Over the past few decades, demographers and historians of women have debated whether economic conditions after the plague helped facilitate a temporary "golden age" for women. In theory, demographic crisis ought to have reduced social inequalities throughout late medieval England, as everyone's labor was valued more highly. Certainly the deaths of between one-third and one-half of the English population enabled modifications to the class structure. While historians' views might differ on the extent to which peasants' social and economic standing was enhanced in the late fourteenth and fifteenth centuries, or the precise decades in which this change took place, few would dispute the characterization of J. E. Thorold Rogers that the fifteenth century was a "golden age" for the English laborer.[13] Yet the effects of demographic crisis on the gender order have proven more controversial: some suggest that women's status was improved, whereas others see more continuity than change.

Those historians who argue that women's status was temporarily elevated after the Black Death have suggested two main loci for enhanced female agency. First, J. E. Thorold Rogers, William Beveridge, Rodney Hilton, Simon Penn, and others have argued that the postplague wages of rural women increased relative to those of men. Indeed, some historians have even claimed that women's wages were temporarily equal to men's wages. The lack of information on postplague wage rates makes it very difficult to compare directly the wages of male and female workers, but I have argued elsewhere that the relative rates of men's and women's wages remained eerily constant throughout the fourteenth and early fifteenth centuries. In the few instances where male and female wages appear equivalent, able-bodied women were probably being compared to boys, old men, or men with disabilities who were not paid as much as healthy adult men.[14] Second, some historians have suggested that the towns of late medieval England, particularly London and York, were spaces of opportunity for women. Caroline Barron has suggested that the lifestyle of women in fourteenth- and fifteenth-century London was "quite rosy" and differed only slightly from that of men at equivalent levels of prosperity. In her later work, however, she has revised this thesis; insofar as the medieval period was a golden age for women, she has argued, it was a golden age confined to towns (possibly even just to London and York) and limited to c. 1370–1470. It was also, by implication, accessible primarily to widows.[15] In his work on women in York and Yorkshire, P. J. P. Goldberg has also identified towns as a locus for enhanced female agency. Women, he has argued, were more independent not only in an economic sense but also, as a result, in an emotional sense. With regard to marriage, in particular, they had more control in both choosing a partner and deciding when to marry.[16] Maryanne Kowaleski has built on Goldberg's theory, arguing that scolding presentments became common in the postplague era as a kind of backlash against women's increased economic and emotional autonomy. Drawing on records from the town of Exeter, she has posited that resentful employers saw scolding presentments as a way to unleash anxieties about the newfound independence of urban women.[17] The prime determinant in arguments for a postplague "golden age" for women has thus been women's economic power, but any increase in female earnings (rural or urban) relative to those of men has yet to be proven. While it certainly makes sense that women's status ought to have improved in a period of economic and demographic demand, little evidence supports such arguments.

Indeed, the lack of evidence for women's postplague enrichment is itself suggestive. In a period in which chroniclers, poets, balladeers, lawmakers, and authors of sermons were acutely sensitive to disproportionate elevation in the status of any estate, mentions of women's improved fortunes are mysteriously absent. While peasants who took advantage of demographic disaster to claim higher wages were condemned as "malic[ious]" and "idle," lazy and avaricious, the worst complaint that chroniclers made about women in relation to the plague was that widows of plague victims remarried men too far beneath them in status.[18] Late medieval English authors were not shy about lambasting women for their speech, their dress, or their perceived sexual appetites, yet they conspicuously did not attack them for an increase in economic power in the decades following the plague. While English laborers experienced a "golden age" relative to their employers, then, women's postplague experience relative to men was decidedly less golden. Disruption in socioeconomic hierarchies prompted some elites to worry that the world was tumbling into chaos and disorder, but little evidence survives of a comparable threat to hierarchies of gender. And while discourses that marginalized the voices of unruly peasants and laborers were certainly employed against women, such slippage does not indicate that the gender order as a whole was under any meaningful threat. Indeed, the catchcry of rebels in 1381 might be interpreted as evidence of the very resilience of late medieval gender hierarchies. When peasants and townspeople asked, "When Adam delved and Eve span, Who was then a gentleman?" they questioned the very notion of a class order by asking, "What is natural or God-given about the status of the gentleman?" But at the same time, they reinscribed the perceived naturalness of gender distinctions in work: Adam, as the man, dug the soil, while Eve, as the woman, spun yarn.[19]

While women's status ought theoretically to have risen, therefore, the lack of evidence for a postplague increase in status suggests that the theory is built on a house of cards. While convenient in explaining everything from a later age of marriage to the rise of scolding presentments, the data does not support the arguments. In place of the "golden age" theory, Judith M. Bennett has proposed that we might explain the relative status of women and men across time through the model of a "patriarchal equilibrium."[20] According to Bennett's model, positive changes in some aspects of women's historical experience have typically been balanced by negative changes in other aspects of their experience, resulting in little or no transformation in women's status relative to that of men. In her study of women who brewed ale in late medieval England, Bennett has demonstrated how women's position in the brewing industry remained remarkably constant between 1300 and 1600, despite major changes in the trade and women's place within it. Forces that *might* have improved women's status, such as increased profitability within the brewing trade, were counteracted by other forces, such as negative representations of brewsters (women brewers), new guild regulations that sought to preclude single women from the brewing trade, and increasing insistence that men should control the work of the household. Brewsters' experiences thus changed, but their status as low-paid workers remained consistent.[21] The model of the "patriarchal equilibrium" thus helps explain why women's work status remained static during the late Middle Ages, an era in which we might have expected their status to rise if there had indeed been a "golden age" for women.

Women's earning power is important because it correlates closely with their status within both the household and the community at large, but it is not the only component of women's status. Also vital in determining women's experiences, quality of life, and autonomy were the ways in which they were perceived and represented within late medieval society. Indeed, cultural and discursive factors are sometimes overlooked in historians' examinations of women's status. More difficult to measure and more ambiguous to interpret, representations of women and attitudes toward their behavior nonetheless played an important role in shaping their lives. In particular, representations of women's speech sent important messages about their power, or lack thereof. Anyone could use the "tongue that is your sword," but when women did so it was more likely to be perceived as an illegitimate weapon. The cultural category of the scolding, gossiping, disorderly woman was one of several factors that helped counterbalance demographic and economic forces, ensuring that the overall equilibrium of women's status remained constant and that late medieval women did not experience any "golden age."

Scholarship on Speech and Scolding

Medievalists have recently rediscovered the importance of speech and its representations, and work in this field is vibrant and interesting. Historians have examined records of both church and secular courts for traces of defamation, treason, heretical speech, and scolding, while literary scholars have paid particular attention to representations and performances of the spoken word in texts such as those of Chaucer, Langland, and Margery Kempe. Interdisciplinary conference proceedings and collections of essays attest to the importance of illicit speech and to its role in the construction of honor and reputation.[22] Scholars of speech in late medieval England owe much to the recent monograph of Edwin D. Craun, *Lies, Slander, and Obscenity in Medieval English Literature: Pastoral Rhetoric and the Deviant Speaker.* Craun suggested that late medieval authors drew heavily on a discourse initiated earlier concerning the "sins of the tongue." From the late fourteenth century, he argued, writers such as Chaucer, Gower, Langland, and the *Patience* poet were increasingly familiar with this discourse and sought to model examples of proper speech at the same time that they condemned deviant speech. Craun's argument was well reasoned and based on careful examination of both Latin treatises and Middle English literature. He was less concerned, however, with the ways in which this discourse was gendered or with the influence of events outside the strictly discursive, such as political anxiety about heresy and treason, and economic and social disruptions caused by the Black Death.[23]

While Craun's work does not focus particularly on the gendering of deviant speech, other scholarship has focused more closely on the relationship between illicit words and women. L. R. Poos and Laura Gowing have highlighted women's close association with defamation—as both defamers and defamed—in church courts of the late medieval and early modern periods respectively, while Steve Hindle has examined a well-documented case of gossip in early modern Cheshire. Karma Lochrie, in her study of medieval secrecy, has focused on women's association with gossip in texts and sermons of the late Middle Ages, emphasizing continuities between the practice of confession and the practice of gossip. Joy Wiltenburg has also examined representations of disorderly women, looking particularly at early modern English and German ballads and pamphlets. She has suggested that while texts ridiculing contentious wives served to warn women against shrewishness, they might also have served a liberating function. Women, she has argued, need not have shared the dominant cultural devaluation of their role, and they could have interpreted the figure of the disorderly woman in an empowering way. Popular literature could thus nurture self-respect among women even at the same time as it bolstered patriarchal interests.[24] Bernard Capp and Pamela Allen Brown have raised similar arguments about the ways in which gossip and stereotypical depictions of scolding or shrewlike women could prove empowering to women in early modern England.[25] Such work reminds us that those punished for deviant speech were not simply victims of an authoritarian class and gender regime. In addition to their victimhood, they may have claimed an authority of their own, however successful or unsuccessful.

While both historians and literary scholars have addressed gossip, defamation, and the "sins of the tongue" in general, the crime of scolding has received less sustained attention. Antiquarians of the late nineteenth and early twentieth centuries described scolding—and particularly its punishments—in detail, but they tended to regard it as a quaint peculiarity of the medieval period and an occasion for self-congratulation about modernity's retreat from barbaric castigations. Despite such problems in antiquarians' treatments of scolding, their work is often helpful for its preservation of scolding presentment records and evidence of instruments of punishment.[26]

Modern treatments of scolding have revolved around two main issues: the extent to which scolding prosecutions varied over time and the broader social changes that scolding prosecutions reflect. First, the chronological contours of scolding prosecutions in the courts have sparked considerable debate. David Underdown, the first modern historian to focus on scolding, argued in a 1986 article that scolds were seldom prosecuted until the sixteenth century. His chronology was soon disputed by Martin Ingram, who argued that scolding prosecutions were common in many jurisdictions from the fourteenth century and that evidence for greater concern in the sixteenth and seventeenth centuries was insubstantial. Ingram conceded that scolding presentments may have been more visible in the sixteenth century, but suggested that this was the result of a general trend toward legal definition and uniformity in local jurisdictions. Marjorie McIntosh's 1998 study of misbehavior in late medieval and early modern England confirmed that scolding was an earlier phenomenon than Underdown had supposed. McIntosh included scolding, along with eavesdropping and nightwalking (wandering about at night without a lawful excuse), among crimes that threatened communal harmony. Such crimes, she argued, increased in the fifteenth century with high levels of population growth and migration. McIntosh surveyed 267 jurisdictions, beginning in the 1370s, and found that scolding presentments peaked in the first half of the fifteenth century and again in the 1520s and 1530s. McIntosh's work has provided the best attempt yet to set out a picture of the periods in which scolding attracted most concern. Her chronology was somewhat limited, however, by her method. McIntosh charted the number of jurisdictions within her sample that prosecuted at least one scold during two or three sample years per twenty-year period. She did not take account of increasing numbers of presentments within any one jurisdiction, and because she chose only a few sample years within each twenty-year period, she almost certainly undercounted the number of jurisdictions that presented scolds. Nonetheless, the breadth of her study, in terms of chronology, geography, and the numbers and types of courts surveyed, has provided ample corrective to Underdown's claim that scolding was primarily an early modern phenomenon. The most recent publication on scolding in medieval and early modern England involved a reexamination of the Underdown-Ingram debate by Karen Jones and Michael Zell. In their analysis of thirty-seven scolding presentments from the biannual courts of the small borough of Fordwich (Kent) between 1450 and 1570, Jones and Zell found that concern about women's speech in Fordwich peaked around 1500, a century earlier than Underdown had suggested, and between the peaks identified by McIntosh. In other words, while recent work has demonstrated conclusively that scolding predated the sixteenth century, scholars do not agree on the patterns of concern about scolding throughout the late Middle Ages. Maryanne Kowaleski's forthcoming article will address some of these concerns as she discusses evidence and possible reasons for the origins of scolding prosecutions in English local courts. Aside from Jones and Zell and Kowaleski, historians have paid minimal attention to patterns of prosecutions within individual jurisdictions and the correlation of scolding with local conditions. Work on the chronological contours of scolding is thus promising but leaves a number of questions unanswered.[27]

In addition to examining chronology, historians have claimed scolding as symptomatic of a variety of broader social changes. For Underdown, scolding was a by-product of the onset of capitalism and a corresponding decline in social harmony and good neighborliness. He argued that scolding should thus be viewed alongside witchcraft accusations and charivari as part of a sixteenth- and seventeenth-century crisis in gender relations. Ingram disagreed, focusing more closely on the characteristics of alleged scolds themselves. Sixteenth-century scolds, he suggested, were usually women who were poor or old and had a long history of "troublesome" or "antisocial" behavior. Their prosecution, he argued, was due more to personal circumstances and individual psychology, even mental illness, than to a general crisis of gender relations. Scolds, Ingram claimed, were "dismal negotiators of social relationships" and "temperamentally inclined to confrontation rather than compromise." McIntosh, on the other hand, paid less attention to the personalities of individual scolds or the dynamics involved in their prosecution; rather, her concern with scolding reflected her broader interest in issues of local governance in late medieval and early modern England. For McIntosh, scolding was a crime that threatened communal harmony, reflecting late medieval social dislocation in a period of population growth and high migration. Social dislocation and migration played a role in Kowaleski's assessment too: in particular, Kowaleski argued, scolding prosecutions reflected the concern of urban officials about the immigration into towns of young single women outside the control of men. A significant minority of Exeter scolds consisted of unmarried servants, and Kowaleski has suggested that high levels of scolding prosecution might reflect unease and resentment on the part of employers who found themselves paying higher wages in the wake of the Black Death. For each of these historians, therefore, scolding prosecutions serve as evidence for a broader agenda. Only Jones and Zell have considered scolding on its own terms, but their data is limited to thirty-seven presentments within one jurisdiction and they do not speculate about the reasons for the emergence of scolding as a phenomenon.

This book owes much to the foundational work of Underdown, Ingram, McIntosh, Jones and Zell, and Kowaleski. Yet, because I focus more closely on scolding and its relationship to other types of deviant speech, I hope that I can also address scolding more firmly on its own terms. In order to understand better the phenomenon of scolding presentments, we need more thorough examination of when, why, and how scolding prosecutions first appeared. While the dynamic of scolding was not static across the late Middle Ages, and while it was certainly adapted to suit local conditions, prosecutions must nonetheless be considered in the light of a preexisting and pervasive discourse about the dangers of speech. As part of the discourse on the "sins of the tongue," scolding existed in literary texts before it was prosecuted in courts, and it continued to be addressed by contemporary authors throughout the fourteenth to seventeenth centuries. Historians' examinations of literary texts about dangerous speech in general and scolding in particular have either been confined to the early modern period or have considered a relatively superficial selection of materials. Certainly social and economic changes played an important role in the rise of scolding prosecutions—the demographic crisis of the Black Death was crucial in propagating concern about the "sins of the tongue"—but discursive factors played an important role too, and these have sometimes been overlooked by historians. Further, the role of gender in scolding prosecutions deserves more rigorous study. To say that women outnumbered men is not enough, since not every woman was accused of scolding. What was it about certain women (and indeed, certain men) that made them liable to scolding charges? And what role did scolding play in the construction of medieval manhood and womanhood?

How We Know about Illicit Speech

In seeking to answer these questions, this book adopts an interdisciplinary approach, examining legal records alongside literary and artistic sources. Each source—whether a court record, a literary characterization, or a wall painting—represents only one aspect of the cultural meanings of illicit speech and the fullest (if always necessarily incomplete) picture will result from consideration of multiple types of construction. In late medieval England, as in modern society, people gathered their ideas and information from many different media.

First, this study draws on data about legal prosecutions of problematic speech. The justice system of late medieval England was eccentric and complicated, consisting of three main systems of courts: local, royal, and ecclesiastical. Ordinary people dealt most often with local courts, courts theoretically under the control of the feudal elite but in practice run largely by local communities themselves. Local courts were held regularly, which could be once every two to three weeks, once a month, once every six months, or at some other interval. A large proportion of each community regularly attended court sessions. On manors, attendance was obligatory for all unfree tenants and most free peasants, while in boroughs the obligations varied. Local courts dealt primarily with people who were charged with such petty crimes as cheating customers, committing assault (where this did not result in serious injury), or acting as a general nuisance to the community in some way. Punishments typically took the form of monetary fines, although repeated offenders were sometimes subjected to humiliating physical punishments, such as public confinement in the stocks. Local courts were about more than the punishment of crimes, however: they also served as sites for collection of fees, rents, and taxes, for ensuring that all roads were kept clear, for the pursuit of grievances among individuals, for the appointment of local government officers, and for dealing with many other mundane details. In addition, they provided something of an occasion for local people to group together—to observe each other, to gossip, and to catch up on community news—in a way that was matched only by weekly gatherings in parish churches. Indeed, those who distracted others with their gossip during court sessions were sometimes punished by the court, just as those who gossiped in church drew censure from the priest or ecclesiastical courts. In some places, such as Middlewich (Cheshire), courts were held in the purpose-built moothall, but elsewhere they were held on the village green, in the manor house, in the nave of the church, or in some other spacious location.[28]

On rare occasions, crimes such as scolding were presented to local courts in civil cases, in which one individual brought a suit against another, but more typically they came to the courts' attention in two main ways.[29] First, juries of presentment, composed of twelve or more men of relatively high local status (that is, wealthier peasants or townspeople, but not usually members of the gentry) might include scolds among their lists of recent offenders. Juries of presentment were theoretically guided by a charge, which stated the kinds of crimes they should bring to the court's attention. Some charges, for instance, specified that jurors should look out for tavern-keepers who allowed disorderly behavior, while others emphasized the need to punish people who wandered around at night without a lawful excuse.[30] The earliest surviving charge in which scolds were mentioned explicitly dates to 1536. But, as with all legal processes, space existed for wide variations in interpretation of charges, and juries often went beyond their explicit directions.[31] Some juries appear to have regarded scolding as falling under their jurisdiction, while others did not. Juries of presentment generally met only a few times a year, at courts known as leet courts, great courts, legal courts, courts with views of frankpledge, or other such titles. Their purpose was to deal with a wide range of petty disturbances and payments of fees.[32] While accused individuals had the right to defend themselves, the lists compiled by jurors were generally accepted, and punishments were determined. Second, scolding cases might come to the courts' attention at the more regular courts that met in between the leets, due to reports by local officers appointed to regulate community peace. In Dunster (Somerset), for instance, most scolds were presented by juries of presentment at six-monthly "legal courts," but two specially appointed "constables of the peace" occasionally presented scolds at sessions in between.[33] In Middlewich, scolds were seldom charged at sessions headed by juries of presentment but were instead presented by bailiffs at the court sessions held once every three weeks.

Local courts, therefore, presented opportunities for variation and even innovation within a traditional system. Jurors, bailiffs, and constables were bound to some extent by precedents and conventions, but they also had flexibility to respond both to new behaviors and to new anxieties about old behaviors. While these officers relied heavily on reports from other members of the public, they also exercised a degree of discretion over which offenses were worth pursuing and which were not. Anne DeWindt has described medieval juries and their communities as engaged in a dialogue in which each group responded continually to reactions it inspired in the other.[34] Because this dialogue depended heavily on the personalities and dynamics at play in each locale, constructions of crimes played out differently in different jurisdictions. Scolds presented in the town of Congleton (Cheshire) in 1422, for instance, were typically described as "common scolds" (*communes litigatrices*) and charged by juries of presentment, while alleged scolds in nearby Halton in the same year were brought before the court by appointed bailiffs and accused of specific instances of scolding (for example, Agnes Bathe "scolded" [*litigauit cum*] William Pole and called him a thief).[35] In other jurisdictions, other conventions applied, and within each jurisdiction, conventions changed over time.

For secular issues, most peasants and townspeople dealt only with local courts. Occasionally, however, they might find themselves facing one or another of the multiple layers of royal courts. The king's courts—such as those of the itinerant eyre justices or the county courts—heard weightier matters, both civil and criminal.[36] In particular, they dealt with cases of felony, such as murder, treason, or more serious assaults that resulted in the shedding of blood. Cases involving illicit speech came to the attention of such courts in two ways. First, the king's courts punished those committing treasonous speech, barrators (those who created trouble or wasted the court's time with spurious court cases), and those who started or spread rumors that directly affected the king himself or his chief officials. Second, on rare occasions, the king's courts heard cases of scolding. Usually scolding was not the primary purpose of such cases being brought before the courts, but people accused of other crimes were sometimes also accused of scolding or of scoldlike behavior in addition to their primary offense. In 1407, for instance, when a woman from the town of Hurdesford (Cheshire) was presented before the county court for assault, it was recorded that she was also "a common scold [*communis litigatrix*] among her neighbors, . . . telling malicious stories . . ."[37] The king's courts had the power to execute felons, but those committing more minor offenses were typically fined.

In addition to local courts and royal courts, late medieval English people were also subject to the jurisdiction of the church. Ecclesiastical courts, with an elaborate hierarchy of their own, claimed responsibility for the sexual and moral behavior of all English people, both clergy and laity.[38] Defining morality, however, was not always easy, and the contours of church jurisdiction do not always make absolute sense to us today. Much of the business of lower-level church courts was taken up with allegations of adultery and fornication. The church also adjudicated disputes involving marriage, such as breaches of contract or allegations of bigamy. In addition, it sometimes heard cases of defamation and—perhaps by extension—of scolding.

Scolding, defamation, and other crimes involving speech were generally the preserve of lower-level church courts, such as consistory courts and visitations (in which bishops or other church officials would tour their dioceses, hearing complaints against laity and clergy alike). Cases were brought to the courts' attention either in the form of instance litigation (suits between plaintiffs and defendants) or as ex officio cases presented by local jurors or other committees convened for the purpose. By the late fourteenth century, these local committees were asked explicitly to present scolds, along with perjurers, heretics, adulterers, and other such sinners, and by the early sixteenth century, bishops also specified the need to present those who gossiped during church services.[39] Church courts did not levy fines per se; rather, individuals were offered the opportunity of compurgation, the chance to swear to their innocence with their testimony supported by the oaths of fellow parishioners. Those who admitted guilt, and those failing to find the requisite number of people prepared to testify to their innocence, were required to do penance. In 1499, for instance, Agnes Rawson of Haverhill (Suffolk) was charged as a "common reviler of her neighbors" and instructed to bring four of her neighbors as compurgators to the next court. Apparently Agnes's neighbors either saw the charge as justified or lacked sympathy for her cause, for she failed in her compurgation. The judge thus found her guilty and ordered her to offer two candles, presumably before the altar in her parish church.[40] Other scolds convicted in church courts received physical punishments such as public floggings, or they were required to process around the church barefoot, dressed in penitents' garments. On some occasions, however, these corporal punishments or humiliations were remitted in favor of monetary payments. Church courts also oversaw the behavior of the clergy, hearing cases about priests who neglected their parishes, revealed secrets of their parishioners, or otherwise behaved in an immoral fashion.

Although theoretically separate, the three systems of local courts, king's courts, and church courts sometimes overlapped in terms of jurisdiction. Theft, for instance, was a felony and ought to have been reserved for the king's courts, but petty theft was often punished by local courts and theft of church property was often considered by church courts. Scolding was a crime against public order and therefore fell under the jurisdiction of local courts, yet cases were often heard in church courts and occasionally in royal courts. Indeed, the lines between secular and ecclesiastical control over cases such as scolding were not always clear. In 1425, for instance, the regular three-weekly court of Middlewich dealt with a case that sounded much like it belonged in the church courts. Alice, wife of Hugh Wytton, was accused of having scolded (*obiurgata fuit*) Margaret, wife of Richard Shene, and of having defamed her enormously in church, "disturbing divine services in contempt of the lord king and of divine Christ." For several weeks, Alice did not appear to face the charges, but when she did she was fined the heavy sum of 16d.[41] Disturbance of church services was typically a matter for the ecclesiastical courts, but it is possible that if the nearest church court was at Chester—twenty miles away—it was easier and quicker for Alice's case to be heard and punished in the local court. Court systems, therefore, were multiple and overlapping. Some individuals were able to use these fuzzy boundaries to their advantage by making strategic choices about where to take cases, weighing the advantages and disadvantages of the frequency of sittings, the composition of the jury, and the costs involved in litigation.[42]

Investigation of illicit speech in late medieval English courts thus requires a broad array of sources. To study both general patterns among court presentments and variations over time, place, and jurisdiction, I collected more than six hundred cases of individuals accused of scolding between 1311 and 1530. These come from more than forty jurisdictions, both secular and ecclesiastical, and enable assessment of the various ways in which the crime of scolding was recorded, the amounts of fines assessed of convicted scolds, the ratio of women to men accused of scolding, and something of the chronology and geography of scold prosecution. They also enable comparison of the presentment and punishment of scolds in secular courts to those in ecclesiastical courts. I have also surveyed a comparable number of records for other offenses involving speech, such as defamation, abuse of community officials, disruptive speech in the courtroom and church, and the raising of false hues (explained in Chapter 1). Readers may notice a number of examples drawn from the courts of Battle (Sussex), Bridgwater (Somerset), Chedzoy (Somerset), Clare (Suffolk), Colchester (Essex), Crowle (Lincolnshire), Dunster (Somerset), Halton, Congleton, Widnes and related jurisdictions (Cheshire and Lancashire), Methwold (Norfolk), Pleshey, High Easter, and related jurisdictions (Essex), Ramsey (Huntingdonshire), Wakefield (Yorkshire), and Yeadon (Yorkshire).

In order to understand the dynamic of scolding accusations within local, marital, occupational, and social contexts, I also undertook a more detailed investigation of one jurisdiction, that of the town of Middlewich, in the palatine county of Chester, in the first half of the fif-

Map 1. Places Mentioned Frequently in the Text

teenth century.[43] Middlewich was located on an important road between London and Lancashire and served to connect the busy county town of Chester with a network of late medieval highways. The core of the local economy was the trade in boiling and marketing salt from the brine springs at the town center, but two competing salt towns—Northwich and Nantwich—lay within a ten-mile radius.[44] The fourteenth and early fifteenth centuries were difficult years for the town: Middlewich and surrounding villages lost many residents in the Black Death of 1348–9, and fluctuations in the salt trade, combined with periodic disruption along the nearby Welsh border, kept the local economy unstable.[45] Middlewich prosecuted seventy-eight incidents of scolding in 196 surviving courts between 1413 and 1443. While the numbers of scolds presented in Middlewich were higher than in most jurisdictions, Middlewich scolds were representative in other respects: they were fined at similar rates to scolds elsewhere, the ratio of male to female scolds (1:13) was well within the range of other jurisdictions, and—with only one or two exceptions—the words allegedly spoken by Middlewich scolds were every bit as formulaic as those most often used by scolds elsewhere.[46] From borough court records, sheriffs' tourns, eyre courts, county courts, ministers' accounts, land deeds, rentals, wills, and other sources, I compiled a database of 799 residents of Middlewich and its surrounding villages between 1400 and 1450, which I used to locate scolds and other deviant speakers within their familial and socioeconomic contexts.

Traditional legal sources are the basis for a large part of this book, but I also draw heavily on literary representations of troublesome speech. In England, as elsewhere in Europe, the late Middle Ages witnessed the blossoming of vernacular literature. In addition to well-known works by Chaucer, Langland, Gower, and others, we possess far more texts by lesser-known and anonymous poets. Plays and ballads which would have been seen and heard by ordinary people also survive in significant numbers. These provide historians and literary scholars alike much more insight into late medieval popular culture than we can glean from surviving texts of the high Middle Ages. Anonymous stories, poems, and advice literature were often collected and written into commonplace books, and the proliferation of certain texts gives us a sense that—even prior to the invention of the printing press in the mid-fifteenth century—some texts were well known throughout England. Devotional literature was written and circulated more readily in the late Middle Ages too: manuals of lay piety, collections of sermons, and treatises on religious topics were eagerly consumed by both urban and rural audiences. Some of these works were translations of Latin or French originals; others were composed—either by clerics or members of the laity—in response to local demands. As Janet Coleman has pointed out, the mid-fourteenth-century treatise *The Pricke of Conscience* survives in more than 114 handwritten manuscripts, pointing to the broad dispersion of devotional literature.[47] Mystery plays, discussed further in Chapter 2, provided opportunities to link religious stories with local dynamics and concerns and reached an even broader audience with their annual performances.

These texts and their contexts are closely interwoven. Just as the speech of medieval people influenced the ways in which it was represented, so too the representations of speech influenced how ordinary people spoke and how they interpreted the speech of others. Laura Gowing's work on women and slander in early modern England, for instance, has identified ways in which legal narratives were shaped by stock plots in ballads and other popular literature.[48] Gowing, an historian, thus recognizes the ways in which literature helped to constitute reality, rather than merely reflecting it. Literary scholars have shown that they have much to teach historians about the cultural environment of late medieval England. For instance, Felicity Riddy's careful analysis of the fourteenth-century "How the Good Wife Taught Her Daughter" (a text which I discuss in more detail in Chapter 2) has shown how we can glean insight from the poem into what she terms the "bourgeois ethos" of late medieval towns.[49] Much recent scholarship has been influenced by the New Historicist approach to literary analysis, with its emphasis on context and on the ways in which conflicts and anxieties manifest in contemporary texts. For the postplague era, when English society struggled to restore social and economic equilibrium and coped with problems in the ongoing war against France, these conflicts and anxieties are not difficult to find: indeed, the late Middle Ages saw the flowering of an "abuses of the age genre" or a "literature of complaint." More than three hundred surviving late medieval poems deal in some way with contemporary conditions, whether political, religious, or social.[50] This readiness to lament the "abuses of the age" pervaded other genres besides poems: late medieval authors of sermons, plays, and advice literature sometimes sound remarkably like editorial writers of the modern era. Among their complaints, as Chapter 1 will explain, was concern about deviant speech.

In examining late medieval texts, I have limited material to sources in Middle English, rather than including materials in Latin (the language of the medieval church) or Old French (the language of the English aristocracy in the high Middle Ages). Although I have tried to do justice to literary context, I admit to an historian's bias in the use of these texts: my interest is primarily what we can learn about speech, rather than what we can learn about the development of literature. In particular, I have concentrated on the ways in which women's speech was constructed in comparison to the speech of men. While men were often singled out in warnings about the dangers of cursing and swearing, women were identified as the main culprits of gossip, slander, and scolding. The ambivalence and richness of literary sources provide a welcome balance to what are sometimes fairly terse condemnations of deviant speech in presentments before the courts.

Artistic representations of illicit speech add further to the richness of literary texts. For many medieval people, artistic "texts" were the most accessible of all. The interiors of parish churches, for instance, were routinely covered with colorful wall paintings, so that people who could not read or had no access to written texts would nonetheless have interacted with images on a regular basis. These sources played an important role in constituting the cultural environment of late medieval England: just as literary texts not only reflected but also helped comprise discourses, so too artistic representations played this double role. Indeed, contemporaries were well aware of the power that images could have: throughout the Middle Ages, moralists worried that ordinary people might come to revere (or—worse still—worship) artistic representations for their own sake.[51] Others argued that, in the words of Pope Gregory the Great, images were the "book of the illiterate," and thus played an essential didactic function.

Whether benignly didactic or dangerously powerful, images participated in local discourses about morals, virtues, and sins. In the words of Miriam Gill, "Every wall painting, however conventional its subject matter and position, represents individual or communal choice."[52] In the process of making such choices, individuals and communities sent powerful messages about their own concerns. They also demonstrated their familiarity with other forms of discourse. As recent work by literary scholars and art historians has emphasized, medieval artists and authors incorporated aspects of each other's work. Themes from *Piers Plowman* made their way into wall paintings, sermons and devotional materials were depicted in stained-glass windows, and preachers referenced church art as part of their sermons.[53] With regard to the discourse on inappropriate speech, artistic sources contribute recurrent images of deviant speakers gossiping, swearing, or being punished for their verbal improprieties.

Wall paintings from parish churches are a particularly useful source because of their ubiquity and the fact that they were viewed, on a regular basis, by people of all social statuses. Hundreds of late medieval wall paintings survive, and these are just a fraction of the number that once existed: the vast majority of medieval wall paintings have eroded or been destroyed. Ironically, early modern Puritans who whitewashed walls in an effort to simplify church interiors sometimes ended up preserving paintings, enabling them now to be restored.[54] Painted in an era before the Renaissance conception of the artist as genius, medieval wall paintings are almost all anonymous. The craftspeople who painted church walls commented on illicit speech particularly in images of gossiping women and swearing men (discussed in Chapters 2 and 4, respectively).

Another particularly interesting genre is that of misericords, ledges on the underside of hinged seats in the choirs of churches. Once the seat was lifted, these ledges provided relief to priests, monks, and nuns by enabling them to lean back and give the general impression that they were standing up (much as lecturers sometimes prop themselves against the edge of a table today). By the mid-fourteenth century, the ledges and the area beneath the ledges had become sites of intricate carvings, both religious and secular in theme. Misericords were usually found in larger parish churches or in cathedrals, and thus may not have been seen frequently by members of the laity. Their creators, however, were almost certainly lay craftspeople (who sometimes satirized the clergy in their carvings). The "marginal art" of misericords, present in a religious context but not readily visible, provided an opportunity for humorous and even subversive images. Among the more common of these were women beating men, scatological imagery, and representations of fools and folly.[55] As will be discussed, misericords also sometimes depicted illicit speech, representing gossiping women (see Figure 3) or demons trying to close women's mouths.

Most of the art considered in this study was commissioned to appear in public spaces, especially parish churches, rather than in the homes of elite patrons. This emphasis on popular and vernacular art, rather than, for example, the art that ornamented manuscripts designed for members of the elite, parallels my concentration on literary works in Middle English. Whereas literary scholars have long been mindful of representations of illicit speech, art historians have generally paid it less attention.[56] As with my use of literature, my approach has been to focus on what images tell us about medieval views toward speech rather than to trace the development of art for its own sake. Despite the invisibility of spoken words themselves, orality (and especially illicit orality) was such a critical part of the culture of late medieval England that wood carvers, painters, and even stonemasons and glaziers found multiple ways in which to depict deviant speech.

While I sometimes discuss these different genres—legal, literary, and artistic—under separate categories, I have aimed wherever possible to integrate and combine them while remaining conscious of the conventions involved in the interpretation of each. The gaps between constructions of deviant speech in different sources are perhaps some of the most fruitful points for considering its meanings for late medieval people. Court records and borough ordinances, for instance, almost universally condemned scolds and those who verbally abused local officials. While alleged scolds or abusers were sometimes deemed innocent, dangerous speech itself was repeatedly vilified and punished. Court records also serve as reminders that scolding and verbal abuse had very real consequences—economic, social, and sometimes physical—for those judged guilty. Artistic and literary sources similarly condemn disruptive speech, yet they also hint at moments of ambivalence. The character of the Wife of Bath may have flaunted many social conventions concerning speech and sexuality, yet she was ambiguously celebrated for her spirit rather than being wholeheartedly vilified. Representations of women gossiping in church emphasized women's connections with the demonic, but the women depicted often look young and seem to take joy in one another's company; they were not the ugly and bitter crones associated with gossip in other contexts. These overlaps and contradictions suggest that something about transgressive speech both horrified and attracted late medieval townspeople and villagers. Verbal insubordination captured the popular imagination and lent itself to more general resistance to hierarchical constraints in a similar way, perhaps, to the romanticization of highway robbery in the seventeenth century or smuggling in the nineteenth century. Whereas the condemnation of deviant speech helped perpetuate local power, it also served as something of a focus (indeed a voice) for resistance to hierarchy and delight in the deviant.

The first chapter, "'Sins of the Tongue' and Social Change," examines the rising tide of concern about speech in the late Middle Ages, focusing on the ways that people at all social levels adopted and adapted the ecclesiastical discourse on the "sins of the tongue." As we shall see, the discourse proved useful for any group that sought to underscore or promote its own power, particularly during an era of social dislocation. Chapter 2, "The Sins of Women's Tongues in Literature and Art," shows how this newly laicized and popularized discourse on the evils of speech came to be associated particularly with women. During the late Middle Ages, poets, playwrights, stone and wood carvers, wall painters, and others vilified female speech in particular. It is no accident, I argue, that the stereotypical gossipy character best known in the guise of Noah's Wife and Chaucer's Wife of Bath emerged during these centuries.

Chapter 3, "Women's Voices and the Law," shows how the same concern about female speech played out not just in literary and artistic contexts but also in the courtroom. From the late fourteenth century on, women lost access to the hue and cry—a means of community policing that had previously empowered female voices—and they were increasingly charged with disruptive speech in the forms of defamation and scolding. In Chapter 4, "Men's Voices," I examine the consequences for men of this legal and cultural discourse about women's words. Whereas men who spoke in problematic ways risked being seen as effeminate, certain categories of male speakers and certain individual men were able to overcome this association with womanliness.

The final two chapters focus more closely on the crime of scolding. In Chapter 5, "Communities and Scolding," I examine definitions and elements of the crime of scolding. I also discuss the ways in which scolding varied according to jurisdiction, arguing that the key factors were the presence of individuals invested in prosecuting scolds and geographical and jurisdictional connections with other scold-prosecuting courts. Chapter 6, "Who Was a Scold?" explains the backgrounds of individuals charged with the offense. Whereas scolds were more likely to be single or married than widowed, and more likely to be associated with certain other crimes, nonetheless the label remained flexible and applicable to almost anyone. Indeed, the flexibility of the crime meant that jurisdictions could exercise considerable latitude in deciding who best fit the label of "scold." Whereas poor women were most likely to be charged in some places, other jurisdictions charged women of all socioeconomic levels below that of the gentry. The conclusion, "Consequences of the Feminization of Deviant Speech," explores the significance of the late medieval association between illicit words and women, both for individual women and for society as a whole. It also discusses why concern about women's speech emerged when it did and why it has survived.

The history of efforts to control speech is simultaneously part of the history of sin and the history of power, for regulation of speech involved condemnation of particular words, modes of speech, and speakers. It is also closely tied to the history of gender: when the Wife of Bath claimed that "half so boldly can no man / Swear and lie, as a woman can," she simultaneously associated women with problematic speech and implicitly associated problematic speakers (both male *and* female) with womanliness.[57] During the fourteenth and fifteenth centuries, English people began to think and talk about speech in a different kind of way. As they did so, they changed the ways in which they constructed gender. By the fifteenth century, women were to words as geese were to excrement. Women were gossips and chatterers, scolds and shrews, and gossipy or scolding men were like women.

Chapter 1

"Sins of the Tongue" and Social Change

The entrance to hell, according to medieval artists, was an enormous gaping mouth. In wall paintings, stained-glass windows, carvings, and manuscript illuminations, sinners were cast through this ignoble opening, propelled by demons of all shapes, sizes, and colors. Some of the damned were rounded up with ropes and dragged toward hellmouth, while others were pushed in wheelbarrows or threatened with pitchforks. The point was reinforced in elaborately staged mystery plays which included a hellmouth in their stage props, ready to swallow sinners who deserved damnation. While hellmouth images had been around since as early as the eleventh century, they were greatly elaborated during the fourteenth century, complete with glaring eyes, wide jaws, and sharp teeth. By the late Middle Ages, everyone understood the metaphor: the mouth could be a site of evil, an entrance to hell, just as speech could be a form of sin.[1]

Christian moralists had long encouraged people to speak the truth and refrain from malicious gossip, but their efforts were redoubled from the early thirteenth century on. Speech, preachers cautioned, was open to abuse and should be employed sparingly. Edwin D. Craun has done much to draw our attention to this developing discourse on the "sins of the tongue" and the ways in which it spread from clerical to lay literature in fourteenth- and fifteenth-century England. Here, I build on Craun's argument by proposing that—especially from the late fourteenth century—the discourse spread also among non-literate, ordinary English men and women and that it spread into contexts beyond the literary. That is, the discourse on the "sins of the tongue" was not only laicized but also popularized and woven more securely into the fabric of everyday life. By the late fourteenth century, it permeated not only poetry and sermons but also the law courts (whether ecclesiastical, royal, or local), popular ballads and plays, regulations of manors, boroughs, and guilds, and visual representations. Presumably, it also reached places for which we do not have records: conversations between parents and children in the home, for example, or between neighbors in the village tavern. In late medieval England, the discourse on the "sins of the tongue" was thus one of multiple, mutually reinforcing, strands: jurors deciding scolding or defamation cases listened to sermons and poetry, priests wrote homilies in response to legal prosecutions of deviant speakers, and wall painters and carvers chose representations of evil speech to address community concerns. This chapter focuses particularly on how the discourse on evil speech was developed beyond the literary and artistic spheres, but we should not forget the ways in which literature, art, court prosecutions, and everyday interactions participated in an ongoing feedback loop, each strand reflecting and helping to construct the others.

The late medieval discourse about evil speech was grounded in the church. After the Fourth Lateran Council of 1215 established that all Christians were required to attend confession at least once a year, texts identifying and categorizing vices proliferated. In order to hear confessions and dispense appropriate penances, priests needed to understand the different types of sins and to locate each sin in relation to others in a hierarchy of evil. Among these closely scrutinized and annotated sins were the "sins of the tongue," regularly granted a chapter or more in the expansive and encyclopedic pastoral manuscripts that proliferated from the early thirteenth century. Guillaume Peyraut's *Summa de vitiis*, for instance, included no fewer than twenty-four chapters on specific oral sins, among which were blasphemy, hypocrisy, boasting, rumor, lying, flattery, mocking of good people, and sowing of discord. Due to its popularity both on the Continent and in England, Peyraut's *Summa* continued to propagate the discourse on the "sins of the tongue" throughout the late Middle Ages.[2] As Craun has shown, this ecclesiastical discourse on the "sins of the tongue" continued throughout the fourteenth and fifteenth centuries to draw heavily on a scholastic theology laid down in the thirteenth century.[3] But the discourse also found its way into places not perhaps envisioned by the authors of penitential manuals and works of lay piety. Indeed, by the end of the fourteenth century, the discourse on the "sins of the tongue" had become a regular and important part of everyday English life.

This chapter argues that the laicized and popularized discourse on the evils of speech was employed particularly to establish, enforce, or extend authority. By asserting power over speech, people who sought to bolster their status found that they could silence or even punish the voices of their detractors. This strategy was especially useful during periods of social change, and the late fourteenth century, with its demographic crises and subsequent social readjustments, was certainly such an era.

"Sins of the Tongue" and the State

As Craun has explained, vernacular poets such as Chaucer, Gower, Langland, and the *Patience* poet picked up on clerical discussions of the "sins of the tongue" and modeled both good and bad speech in their poetry. But the concern with the "sins of the tongue" was also reflected in the law courts, as secular legislators expressed heightened anxieties about speech. In 1275 and 1276, English statutes specifically prohibited rumors and slanders concerning the king or great nobles and expressed concern that justice in royal courts was impeded by barrators, those who indulged in wasteful litigation. During the fourteenth and fifteenth centuries, the jurisdiction of royal courts over speech crimes was solidified by repeated statutes not only against treason but also against rumors and lies about the aristocracy.[4] Yet not all deviant speech or speakers were considered worthy of concern: rather, the king and his counselors sought primarily to protect their own interests and reputations.

The notion of defamation—the act of speaking false words that harmed the reputations of others—had been a part of English secular law from at least the Anglo-Saxon period, but, like many other legal matters, it received greater attention from the thirteenth century onward. The son of an insecure king, Edward I moved quickly to outlaw defamation after his accession in 1272. The Statutes of Westminster of 1275, for instance, complained that "devisors of tales" had often caused conflict between the king and his subjects. From henceforth, it was decreed, no one may "tell or publicize any false news or tales, from which discord or occasion of discord or slander may grow between the king and his people or the great men of the realm, and . . . he that tells such tales shall be taken and kept in prison until he had brought into the court the first author of the tale."[5] The king, in other words, was interested in prosecuting defamation when it directly concerned him or other magnates. He was less interested in other kinds of defamation. The Statute of Circumspecte Agatis in 1285 explicitly stated defamation to be the preserve of the church courts, not the royal courts, in cases when no monetary damages were sought, and when Irish magnates approached Parliament to help resolve a dispute ten years later, they were told that royal courts did not administer defamation actions.[6] Nonetheless, the effort to prevent defamation of the king and his officers persisted, and subsequent litigation reiterated portions of the Statutes of Westminster involving illicit speech. Chapter five of the Statute of Gloucester of 1378, for instance, specifically forbade the speaking of lies, slander, and false news against great officers of the realm.[7]

The ban on high-level gossip proved useful over the ensuing centuries in maintaining authority in periods of political uncertainty, ensuring that the king's information sources were reliable, and punishing those who used their power of speech in devious ways. In January 1432, for instance, Andrew de Holes, parson of the church of Davenham (Cheshire), was charged in the county court with having told the king "various false stories" about Richard de Bulkeley of the nearby town of Middlewich. Andrew, it was alleged, had told Henry VI that Richard was a disrupter of the peace. These stories were said to have caused "great scandal and discord" to grow up between Richard and his king, and Andrew was charged with having thus transgressed against a statute.[8] A few months later, George de Wever was accused in the same court of telling false stories about two other members of the gentry to Henry, bishop of Winchester, a member of the king's council. George's words were said to have caused the growth of "scandal and discord" between the king and the slandered men, so George too was alleged to have transgressed the statute.[9] In each instance, the alleged slanderer was acquitted, yet these cases nonetheless point to a continuing concern to monitor and purify information received by the king. Perhaps even more telling is the context in which these cases emerged: in their constant disputes during the fifteenth century, members of the Cheshire nobility not only engaged in out-and-out violence but also attacked one another's reputations. Lying and speaking ill of others was more than just a matter of conscience, however, when the king was involved, and the discourse on malicious speech might thus be used to prosecute slanderous words.

By the late fifteenth century, the interests of the royal courts were growing, and the crown's jurists began to rethink their policy of dealing only with defamations of the king and other "great men." Whereas the crown had conceded jurisdiction over defamation to church courts in the late thirteenth century with remarkably little tension, the royal courts two centuries later asserted authority over all defamation cases that involved accusations of secular crimes. Defamation cases heard in church courts were slowly confined to slurs about spiritual offenses, especially sexual transgressions.[10] Defamation, by the late fifteenth century, was more than a sin; it was also a crime, and a crime for which the king could justify collecting fees for adjudication.

At the same time that the crown sought to extend its control over defamation, a new kind of speech crime was emerging. Associated first with the general extension of royal jurisdiction, barratry originally involved the offense of pursuing spurious court cases that wasted the time of judges. The Middle English noun "barat" or "baret" meant both deception and trouble or fighting, and those who brought litigation before the courts without sufficient cause were regarded as both deceitful and troublesome for they created social tension, deceived the court with weak claims, and subverted judicial attention from more important issues. Local courts had long fined individuals who made false claims by bringing weak suits against others, but during the fourteenth and fifteenth centuries the act of bringing such cases acquired the more specific label of barratry. Moreover, between the thirteenth and fifteenth centuries, the meaning of barratry expanded, both in terms of the behavior it described and the social classes to whom the label was applied. By the early sixteenth century, barratry could mean troublemaking in the most general sense, both within courts and within the community at large.

Two statutes passed in the mid-1270s expressed concern that barrators were impeding justice by clogging the royal courts with lengthy cases and usurping the king's jurisdiction by claiming authority to pronounce judgments. The Statutes of Westminster of 1275, for instance, instructed sheriffs, "It is provided that no sheriff shall suffer barretors [or maintainers of] quarrels in their shires. Neither stewards of great lords, nor any other unless he is attorney for his lord, may make suit or give judgment in the counties or pronounce the judgment unless he be specially required and prayed of all the suitors, and attornies of the suitors, who shall be at the court."[11] The intention of this law was to regulate ways in which members of the nobility might use the royal courts in their dealings with each other. Barratry, then, signified noble litigiousness and legal meddling. Over the next century, however, the meaning expanded. A statute of 1361 empowered specially appointed magnates in the countryside with the power to restrain "offenders, rioters, and other barrators," and in 1396, Richard II, fearing "conspiracy of the people," sent a commission into Cheshire in search of "barrators and rioters."[12] Barratry was thus no longer a crime committed primarily by members of the elite in their constant legal struggles against each other but could also imply any kind of local disturbance, of which verbal offense and riot were two instances.

Overlapping with both defamation and barratry was the offense of treason. Medieval English concepts of treason combined the ancient Germanic notion of betrayal with the Roman notion of insult to those with public authority. Treason could thus involve both deeds and words, and legal constructions of treason throughout the medieval period emphatically included both physical and verbal rebellion. Prior to the mid-fourteenth century, the category of treason covered a wide and somewhat vague range of behaviors directed both against the king (and his family) and against others in positions of power. Treason could include killing one's king, plotting (or assenting to a plot) to kill the king, killing one's lord, killing one's husband, violating the wife or daughters of the king or lord, counterfeiting coins, clipping metal from good coins, falsifying the king's seal, or betraying the king's army. Yet, as J. G. Bellamy has argued in his authoritative work on medieval English treason law, concepts of treason correlated strongly with the prevailing system of government. The decline of the personal loyalties that were fundamental to feudalism and the development of more abstract loyalties to state or king necessitated new articulations of treason law.[13]

These new articulations occurred especially during the reign of Edward III with the Great Statute of Treasons of 1352. The Great Statute tightened significantly the varieties of treason, at the same time as it asserted the claim of the monarch to represent law and order in the kingdom. For the most part, the Great Statute of Treasons and the cases that fell under it dealt with treasonous deeds, rather than words. Indeed, the statute itself insisted that treason had to consist of "overt acts," although it did include the crime of "imagining" the death of the king, queen, or royal heir among such acts. From the early fifteenth century, this provision was interpreted strategically by those concerned about the security of royal power. The distinction between treason and defamation of the king was sometimes hard to call. Henry IV's usurpation of the throne from Richard II provides a case in point. Several dozen individuals known to support Richard II were punished in the Cheshire county court in 1400 for speaking "malicious words" against their new king, although their speech was not constructed explicitly as treason.[14] Yet in 1402, at least five cases of "imagining the king's death" were prosecuted under the Great Statute of Treasons, four of which involved circulation of rumors that Richard II was still alive and sought to regain his throne from Henry IV. Henry IV was right to be concerned: in 1403, Sir Henry Percy (Hotspur) used the rumor to fuel a revolt against the king. Although the rebels were defeated at the Battle of Shrewsbury, Henry IV's sensitivity about the power of speech persisted, and in 1404, men were appointed to inquire throughout Cheshire about "false rumors" circulating among the people and disturbing the peace.[15] Over the fifteenth century, several people were executed on charges of "imagining." In 1441, one of the king's justices ruled explicitly that mere thoughts—without deeds—were enough to render someone a traitor. Of course, in order for these thoughts to be known and hence dangerous, they needed first to be spoken: treason, from the late fourteenth century, had become increasingly associated with the evils of the tongue and with speech in general.[16]

The Great Statute of Treasons and the cases pursued in its aftermath were in large measure aimed at members of the upper classes. Several cases of "imagining the king's death" involved friars; others involved gentlemen, yeomen, and members of the aristocracy. As a rule, the king and his ministers made little effort to police what was said about them by ordinary people, who were seldom subject to charges of treason. But there was one important exception: the Revolt of 1381.

The changing socioeconomic background of the fourteenth century is vital to an understanding of the 1381 uprising. At the beginning of the fourteenth century, England's population suffered food shortages, unemployment, and overcrowding. So tenuous was the balance between population and resources that a change in climate—and its corresponding drop in productivity—could lead to mass starvation, as occurred during the Great Famine of 1317. Such a situation favored England's nobility, the landowners who were able to charge steep rents on scarce land and pay low wages to the many peasants competing for employment. Within a few decades, however, all this changed. The Black Death spread throughout England in 1348–49, killing as much as one-third of the population in its initial outbreak. Subsequent visitations of the plague killed more still, and the population did not begin to recover until the mid- to late fifteenth century. For landowners, this was a disaster because—much as they resisted economic forces—they were forced to pay higher wages and to charge lower rents.[17] Members of the nobility needed to work overtime to maintain the hegemonic discourse about the importance of everyone keeping to their social station. They also used the courts: they legislated for and tried to enforce a wage freeze, they reinstated old manorial dues that had been allowed to lapse, and they resisted efforts on the part of serfs to rid themselves of the bonds of villeinage.

The power of peasant voices in spreading resistance to nobles' demands was demonstrated by the "Great Rumour" of 1377, which prompted peasants from more than forty villages in the south of England to refuse to bring in the harvest because they claimed freedom from labor services to landowners.[18] Concerned by such rumors, landowners brought a petition to Parliament, speaking of fears about treason, civil war, and peasant rebellion.[19] Peasant rumors about freedom added fuel to noble suspicion and resulted in the establishment of special commissions inquiring into peasant insubordination. These attempts to undercut peasant resistance, however, were unsuccessful. Tension was further increased by governmental efforts to collect taxation. Social pressures were finally ignited by the attempt in 1381 to collect the third heavy poll tax in four years. In Essex and Kent, peasants (including village leaders), priests, and other supporters gathered and marched toward London, where they were joined by disgruntled townspeople. Rebels killed the Archbishop of Canterbury and several other important government officials, and they burned and looted property before being dispersed. Similar uprisings took place in the town of St. Albans (Hertfordshire), in Suffolk, Norfolk, and Cambridgeshire.[20]

In the wake of these unsuccessful revolts, the legal concept of treason was quickly extended to ordinary people, both by justices and by chroniclers. As Bellamy has pointed out, the distinction between felony and treason was often unclear when rebels of 1381 were convicted, and the late medieval category of treason perhaps assumed its widest proportions in the years immediately following the revolt. In some places, jurors accused rebels of acting feloniously; in other places, they were described as both felonious and treacherous. For rebels, the consequence of conviction was the same (death), but the application of the label "traitor" to ordinary people temporarily expanded the legal meaning of treason. In November 1381, Parliament passed an act specifically prohibiting popular uprisings, and rebels of future insurrections were dealt with under that law, rather than under the 1352 Great Statute of Treasons.[21]

While the legal meaning of treason was extended to rebels of ordinary status only temporarily, cultural connections between treason and the peasantry (the group most closely associated with the revolt) persisted. Indeed, chroniclers of the time had much to say about the treacherous words and voices of peasants. Contemporary accounts characterized rebels as animals, lacking both reason and direction, and certainly not qualified to question their social superiors. By describing participants in the 1381 uprising as members of an uncontrollable, bestial mob, chroniclers and poets were able both to belittle peasant motivations for revolt and to distinguish themselves as separate, superior beings. As Paul Strohm has pointed out, the first book of the outraged poet John Gower's *Vox Clamantis* represents rebels as asses, oxen, swine, dogs, cats, foxes, birds, flies, and frogs.[22] Ralph Hanna has drawn particular attention to chroniclers' constructions of peasant words as the bleating of sheep or the devilish voices of peacocks.[23] Archbishop Simon Sudbury described the peasant leader John Ball as a fox trying to evade the huntsmen (and implicitly preying upon the peasant poultry, a metaphor familiar to medieval people since it was sometimes used to portray the preaching of friars).[24] By characterizing rebel voices as animal-like, chroniclers and poets simultaneously cast them as traitors to order and propriety. Like animals, peasants did not possess legitimate voices, and by implication they belonged at home on the pastures, not involved in affairs of governance.

Because they threatened the stability and order of the entire ruling class, the events of 1381 both heightened anxiety about treason and extended the ways in which it was constructed. Anyone who, in words or deeds, posed a significant threat to accepted authority was liable to be charged, in popular discourse if not in courts, with treason. Rebels also sometimes used this discourse of treachery to their own ends. In their eyes, the king's bad advisors were the true traitors, betraying the kingdom with unwise advice, and the young king Richard II was their innocent victim.[25] Treason, in late medieval England, was a crime that could excite considerable anxiety in many different social groups. While treason typically involved deeds as well as words, its verbal nature remained important to constructions of the offense in the fourteenth and fifteenth centuries.

The discourse on the "sins of the tongue" was thus readily sponsored outside its original church setting. The crown adopted the discourse eagerly to defend against threats, imaginary and real, to the king and his chief officers. Members of the nobility read poems that vilified deviant speakers and used the courts of law to charge one another as spreaders of rumors and barrators and to prosecute peasant rebels as traitors. By the late fourteenth century, the "sins of the tongue" were thus thoroughly vernacularized and entrenched in courts as well as in literature. The discourse on the "sins of the tongue," as the king and members of the nobility had discovered, was a useful device indeed to silence detractors and underline the authority of its promulgators.

The Popularization of the "Sins of the Tongue"

By the late fourteenth century, the discourse on the "sins of the tongue" had made its way also to the local level, to relationships among peasants and townspeople. Over the next couple of centuries, it was further adapted and popularized, functioning as a tool in support of any group looking to establish, protect, or enhance its own authority. In particular, it was wielded by the rising local elites, men and women whose status did not yet approach that of the gentry but who garnered local-level power and exercised their influence in manorial, borough, and lower-level ecclesiastical courts. The Black Death certainly benefited peasants and townspeople in an economic sense, but it did not benefit all in equal measure. Particularly advantaged were the richer peasant families who were in a position to capitalize on cheap rents and expand their socioeconomic roles at a local level. Along with accumulating land and material goods, social mobility might be achieved by occupying positions of local authority such as those enjoyed by jurors, chamberlains, and bailiffs in manorial or borough courts and *inquisitores* responsible for bringing ex officio cases in church courts. A discourse about appropriate and inappropriate speech served to silence resentful subordinates, distinguish the prosecutors from the insubordinate mob, and add another series of matters to the increasing business (and, hence, authority) of the local courts.[26]

During the fourteenth and fifteenth centuries, ordinances against abusive speech were passed in many manorial and borough courts, and those who insulted court officials were increasingly likely to be prosecuted. In the villages of Wolveston and East Merrington (Durham) in 1379, for instance, ordinances warned tenants against harming others in either words or deeds.[27] Parish and trade guilds passed similar ordinances prohibiting "debate with another," or anyone "who is a rebel of his tongue," fining and even expelling those who transgressed. Ordinances from a guild at Watlington (Norfolk) in the 1380s, for instance, insisted that any conflicts that had arisen between members be settled at fraternity feasts and that conversation at such feasts should be "all of peace and love."[28] Precisely who initiated such ordinances cannot be recovered from the minimalistic court rolls and guild documents, which recorded these new rules as a fait accompli.[29] The power structures of both local courts and guilds, however, would suggest that ordinances were unlikely to be passed without the support of local leaders. Clearly, a generalized verbal propriety was becoming increasingly important.

Just like royal courts, local courts and guilds also identified and punished specific types of illicit speech. Local courts expanded further the category of barratry, and the term "common barrator," with its implications of a threat to the "common peace," entered popular parlance. Similarly, several guilds specifically prohibited barratry in order both to protect their reputations and to limit their liability in supporting members who pursued court cases. A London guild, for instance, set out that "if any brother or sister, . . . become of evil fame or of evil name, as thief, or common barrator, or common questmonger . . . that at once he be put out of the fraternity and nevermore come therein in no manner." Similarly, the Guild of the Lord's Prayer of York included in its rules in 1389 that any brother who was "forward in getting into lawsuit or quarrel, or in upholding any wrongful cause whatever" in the expectation of help from his brethren risked losing all guild support.[30]

Surviving court cases from early fifteenth-century London also indicate that the meaning of barratry was expanding, both in terms of behavior and in terms of those accused of the crime. No longer an elite offense, barratry was pursued and punished at all social levels. A secular court of 1421, for instance, described John Scarle, parson of St. Leonard's in Fasterlane, as a barrator, a scold, and a common ribald of his tongue. Among Scarle's many verbal offenses, according to the court record, was his habit of revealing the confessions of his female parishioners if they did not agree to commit adultery with him. The following year, John Kempe, a carter, was presented as a barrator and a scold, and in 1423 Lambo the Boatman was accused of being a chider, a barrator with his neighbors, and a rebel against the king's officers.[31] As tradesmen, Kempe and Lambo were of inferior social status to Scarle, the parson. Their prosecution demonstrates that, by the early fifteenth century, the label of barrator was applied at a range of social levels in a range of situations.[32] The prosecutions of Scarle, Kempe, and Lambo—each charged with multiple verbal offenses—also suggest that the meaning of barratry was no longer confined to litigiousness. Rather, it implied a more general verbal disorder.

Overlapping with barratry in the local courts was the crime of abusing community officials and institutions, which was increasingly prosecuted in both manors and boroughs after the plague. Anne DeWindt and J. A. Raftis, in their studies of Ramsey and Warboys (both in Huntingdonshire) respectively, both noted an increase in charges of rebelliousness after the Black Death. In Ramsey, at least, this continued into the early fifteenth century. In 1429 and again in 1430, the town passed ordinances against such rebelliousness toward the constables, under the steep penalty of 6s. 8d.[33] The types of behavior considered rebellious were various. A manorial official in the village of Halton (Cheshire) objected, for example, when two local men allegedly called him a thief as he collected rents for the lord in 1357.[34] In nearby Middlewich in 1361, William, son of Thomas Luycesonne, was presented for having obstructed and abused the bailiff as he carried out his duties. In the following year, the same court heard three similar cases involving abuse of the bailiff, and fined another man 12d. for lying in court.[35] In other jurisdictions, such as Walworth (Surrey) in 1369, individuals were described as rebels against the constables of the local lord.[36] The hierarchy of governance was sometimes reflected in fines for insulting or rebellious behavior: those who abused the common sergeant in Beverley (Yorkshire) in 1405 were liable for a fine of 3s. 4d., those who abused the town clerk were fined 6s. 8d., whereas those who abused one of the twelve keepers of the town might face a fine of 40s.[37] Like the Germanic system of *wergild*, whereby fines varied according to the status of victims of violence, so too the varying fines for abusing officials in Beverley underscored their status.

Disrespectful and rebellious behavior was often described in the context of the courtroom itself: individuals were charged with contempt of court or were punished for gossiping or creating disturbances during court sessions. Between 1368 and 1370 alone, the court of Methwold (Norfolk) heard fifteen charges of gossiping (*garulandi*), creating disruptions (*tumultum faciendi*), abusing others (*maledicendi*), and murmuring (*murmerandi*), a word with connotations of gossip and rumor spreading, all during court sessions.[38] In some cases of inappropriate courtroom speech, the precipitating event can be presumed from context. Nicholas Colleson of Crowle was fined 12d. in 1381 because he apparently spoke evil about (*maledixit*) his neighbors and the lord, immediately after they elected him to the position of reeve.[39] Defendants who disagreed with jurors' verdicts also had to be especially careful about how they vented their reactions: otherwise, like John de Konynghal of Methwold in 1382 or John Webster of Ramsey in 1422, they might find themselves facing additional charges for claiming that the jurors were false (which in this context meant that the jurors were liars).[40]

Those who muttered in the courtroom had much in common with those who gossiped during church services (discussed further in Chapter 4). Medieval people were required to attend church on Sundays and certain feast days, and ecclesiastical court presentments of those who skipped services tell us that this obligation was sometimes resisted. A slightly subtler means of resistance involved showing up but chattering throughout the church service. Priests employed sermons and exempla to warn people about the spiritual consequences of inattention. As the author of a late medieval poem explained, dire fates could befall both the individual sinner and the world as a whole if mass were to be neglected. Through their neglect, the parishioners might anger a vengeful God, with the result that "all this world might fare the worse."[41] Churchwardens and parish notables tried also to enforce this message by sponsoring wall paintings depicting gossiping women overshadowed by a demon (as discussed in more detail in Chapter 2). Persistent chatterers, however, were reported to lower-level ecclesiastical courts, by priests and local elites serving as *inquisitores*, and found themselves hauled before archdeacons, deans, and bishops. The message was clear: in the public setting of the church or the court, one was expected to be silent and subordinate, and those who were disruptive could expect to be punished.[42]

Offenses involving disrespectful and disruptive speech increased markedly during the postplague decades. Certainly such offenses occurred in earlier and later periods—in 1294, for instance, a Ramsey man accused of forestalling was deemed in contempt of court for saying "outrageous things" to the jurors—but the last decades of the fourteenth and first decades of the fifteenth centuries seem to have been a period of particular hostility *toward* local officials, particular sensitivity *by* local officials, or both.[43] It is tempting to read these cases, especially those in the secular court setting, as indicative of an enhanced resistance both to the authority of local elites and to the authority of manorial officials working on behalf of landowners. Yet if murmuring and abuse of officials does indeed indicate that postplague peasants and townspeople thought less of local elites, that feeling was reciprocal. Changes were taking place in the ways in which crimes were brought to the attention of the courts, and the net result was to disempower the voices of ordinary people and vest more authority with bailiffs, constables, *inquisitores* and presentment juries. Emboldened by the discourse on the "sins of the tongue," local officials were more conscious of their own authority and of the need for appropriate, contained, and respectful speech.

One manifestation of this change was the declining use of the hue and cry. If someone made an illegal attack on another's property or person in late medieval England, the local courts could be used to seek retribution in one of several ways. One option was to bring a private suit against the offender. This would give the victim the satisfaction of seeing the assailant dragged into court, but it would cost money: courts charged a small fee for dispensing justice, and those most likely to bring private suits were people from wealthier and more established families.[44] A second option for bringing crimes to the court's attention was by convincing local jurors or constables—again, members of the wealthier and more established families—that the matter was worthy of community concern. The mechanism of the hue and cry, however, offered a third, more direct way of bringing a case to the court's attention, a means of short-circuiting the justice system that required neither money nor political clout. When someone saw an offense being committed, he or she was expected to shout out to those nearby, rousing them to pursue the offender. Anyone within earshot who did not respond to the hue and cry could be—and sometimes was—punished in the local court.[45] But local courts also considered the legitimacy of each hue raised: if it was decided that the hue was justified, the person on whom it was raised paid an extra fine, in addition to that levied for his or her crime. If the hue was deemed unjust, however, the court punished the hue-raiser. Because the court had to judge every hue raised, the hue represented a situation in which each person who was able to speak—whether a woman, a man, or a child, whether of high or low status—had the potential to muster others in pursuit of an alleged offender. True, the court might take the hue-caller's wealth and status into account when judging the hue, but the matter would get into the court nonetheless. Hues and cries were considered in manor courts from as far back as court records stretch—and the earliest substantial collections of surviving manorial court records come from the late thirteenth century.[46]

Hue-raising as a means of communal policing, however, declined in popularity throughout England from the mid-fourteenth century onward. Hues and cries, both just and unjust, were particularly frequent between the famine of the 1310s to 1320s and the immediate aftermath of the Black Death of 1348–49. In most places, they declined during the second half of the fourteenth century and began to fade away altogether during the early 1400s. Clare Burgus (Suffolk) provides a case in point: as Figure 1 shows, the courts of Clare heard an average of 14.1 hue cases

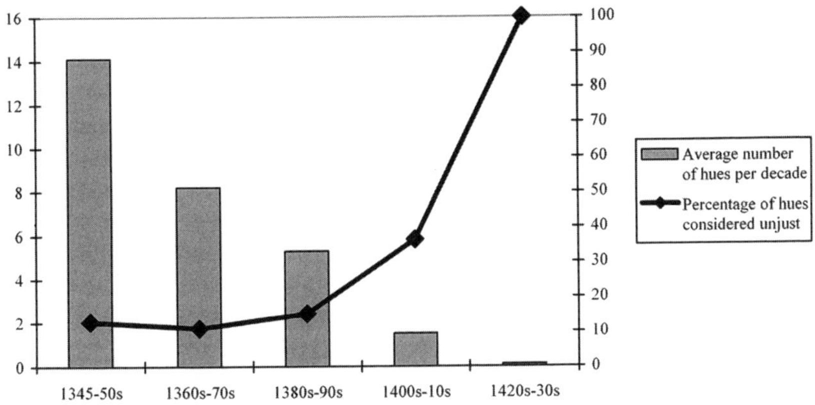

Figure 1. Presentments of the Hue and Cry in Clare Burgus, 1345–1439. Hues were typically considered in the annual leet court in April or May, although the business of the leet (including hue presentments) sometimes carried over into the subsequent regular court. Data is included only for years with complete, legible records—hue presentments in courts that are only partially legible are not included. Years for which complete, legible records survive are 1345–46, 1348, 1351–53, 1356–59, 1361–68, 1371–72, 1374–75, 1377, 1380, 1382, 1388–89, 1390, 1399, 1400–1401, 1404–5, 1407, 1412–13, 1417, 1420, 1422–23, 1425, 1430–32, 1437–39. TNA: PRO SC 2 203/45–70.

every year between 1345 and 1359. This average dropped markedly over the next several decades until, in the early 1400s, hues were seldom considered by the court. The last case recorded in surviving records comes from 1420.

Sherri Olson has noted similar patterns in the villages of Upwood and Ellington (Huntingdonshire), where the average number of hue citations per court roll increased from the 1280s to the 1350s, but dropped off thereafter, with "an ambiguous and uneven withering away" in the early fifteenth century.[47] Although the occasional hue can be found as late as the 1470s, the general pattern was that hues as a means of community control were phased out by the early fifteenth century.[48] In part, this decline may have been a function of a changing community dynamic. After the Black Death, peasants were able—legally or illegally—to exercise much greater freedom of movement, since their labor was in high demand. In an age of increased mobility, people were less likely to know their neighbors and perhaps less likely to pursue a hue called by someone they did not know or trust. Nonetheless, hues called by "strangers" were in fact several times pursued and upheld as just by the court of Clare. Between 1345 and 1390, strangers who had been attacked by local people called at least nine hues, and in each case the hue was deemed justified.[49] While whole villages or towns were sometimes amerced for their failure to pursue hues, surviving records from Clare suggest no such dereliction of the responsibility for pursuit. The reasons that hues were called—usually in instances of assault or theft—remained pressing. In Clare, 90 percent of all hues deemed just resulted from physical assaults, either on the hue-raiser or on someone else. Yet assaults and thefts were still prosecuted by the courts after the decline of the hue. Instead of relying on the old system, whereby everyone had the power to summon their fellows, fifteenth-century cases of assault and theft were increasingly introduced into court by the bailiffs, constables, and jurors.

Indeed, by the last few decades of hue presentments, hues seem to have been considered more of a *disruptive* than a constructive force in the local community. As Figure 1 shows, the percentage of hues deemed unjust rose in later decades, suggesting a shift in the ways in which they were viewed by the court. By the last decades of the fourteenth century, in other words, unjust or annoying hues were perhaps more likely to attract the court's attention. Some individuals even found themselves prosecuted for raising the hue "on everyone" or for being "common hue-raisers," and were fined for disturbing (rather than promoting) the king's peace. In Chedzoy (Somerset) in 1372, for instance, Alice, wife of Richard Raules, was presented as a "common hue-raiser and disturber of the peace of the lord King and of her neighbors." Alice and her husband were jointly charged the heavy fine of 40d. Alice's offense was constructed not as a specific behavior, but as an identity, an ongoing part of her personality, that had negative consequences for the people of Chedzoy.[50] By raising hues, Alice may also have been seen as usurping a role that local elites preferred to regard as their own responsibility.

Local courts were not, however, the only arena for dealing with people who usurped the power to label others. By the late fourteenth century, cases of defamation were largely the preserve of the church courts, and the same members of the local elite who cited the bad behavior of others in manorial and borough courts also presented ex officio cases of defamation before ecclesiastical venues.[51] The church's jurisdiction over defamation was something of an anomaly. Although minor defamation cases (cases among ordinary people, rather than those involving the king or his magnates) were the business of local courts until the early fourteenth century, they were increasingly taken over by church courts thereafter.[52] Defamation remained an ecclesiastical matter until the late fifteenth century when, as noted above, the royal courts began to claim jurisdictional rights over defamation too.[53] Defamation cases heard in church courts were slowly confined to slurs about spiritual offenses, especially sexual transgressions. Since defamation about sexual misconduct accounted for a large proportion of cases anyway, this meant no great loss of business, and the ecclesiastical courts continued to do a lively trade in the regulation of speech, even beyond the Reformation.[54] The patchy survival of church court records, combined with a complicated and idiosyncratic system of jurisdictional responsibilities, makes it difficult to determine how many cases church courts typically judged in a given year. By the fifteenth century, however, it was more than a mere few: in his work on gossip networks and defamation regarding illicit sex, L. R. Poos identified 138 parties in defamation cases heard by the Deanery of Wisbech court in the Diocese of Ely between 1460 and 1479, 53 from the prior and convent of Durham peculiars between 1436–56 and 1487–98, and 103 from the Middlesex and Barking deaneries of the commissary court of London in 1496–97.[55] While the royal courts of the fourteenth and early fifteenth centuries confined themselves to matters of defamation involving the nobility, the speech of ordinary people was thus subject to scrutiny in the church courts.

By the fifteenth century, therefore, the discourse on the "sins of the tongue" was not only promulgated by the church and the nobility but had also entrenched itself firmly in local courts, both secular and ecclesiastical. Barrators and those who mouthed off at officials were more likely to be censured for their insubordinate speech, and those who muttered during court sessions or gossiped in church were more likely to find themselves in trouble for their disrespectful words. In addition, women who engaged in loud public arguments were liable to be charged as scolds, as Chapter 3 will explain. Yet at the same time, those who employed traditional means of voicing grievances, such as raising hues, were less likely to be heard. Why did the discourse on the "sins of the tongue" become popular at local levels in the fourteenth and fifteenth centuries? It was by no means inevitable that the discourse on verbal sins initiated in the thirteenth century would cross over from Latin to the vernacular, from elite to local. Indeed, not every ecclesiastical discourse was taken up with such enthusiasm at local, popular levels. As Marjorie McIntosh has shown, jurors in local courts were selective in their application of discourses on sin and crime, choosing those which seemed most applicable to the local setting,[56] and thirteenth-century sermon manuals and exempla collections were bristling with vices and virtues that were not translated into crimes punishable by local, secular courts. The discourse on the "sins of the tongue" succeeded in becoming especially popular, I suggest, precisely because it resonated with a particular group of people in a particular way and at a particular time. For those who were able to capitalize on the economic changes wrought by the Black Death and use local governance as a springboard to higher social status, the discourse on the "sins of the tongue" proved very useful indeed.

Common Associations among "Sins of the Tongue"

While each of the various types of verbal offense discussed above was a crime or sin with its own evolution and history, it was also an element in a broader continuum of anxiety about subversive speech. Irritation at gossip at the back of the courtroom or church, for instance, went beyond a paternalistic concern that someone might miss hearing important wisdom, and fear of treason was about more than political order. Each was concurrently part of a wider discourse about order and control, a discourse that centered on the dangerous potential of spoken words. The discourse of dangerous speech shaped each of these offenses at the same time that it was shaped by them. Overlapping and messy boundaries between defamation and treason or between barratry and abuse of officials demonstrate that distinctions among various verbal sins were not always clear or important to contemporaries. Rather, the discourse of dangerous speech—speech that threatened authority and order—was a phenomenon in and of itself.

At the heart of constructions of "sins of the tongue" in late medieval England was a concern to protect and reinscribe hierarchy. A late medieval verse perhaps best sums up the ways in which constructions of "sins of the tongue" interacted with rank:

If you chide your subject [social inferior]
It is great villainy [shame] to you;
With your fellow if you chide,
Dissension you shall make that time;
And if you chide your sovereign [social superior]
Men may say you are mad, [for] certain.[57]

In other words, any kind of angry speech was wrong, but speech directed at a social superior was not only wrong but also crazy, because it would be punished most severely. Integral to the construction of "sins of the tongue" was the silencing of subordinates and the reinscription of hierarchies.

In addition to protecting and emphasizing authority, the discourse of dangerous speech linked various "sins of the tongue" by means of common metaphors and associations. Following the Black Death, it is perhaps unsurprising that metaphors of disease and contagion were common among constructions of dangerous speech. The spread of the Black Death itself acted as a powerful metaphor for the transmission of evil and dangerous ideas among individuals.[58] In examining constructions of twelfth-century heresies, R. I. Moore drew attention to images of heretical ideas as infectious, poisonous, and contaminating. The image of disease, Moore suggested, provided a consistent and comprehensive model for understanding the spread of heretical ideas.[59] But metaphors of disease must have had even greater resonance in the late fourteenth and early fifteenth centuries and beyond. Survivors of the mid-fourteenth century Black Death and its repeated recurrences would likely have shuddered at anything associated with contagion or pestilence. "Disease, war, sorrow and debate," ran the refrain of a fifteenth-century poem, often stemmed from the same source—the "venomous tongue."[60] Associations between speech crime and disease persisted throughout the late Middle Ages. A sixteenth-century sermon against discord, for instance, advised that "contention, brawling and chiding" were vices most "pernicious and pestilent to common peace and quietness" and that because "a railing tongue is a pestilence so full of contagion," one should avoid eating or drinking with people so infected.[61] To a vulnerable population, the association with contagion must have made deviant speech seem even more dangerous.

A second metaphor common to many "sins of the tongue" involved excessive eating and drinking. Marjorie McIntosh has suggested that court presentments associated with alehouses, taverns, and inns increased in frequency during the fifteenth century.[62] Taverns were increasingly regarded as places that fostered prostitution and the playing of illegal games. Even in the fourteenth century, drunken peasants who disturbed their neighbors, like John Webbe of Pleshey (Essex) in 1374, might occasionally find themselves hauled up before local courts.[63] In literature, the tavern and the unruly activities it encouraged served as a topos for elite condemnations of peasant activity. Taverns, Ralph Hanna has argued, were imagined in the fifteenth century as sites of overindulgence and lack of control in both speech and behavior.[64] A wall painting at Broughton (Buckinghamshire) depicting swearing men includes in it an apparently unrelated scene of two men seated over some kind of board game (see Figure 9). The game seems to have led to tension between them, for one man is striking the other with his sword. The inclusion of this scene has led some scholars to suggest that the main subject of the painting—swearing—should be imagined as taking place in the setting of a tavern.

Overindulgence in food could excite similar concerns. A late medieval verse spuriously attributed to Pope Gregory the Great demonstrated the association:

Large Table and plenteous[ness]
Makes men of jangling surfeitous;
When the body filled-up is,
The tongue is ready to speak amiss.[65]

Guild legislators made similar connections between excessive feasting and problematic speech, setting out penalties for those who made noise during feast-times.[66] Following the Black Death, the notion of overindulgence tapped into additional resentment, as peasants were able to afford better food, in larger quantities, than they had earlier, thus usurping privileges previously reserved for the nobility. As Christopher Dyer has noted, postplague peasants ate more meat and drank more ale than their preplague ancestors, whose diets had been based primarily around bread and pottage. After the plague, peasants still ate bread in large quantities, but the bread was more likely to be made from wheat, and was hence more palatable than bread made from the variety of cheaper grains common before the plague.[67] Their contemporaries were quick to notice this improvement in diet. Langland, for instance, grumbled that peasants were so greedy and finicky that only the finest kinds of bread, ale, and meat were acceptable to them.[68] Peasant indulgence in excessive food and drink demonstrated dramatically to landowners that their former economic power over the peasantry was reduced, and it was perhaps little wonder, then, that fourteenth- and fifteenth-century texts harped on the theme of excess and advised temperance in both food and drink and in speech.

Associations with disease and contagion and with excessive, boundary-spilling eating and drinking served to link "sins of the tongue" into a common discourse about the perils of unruly speech and the need for hierarchical order. While this discourse was initiated in thirteenth- and fourteenth-century pastoral manuals and employed strategically by the English crown and members of the nobility, it reached its fullest vernacular elaboration at a local level only after the serious social and economic upheavals that accompanied the Black Death of 1348–49. Once the discourse was well established, however, it could be adopted and adapted by any individual or group seeking to assert authority over another. Increasingly, as Chapters 2 and 3 will demonstrate, it was associated with the silencing of women.

Chapter 2

The Sins of Women's Tongues in Literature and Art

Speech in general attracted concern in late medieval England, but women's speech was especially problematic. For one thing, women were considered particularly garrulous. "Where women are," claimed a fifteenth-century playwright, "are many words."[1] A similar phrase was reiterated in sixteenth-century aphorisms: the 1542 poem *The School House of Women* commented that "where [there] be women, are many words," and the phrase "Many women many words" was already cited as an "old proverb" in a book of 1600.[2] During the late Middle Ages, the discourse on the "sins of the tongue" was increasingly gendered, with women especially likely to be identified in literature, in art, and in court prosecutions as sinners. This chapter focuses on literary and artistic representations of women's voices, arguing that these both contributed to and reflected a widespread cultural devaluation of late medieval female speech.

Literature and art did not operate in a vacuum, though. To help understand the ongoing and mutually reinforcing connection between the literary and legal contexts, let us try for a moment to view medieval women and men through the eyes of jurors from the town of Middlewich (Cheshire) in the early fifteenth century. Men such as Richard Hycokson and Henry le Vernon, to name just a couple, presented scolds and other miscreants before the borough court. But how did they know what scolding looked like or how scolds behaved? What cultural baggage and expectations did these men, drawn from the wealthier and more established families and described as "yeomen," bring with them to court? Some knowledge and expectations certainly came from the courts themselves. Middlewich courts had heard scolding cases since the 1360s, if not earlier. For as long as they had attended court—perhaps as boys accompanying their fathers, perhaps as young men paying fines for misdemeanors or fees for boiling salt—Middlewich men had watched the prosecution of alleged scolds and had probably registered somewhere that scolding voices were almost always women's voices. Each time a woman was presented in court as a scold, she helped to underline the connection in the minds of local people between her sex and her unruly voice. But other cultural knowledge was produced outside of the courtroom: in literature and art, in sermons, in songs, in sayings and aphorisms, jokes, and conversations. Most has doubtless been lost. In modern culture, for instance, we all know the trope that women are more inclined to gossip and chatter. The stereotype is reiterated and survives in cultural artifacts such as movies, TV shows, and books. Yet most of us probably encountered the cultural connection in situations of which there are no traces—comments made by relatives, friends, or schoolteachers, for instance, about gossiping girls as "chatty Cathys" or about garrulous men as "aunties" or "old women." While acknowledging our loss of such sources for the Middle Ages, we can, nonetheless, find *some* artifacts of cultural knowledge in the images and the literature of everyday medieval life: the ballads people repeated, the plays they watched, the books that people read (or heard read aloud), the sermons they sat through, and the wall paintings and stone and wood carvings that surrounded them in church.

Stereotypes of women's speech as irritating, disruptive, and dangerous have been present in Western culture for at least two millennia. The Greeks and Romans were certainly familiar with the association, and early Christian moralists highlighted women's propensity to gossip in setting down rules for new congregations. The apostle Paul's first letter to Timothy, for example, ordered women to "learn in silence with all submissiveness" and permitted "no woman to teach or to have authority over men; she is to keep silent." Furthermore, young widows should not be a part of the church, Paul suggested, because "they learn to be idlers, gadding about from house to house, and not only idlers but gossips and busybodies, saying what they should not."[3] As a well-worn trope in misogynist texts, depictions of chattering and nagging women appeared all over Europe, both before the Middle Ages and well beyond. But the stereotype was not a consistent one: the vehemence with which female speech was condemned varied over time. The late Middle Ages were a period in which women's words were condemned in a particularly forceful way.

This chapter seeks not to exhaust every link between women and speech in late medieval art and literature but rather to demonstrate the wide-ranging and pervasive nature of cultural connections between women and spoken words.[4] These can be seen especially in two contexts: prescriptive literature and art, and literature and art designed for popular amusement. Both in prescriptive material directed *at* women and men and in representations *of* fictional female characters, women and illicit speech were emphatically connected.

Women's Voices in Prescriptive Literature and Art

Warnings about the dangers of evil speech were certainly not confined to female audiences: men too were admonished to avoid the "sins of the tongue." But women were cautioned about speech both more often and more vehemently. Moreover, advice about speech doled out to men very often warned them less about limiting their own speech than about being careful of the speech of others. Men, in other words, were constructed primarily as listeners and decision makers who ought to be discriminating about whose speech they heard. Women, however, were constructed more often as potentially disruptive speakers, who ought to limit both the quantity and tone of their words.

We do not know exactly how the Middlewich jurors, those who brought scolding cases to court, encountered such literary and artistic representations of women's speech. Many served as witnesses to deeds of land sales, as town chamberlains, or as officials in charge of salt boiling, tasks which may have required some degree of literacy. If some of the jurors were indeed literate, or if members of their households made a practice of reading books aloud, they might have come across the burgeoning devotional and advice literature aimed at the laity. Proliferating during the fourteenth and fifteenth centuries, devotional literature provided a point of connection between the Latinate clerical manuals on sin and the lives of ordinary people. Even wealthier townsmen like the Middlewich jurors, however, could afford no more than one or two devotional works: still copied out by hand, books were expensive. To maximize readership, they were often passed from hand to hand. Perhaps Margaret, wife of Richard Hycokson, exchanged books with Matilda le Vernon, wife of Henry, or with other members of the town elite? Or maybe Richard's mother spent her last years reading conduct books and sharing their contents with her extended family? If she did, she would have found that warnings about the dangers of speech proved an important concern in devotional literature.[5] Guillaume Peyraut's thirteenth-century treatise on the virtues and vices, for example, which included discussion of more than twenty categories of the "sins of the tongue," was translated into Middle English and incorporated into manuscripts such as the fifteenth-century "Book for a Simple and Devout Woman." Richard Hycokson and his family might also have been familiar with the *Ancrene Riwle*, a guide initially compiled in the thirteenth century for anchoresses. Much copied and adapted for all audiences, especially during the fourteenth and fifteenth centuries, the *Ancrene Riwle* expressed considerable concern about women's speech. Holy women, according to the author, should talk as little as possible, even in the company of priests. A chattering woman, he said, is like someone who grinds chaff in preference to grinding wheat: "[H]er two jaws are the two grindstones, and her tongue is the clapper." In particular, anchoresses should be sure that they do not presume to give advice to men: their advice is fit only for women. Not only should anchoresses ensure that they refrain from unnecessary or evil speech, but they ought also to refrain from hearing female gossip. "It is said of anchoresses," the author of the *Ancrene Riwle* complained, "that almost every one of them has some old woman to feed her ears, a gossip who purveys to her all the talk of the countryside, a magpie as it were, that chatters to her about all she has seen and heard . . ." Both the speaking and the hearing of "venomous, foul, and idle" speech thus posed a threat to the soul, and it was a threat to which women seemed especially vulnerable.[6]

If the families of Middlewich jurors did not have access to full-length devotional treatises, they may well have possessed commonplace books in which they copied out passages and poems that they found particularly meaningful. Discussions of speech often appeared in shorter texts that dispensed advice about marriage, especially advice directed toward husbands. The "Proverbs of Alfred," for example, dating from the mid-twelfth century but copied and circulated throughout the late Middle Ages, warned men to refrain from telling wives their secrets. Women, the proverbs warned, were unable to control their tongues, even if they wanted to.[7] Husbands were often cautioned elsewhere, too, to be skeptical about the tales that women told them, particularly tales concerning servants. Instead of responding immediately to their wives' words, men were advised to ascertain the facts for themselves, in order to avoid trouble.[8] Women's mouths could cause serious trouble for men, cautioned a fourteenth-century English translation of an earlier Latin text, since "no man has more woe, than he that has an evil wife, crying and jangling, chiding and scolding."[9] Correspondingly, women who wanted to retain their husbands' love were told to "hold your tongue still," and answer their husbands meekly, not as shrews.[10] Advice about marriage, a common site for reflection on relationships between the sexes, thus characteristically portrayed women as speaking in troublesome ways, both to their spouses and to others, and posed this troublesome speech as a potential problem for men.

Other prescriptive literature is revealing in the differences between advice given to men and that given to women. One such poem of fourteenth-century origin addressed daughters and sons in parallel verses, and the advice pertaining to speech is indicative of medieval views. The poet forbade women the use of a "sharp tongue, nor mouth licorous [gluttonous or self-indulgent]" while warning men to beware of "flatterers," "swearers, extortioners and ragers." While "maidens" were also encouraged in a later verse to "beware bad counsel and idleness," the poem constructed men's and women's primary relationships to speech in quite different ways: women mostly needed to be warned against speaking in troublesome ways; men mostly needed to be warned against listening to troublesome speech.[11]

Different constructions of speech similarly underlie advice to women and men in two poems sometimes regarded as companion pieces. Despite the fact that they were probably composed several decades apart, the fourteenth-century "How the Good Wife Taught Her Daughter" and the early fifteenth-century "How the Wise Man Taught His Son" both take the form of a parent proffering advice to a child. Both poems include advice about appropriate and inappropriate speech, but daughters are warned about it more often and more emphatically. Marjorie McIntosh has argued that, while the fictional Good Wife told her daughter to be "of good tongue," the Wise Man went further in advising his son that "Your own tongue may be your foe," and that words uttered on any one day might return to trouble him in the future.[12] While McIntosh was correct in pointing out that the texts each contain these lines, my reading of the emphases on speech in the two poems is somewhat different. For, if one examines *all* the references to speech in the Good Wife and Wise Man poems, one finds that the Good Wife text emphasizes proper speech both more frequently and in more contexts than its companion piece:

TABLE 1. ADVICE TO DAUGHTERS AND SONS

How the Good Wife Taught Her Daughter	*How the Wise Man Taught His Son*
"When you sit in the church, over your beads bend; Make you no jangling with gossip or with friend. Laugh you to scorn neither old body nor young, But be of fair bearing and of good tongue."	"And son, wherever you go, be not too talkative in any way, Your own tongue may be your foe; Therefore beware what you say, Where, and to whom, by any way, Take good heed if you do say ought, For you might say a word today That 7 years after may be regretted."
"Meekly . . . answer [your husband] and not as an atterling [shrew], So you may slake his mood, and be his dear darling. A fair word and a meek Does anger slake, My dear child."	"Neither false witness [shall] you any bear On no man's matter, all nor part; You were better to be deaf and dumb Than falsely to go upon a quest."
"Fair of speech shall you be, glad and of mild mood, True in word and in deed, and in conscience good."	"And if you shall not your wife displease, Neither call her by no villainous name; And if you do, you are not wise, To call her foul it is your shame; If you your own wife will defame,

"Fare not as a gig [giggling girl], for
anything that may betide.
Laugh you not too loud nor yawn you
not too wide."

"Have not too many words, from
swearing keep aloof,
For all such manners come to an evil
proof.
For he that catches to him an evil
name,
It is to him a foul fame,
My dear child."

"Acquaint you not with each man that
goes by the street,
Though any man speak to you, swiftly
you him greet."

"And if your neighbor's wife has on
rich attire,
Therefore mock not, nor let scorn
burn you as a fire."

"And if your children be rebel[lious]
and will not bow them low,
If any of them misdo, neither curse
them nor blow [scold;]
But take a smart rod and beat them in
a row,
Till they cry mercy and their guilt well
know."

No wonder that another do so,
But soft and fair a man may tame
Both hart and hind, buck and doe."

"And boast not much, it is but waste;
By boasting, men may know fools."

["But I warn you on the other side,
If your wife comes with a complaint
About man or child at any tide,
Be not too hasty to fight and chide,
And do not avenge until you know the
truth,
For in anger you might commit a rash
act
That afterward you both should rue."]

Sources: *The Babees' Book, etc.*, ed. Furnivall, 36–47, 48–53. The translation of "How the Good Wife Taught Her Daughter" used here comes primarily from Edith Rickert's edition of *The Babees' Book: Medieval Manners for the Young* (New York: Cooper Square Publishers, 1966), 31–42, with only minimal changes by me; the translation of "How the Wise Man Taught His Son" is my own.

While sons were warned against spreading tales, bearing false witness, boasting, and calling their wives bad names, daughters were advised against gossiping in church, talking to men on the street, talking shrewishly to their husbands, laughing too loudly and keeping their mouths open, mocking or scorning others, and swearing. Daughters were also cautioned against cursing or scolding their children; beating them was thought more effective. Women's speech, according to these poems, was policed in a wider range of situations. In particular, it was restricted in the public arena—the church and the street—in a way that men's speech was not. Indeed, the public nature of men's speech is suggested by the expectation that they might be drawn into lawsuits and tempted to bear false witness on behalf of their friends. But perhaps the most telling comment on women's speech is in the Wise Man's advice to doubt the speech of women and to find out the truth of a wife's claims before rushing to defend her: women's words were, after all, always open to doubt. A comparison of all references to speech in both poems thus suggests that, while both sexes were certainly cautioned about the evils of improper speech, women were warned both more often and in more contexts by the Good Wife than were men by the Wise Man.[13]

If Middlewich jurors did not encounter ideas about gender and speech in advice literature, they almost certainly heard about them in church. Sermons emphasized women's association with problematic speech, admonishing women to refrain from "ever jangling as a magpie, or a jay."[14] Indeed, even the most traditional binary in medieval representations of women—that of Eve versus Mary—lent itself to a moral lesson about speech. For example, when William Lichfield, an early fifteenth-century preacher at All Hallows the Great in London, sought to illustrate the importance of appropriate speech, he told his parishioners:

> Eve, our oldest mother in paradise, held long talks with the adder, and told him what God had said to her and to her husband about eating the apple; and by her talking, the fiend understood her feebleness and her unstableness, and found a way to bring her to confusion. Our Lady Saint Mary did otherwise. She told the angel no tale, but asked him discretely things she did not know herself. Follow therefore Our Lady in discrete speaking and hearing, and not cackling Eve who both spoke and heard unwisely.[15]

Cackling Eve's propensity to speech was thus cited as a crucial element in humanity's fall from paradise. This cause of expulsion from the Garden of Eden was also referenced (albeit in a more jocular context) by the Nun's Priest in the *Canterbury Tales*:

> Women's counsel brought us first to woe
> And made Adam from paradise to go[16]

Mary, on the other hand, was applauded for her taciturnity. Throughout the late Middle Ages, anchoresses, nuns, and both laywomen and laymen were reminded repeatedly that Mary's speech was recorded in the Bible on only four occasions and on each occasion she spoke "words of great discretion and great might."[17]

At the same time that both women and men were encouraged to emulate the reserve of Mary, the clergy feared that mortal women were much more prone to follow the example of Eve. John Tuchet, parson of Middlewich church in the early fifteenth century, probably warned his parishioners not only about the dangers of women's speech in general, but also about women's propensity to the more specific crime of gossiping during church services. If he did indeed express concerns about women's church-time chatter, he would likely have reinforced these with a much-repeated sermon exemplum about the fate of those who gossiped in church. This story told of a cleric who unexpectedly burst out laughing in the middle of a reading in church. When questioned after the service, the cleric explained what he had seen: behind two chattering women lurked a demon (sometimes named as Tutivillus), writing every word they said on a piece of parchment.[18] These women were so loquacious, however, that the demon soon ran out of space on his scroll. In order to stretch the parchment, he tugged it with his teeth. But in doing so he knocked his head against the wall, prompting the cleric's mirth. In some versions of the tale the noise of the demon's head hitting the wall was heard throughout the church, and later examination found black demon-blood in the place that his head had struck. The women, confronted after the service, were sometimes said to have wept tears of repentance, causing the words on the scroll to be erased. Variations on this exemplum appear from the twelfth century onward, from as far afield as Iceland, Sweden and Estonia. Although it did not originate in late medieval England, the story seems to have had significant cultural currency there: among English sermons, plays, and poems of the thirteenth to sixteenth centuries, it appears in more than forty surviving manuscripts.[19] But whereas some aspects of the story were unstable—the cleric might be identified as the young Saint Brice, Saint Martin, Saint Augustine, or left unnamed, the demon might or might not shed blood after stretching his scroll to make more room for their words—one key detail remained the same: whenever the individuals caught chattering were given a gender, they were always female. An early fifteenth-century poem that made reference to this tale demonstrated both an assumption that the tale was widely known and an assumption that talking in church was an especially feminine vice:

Tutivillus, the devil of hell,
He writes their names truly to tell,
    ad missam garulantes [those gossiping at Mass].
Better it were at home forever,
Than there to serve the devil to pay
    sic vana famulantes [as those serving vanities].
These women that sit the church about
They be all of the devil's gang
    diuina impedientes [impeding the divine service].

The poem went on to describe how Tutivillus would draw these chattering women to hell, concluding with a general exhortation to be silent in church and thus win admission to God's inn and the bliss of heaven.[20] The Tutivillus exemplum illustrates the extent to which excessive and inappropriate speech was identified as a feminine crime. When priests and poets wanted to warn parishioners against chattering in church, they automatically selected women as the transgressors.

As well as listening to sermons and repeating or copying poems, medieval villagers and townspeople also engaged with the Tutivillus story in another, more active, way: by choosing it as a theme to decorate their churches. Literary critics, historians, and art historians have long recognized the connections between the Tutivillus exemplum and representations in church art of a demon hovering behind two talking women. The theme appears in more than a dozen surviving English wall paintings (such as the painting from Peakirk [Northamptonshire] depicted in Figure 2), in a number of small stone carvings on both the interiors and exteriors of parish churches, and on at least seven surviving misericords (such as that of Ely Cathedral in Figure 3).[21] There even survives at Stanford-on-Avon (Northamptonshire) a stained-glass window of the early fourteenth century that shows two gossiping women, with another woman behind them, being tempted by three demons.[22] Artistic representations of Tutivillus survive from the second half of the thirteenth century through the fifteenth century, with a peak in the fourteenth century. They appear throughout England—from Yorkshire to Kent to Somerset.[23] Connections between literary and artistic representations of Tutivillus and the gossiping women have usually been understood in the context of Pope Gregory the Great's characterization of church art in c. 600 as the "book of the illiterate."[24] Gregory and his ecclesiastical successors regarded wall paintings, stone and wood carvings, and stained-glass windows as opportunities for reminding illiterate parishioners about biblical stories and proper religious behavior. Thus depictions of Tutivillus and the gossiping women have been described as "unsubtle moral injunctions,"[25] and "obviously didactic in intention."[26] Scholars have assumed that material representations of the Tutivillus theme functioned primarily to invoke the story as a whole and reinforce messages about paying attention in church.

Yet we might read images of Tutivillus and the women in another way if we pause and think again about the creators of these visual representations of female speech and the messages they might have intended. Representations of Tutivillus and the gossiping women varied slightly according to media, but in each the focus was on the moment of illicit female speech. Wall paintings, such as that of Peakirk, tend to be the most crude and to represent two women, either standing or seated on a rudimentary bench, with a devil hovering above them, putting his hands on their heads or shoulders. Sometimes, as at Colton (Norfolk), ancillary demons perch on each side of the bench. The women's heads are inclined toward each other, and their hands clutch rosary beads or ges-

Figure 2. Wall Painting of Tutivillus and the Gossiping Women from Peakirk (Northamptonshire). Conway Library, Courtauld Institute of Art, United Kingdom.

Figure 3. Misericord of Tutivillus and the Gossiping Women from Ely Cathedral. G.ten, University of Manchester, United Kingdom.

ture toward one another as if explaining their stories. Tutivillus tends to be about the same size as the women, and the supplementary demons are sometimes smaller. On misericords, by contrast, Tutivillus plays the demonic role alone and is larger in size than the chattering women. As Figure 3 demonstrates, he is still positioned above and behind the women but he appears to occupy much more space. The shape of misericords seems to have encouraged carvers to endow the demon with large, outstretched wings or limbs, making his appearance perhaps more threatening than that of the furrier-looking devils of the wall paintings. In the supporting carvings on each side of the central scene, Tutivillus is sometimes depicted alone, writing on his scroll or trying to stretch it. At Ely (Figure 3), we see him doing both.

Despite minor variations between media, the choice to depict the women in the act of transgression seems remarkably consistent. Who made this choice? Surviving evidence suggests that the decision lay less with the clergy than the laity. Wall paintings, in particular, were both commissioned and created by lay parishioners. Parishioners were responsible for the upkeep of the nave in parish churches, and hence for commissioning both stone and wood carvings and wall paintings.[27] While leading parishioners politely sought "the counsel and help" of local priests in the selection of appropriate images for the church, they also saw such images as foci of parochial pride and communal identity.[28] If paintings weren't executed exactly the way they liked them, parish leaders could—and sometimes did—insist on being refunded.[29] The artisans who carved misericords and the painters of church walls also exercised some control over their subject matter. An early thirteenth-century treatise attributed to Adam of Dore, abbot of a Cistercian monastery in Herefordshire, complained about the "criminal presumption of the painters" in choosing designs that were "foolish," "meaningless" and "the faults of excessive levity."[30] The "public art" of the parish church was thus a contested forum, controlled more by parishioners (especially members of the local elite) and by artisans than by the institutional church, and much as Adam of Dore (and his continental counterpart, Bernard of Clairvaux) might fume, they could not overrule the choices of parishioners and artisans.[31] The church at Middlewich contains no medieval wall paintings or carvings and no records of such decorations survive. But they almost certainly existed at some point, and they would have been chosen primarily by artists and by influential parishioners—probably the same men who made up the jury in the borough court and the *inquisitores* in the church court. Men like Richard Hycokson and Henry le Vernon expected to have considerable say over the decoration of their church, which was, after all, at the literal and spiritual center of the town.

The role of the laity in choosing images for church decoration makes the choice of scene more significant. Rather than focus on a scene from the story in which Tutivillus knocks his head, or the women regret their inappropriate speech, artists and influential parishioners chose to represent the demon and the women almost in collaboration, whether the women are aware of it or not. Tutivillus, sometimes wearing an evil and almost-lecherous grin, encircles the gossiping women, putting his arms (or wings) around their shoulders or his hands on their heads, almost as if he is nurturing them in sin. Rather than focus on the moment of divine retribution of the clerical exemplum, in which the women are warned or frightened and Tutivillus is hurt, artistic representations thus linger on the preceding moments, in which the women are still gossiping and neglecting the church service. The didactic message of the exemplum is not forced by carvings, windows, or wall paintings: the scroll is either forgotten or peripheral and the moment of reckoning is postponed. For members of the late medieval laity, images of women's verbal impropriety held more cultural sway than images of women's redemption.

The often-repeated scene of Tutivillus and the gossips thus both reflected and helped constitute a discourse about women's nature and female companionship in late medieval England. A child growing up in the parish of Peakirk in the fourteenth century, for instance, would have viewed the image of the women and the devil from as early as he or she could remember. At some point, that child might also hear the sermon exemplum of Tutivillus, and might learn to link this exemplum with the wall painting. But the child would see the image both before and after hearing the exemplum, and he or she might well have interpreted it in ways other than that intended by the church. For instance, he or she may have regarded it as a celebration of women's friendship. Like contemporary images in which the Virgin Mary and St. Elizabeth share the news of their pregnancies, the Tutivillus paintings depict a close and warm conference between two women. Indeed, the layout of Tutivillus wall paintings and representations of Mary and Elizabeth are often remarkably similar. Might this image have served to empower and pay testament to the value of women's companionship? Or, alternately, might it have underlined women's connection with things demonic and the need for their close supervision? Might it have done both? So far as we know, the Middlewich jurors did not see representations of Tutivillus and the gossips, at least not on a regular basis. The nearest *surviving* painting can be found at Melbourne (Derbyshire), about fifty miles away, although others quite possibly existed in the Cheshire region during the Middle Ages. It is also possible that Middlewich inhabitants saw a misericord from Nantwich (about ten miles to the south) in which a devil tries to force open a woman's mouth. While the Nantwich misericord may or may not have been intended as an invocation of the Tutivillus exemplum, it similarly made the connection between women, the mouth, and the devil in a way that someone like Richard Hycokson or Henry le Vernon could understand.

The sermon exemplum of Tutivillus and the gossiping women sought to regulate the behavior of churchgoers by employing the misogynist device of linking gossip with women. As such it was part of a widespread patriarchal clerical discourse about the disruptive nature of women. But representations of Tutivillus and the gossips in parish churches also reflected another patriarchal discourse: that of peasants, townsfolk, and artisans, especially those who participated in deciding what to paint or carve on church walls. The Middlewich jurors—or those of Peakirk, for that matter—may have little choice but to listen to the sermon exemplum, but they were potentially active participants in the artistic discourse about female company and the devil. No matter the authorship, prescriptive literature and art consistently associated problematic speech with women and constructed female speech as a hazard both for women and for men. In devotional literature, advice poems, sermons, paintings, and wood carvings, women were warned against excessive speech and men were warned that women's words were dangerous and even demonic. It is hard to know how seriously individuals like Richard Hycokson or Henry le Vernon took such messages, but we do know that some medieval men paid close attention and were willing to apply the discourse, when convenient, to their own lives. For example, when Henry Cok of Trottiscliffe and his wife were brought before the bishop of Rochester in 1347 because they were living separately, Henry complained that his wife behaved extremely badly toward him, by means of both her insubordinate speech and other bad deeds. To Henry, a wife who used "contumelious words" provided partial grounds for his adultery and noncohabitation.[32] Just as Eve's speech with the serpent resulted in humanity's fall from paradise, so too the speech of all women threatened to disrupt peace and order in the street, the church, and the home.

Women's Voices in Narrative Art and Literature

The Middlewich jurors encountered the connection between women and troublesome speech not only in prescriptive literature but also in stories, plays, and poems intended for entertainment. The fourteenth and fifteenth centuries saw the development of a stock character who took the form of a loud and gossipy woman. In contrast to monitory texts and images, women's connections with speech were emphasized in fictional literature by archetypal female characters who both enacted evil speech and claimed it as the special preserve of women.

One of the earliest progenitors of the loud woman character was the wife of the biblical Noah. Rebellion by Noah's Wife (never given a first name of her own) was not mentioned in the Bible, but stories about her insubordination appeared in heretical texts as early as the fourth century C.E. While orthodox Christian theologians continued to depict Noah's Wife as virtuous and humble—an Old Testament prototype of Mary—European folk legends and Islamic traditions throughout the Middle Ages associated Noah's Wife with the devil.[33] An eleventh-century illustration, depicting a woman who appears unwilling to board a boat, gives the first hint that the story was known in England.[34] By the thirteenth and fourteenth centuries, her reluctance had shifted to outright rebellion. Noah's Wife, in illustrations from the Ramsey Psalter and Queen Mary's Psalter, is depicted with the devil, who encourages her to stay out of the ark. In Queen Mary's Psalter, she also appears to share Noah's secret (God's charge to him that he build an ark) with the devil, the first hint that her speech was part of her sin.[35] The Middlewich jurors, even the most wealthy, probably never saw manuscripts as richly decorated as Queen Mary's Psalter, but they very likely encountered the character of Noah's Wife in another medium: the English mystery play cycles of the late fourteenth and fifteenth centuries.

The mystery cycles, in which the character of Noah's Wife reached her fullest elaboration, were cycles of plays performed by amateurs from the various occupational guilds on Corpus Christi day in late May or early June.[36] Within each cycle, each guild had the responsibility for a different play. Mystery plays certainly contained an element of the burlesque. All the actors—even those playing female parts—were male, and it seems likely that the plays functioned as a kind of medieval version of talent or variety shows performed by modern service clubs, diverging from the script to lampoon local people or events. The Flood play, often performed by the shipwrights, tells the story of God's instructions to Noah, Noah's building and loading of the ark, and the flood that destroyed all humanity and all animals except those contained on the ark.[37] Four main cycles of English plays survive: York, Towneley (identified as those of the town of Wakefield and often referred to as the Wakefield cycle), Chester, and N-Town (sometimes referred to as the *Ludus Coventriae*). In three of these four—the Towneley, York, and Chester cycles—Noah's Wife disrupts the biblical narrative not only by refusing Noah's order to enter the ark but also by the loudness and insubordination of her refusal.[38] In the Chester play, for instance, she tells Noah to find himself another wife and wishes him evil luck. The Chester Noah's Wife, like her York counterpart, is reluctant to leave her friends and refuses to come on board the ark unless they can come too. But because God's orders were that only Noah, his wife, and their sons and daughters-in-law might survive, Noah sends his sons to drag their mother on board, and her friends are left to drown. We might imagine one of the Middlewich jurors—Richard Hycokson, for example—making the twenty-mile journey to Chester in May or June, perhaps to sell salt or serve in his capacity as county court juror, and taking the opportunity to watch the mystery plays, laughing as he watched a Chester guildsman dressed up in his wife's clothing being hauled onto the ark.

The plays vary in their details, but the basic stock character of Noah's Wife remains the same. The York Noah, for example, begins the play in harmony with his wife, referring to her as a "worthy wife," whereas the Towneley Noah fears his wife's verbosity from the outset.[39] On being instructed by God to build the ark, the Towneley Noah dreads his wife's reaction, warning the audience:

My wife will I ask what she will say,
And I am afraid that we get some fray [uproar]
Between us both,
For she is very teethy [irritable]
For little [cause is] often angry;

If anything wrong be,
Soon she is wroth.[40]

His wife, true to form, is furious on his arrival home and begins abusing him long before he tells her his news about God's instructions. Noah's Wife tells the audience, "[w]e women must be on guard against all bad husbands," and reports that while she supports her husband when he is in trouble, she makes him pay for the privilege. Noah tells his wife to hold her tongue, and the two fall to blows. Noah admits that his wife can "both bite and whine" and laments her "skryke," or shriek.[41] When the flood finally arrives, Noah's Wife in all three cycles initially refuses to enter the newly built ark. The Towneley Noah's Wife changes her mind as the waters draw higher, while the Chester and York Wives are forced on board by their sons. The Towneley Noah's Wife tells the audience that she wishes she were a widow and says to Noah that, like wives in the audience, she would very gladly pay for her husband's funeral. Noah responds by telling the men in the audience that they should chastise their wives' tongues as early as possible. He and his wife brawl again, and are separated only at the begging of their children. In all three cycles, Noah's Wife is either absent or humble for the remainder of the play.

In her interactions with her husband, Noah's Wife personifies the concerns of prescriptive writers who warn of women's excessive and troublesome speech. Her responses to Noah's direct instructions are typically loud and obstreperous. The Towneley Noah's Wife, for instance, wishes her husband were dead, claiming that all women would welcome the opportunity to eat widows' porridge and pay funeral doles for their husbands, while the Chester Wife tells her husband that, because her friends offer her greater support than he does, she would sooner die with them than survive with him. The York Wife, resenting that Noah had not told her about the building of the ark, clouts her husband. Rather than wishing in return for the death of their wives, the Towneley and Chester Noahs lament the failings of wives in general. When the Towneley Noah responds to his wife's statement that all wives wish to be widows, he casts his abuse in the form of the preexisting genre of advice to husbands, recommending that men take control of their wives' speech as soon as possible. Similarly, the Chester Noah, when faced with his wife's insubordination, laments the general ill temper and lack of humility among women. The contrast between husbandly and wifely abuse in the Flood plays is telling: while wives claim to be better off without their husbands, asserting their own independence, husbands focus their aspersions on wives' unruly speech. What is obnoxious about wives, therefore, is less their presence per se (which husbands desire) than their loudness and insubordination. According to the mystery plays, disorderly and insubordinate voices are thus central to the construction of both Noah's Wife and women in general.

Noah's Wife is not only disorderly in her abuse of Noah; she is also disorderly in her attachment to her friends. The York Wife wants to bring her "friends and [her] kinswomen both" onto the ark, and laments that her friends are "over flowing with flood," while the Chester Wife insists that Noah should admit her "gossips" to the ark.[42] The word "gossips," in late medieval England, could mean people attached by the spiritual bond of serving as godparents (hence "god-sibs"), but it also referred to groups of friends (primarily women) who met together to exchange news and conversation. In both the York and Chester plays, the group of friends and relatives that represent Noah's Wife's attachment to the world is implied to be female. (The Towneley Wife does not mention her friends, but instead insists that spinning, the female activity par excellence, is a more compelling occupation than boarding the ark). The "good gossips" even appear as characters in the Chester play, and they sing a song that celebrates their drinking and conversation. A "vessel of wine, good and strong," they sing in some versions of the play, "it will rejoice both heart and tongue."[43] Noah's Wife and her friends are thus forerunners of the women in the popular "gossips' poems" or "alewife poems" of the late fifteenth and sixteenth centuries discussed below; they constitute a community of women separate from the authority of men, a community in which the exchange of words plays a central role. In trying to persuade her husband to allow her friends on board the ark, the Chester Wife tells him:

they loved me full well, by Christ;
unless you will let them in your ark,
row forth, Noah, whether you like or not,
and get yourself a new wife.[44]

Female company is thus depicted as both powerful and dangerous, drawing Noah's Wife away from husbandly (and, by implication, godly) authority. The Chester and York Flood plays both use this device of the community of gossips to underline further the connection between women and disruptive words, and we can infer that this message was not lost on medieval viewers like Richard Hycokson or another of the Middlewich jurors.

As literary scholars have pointed out, the unruly and garrulous Wife of Noah shares many features with the even more disorderly Wife of Bath created by Chaucer in the late fourteenth century.[45] Chaucer's immediate audience was that of the court, but his poems both drew on and contributed to a broader popular culture, and it is not unlikely that a "yeoman" of Cheshire like one of the Middlewich jurors would have some familiarity with his tales. More than any other single character in late medieval English literature, the Wife of Bath both claims verbal disorder as the special preserve of women and enacts that same disorder. In the prologue to her tale, in the tale itself, and in her behavior throughout the telling of the *Canterbury Tales*, the Wife of Bath gossips, boasts, exaggerates, and openly confesses to whining, chattering, revealing secrets, and lying. She describes herself as "of my tongue a true jangleresse [chatterer]" and brags that in arguments with her husbands she could "bite and whine" as well as a horse, even when she knew she was in the wrong.[46] She recounts that she told her fourth husband's secrets to her friends and family since, as she argues in her own tale, women "can hide no counsel."[47] Not only does the Wife of Bath perform these verbal behaviors herself, but she also claims them as typical of all women. "For half so boldly can no man," she asserts, "Swear and lie, as a woman can."[48] The Wife of Bath's claims about women's speech are echoed in the misogynist aphorisms that she cites from her fifth husband's book about the evils of women:

"It is better," said he, "that your habitation
be with a lion or a foul dragon,
Than with a woman accustomed to chiding.
It is better," said he, "that you live high in the roof,
Than with an angry wife down in the house;
They are so wicked and contrary,
They always hate what their husbands love."[49]

Because her prologue is by far the longest of any in the *Canterbury Tales*, because of the complexity of her representation, and because of her insights into medieval gender relations, the Wife of Bath has proven extremely popular among literary critics. One recurring theme in Wife of Bath scholarship has been the Wife's love of words and her skill in their manipulation. As Barbara Gottfried has pointed out, the Wife of Bath's challenge to the authority of the misogynist literature quoted by her fifth husband is simultaneously a challenge to the authority of written texts.[50] The wisdom of books—as the Wife explains—is limited to the prejudice of their authors. And since medieval authors were overwhelmingly male and clerical, their portraits of women were necessarily distorted:

By God, if women had written stories,
As clerks have within their oratories,
They would have written about men more wickedness
Than all the male sex may redress.[51]

Against the legitimacy of male-authored texts, the Wife argues for the authority of "experience" and oral wisdom.[52] Indeed, in the climactic scene in her disputes with her fifth husband, she persuades him to burn his book of wicked wives, symbolizing the destruction of both the book's authority and her husband's authority. She also seems to challenge the authority of the church: both the Friar and the Pardoner refer to the Wife as a preacher, implying that in her arguments about how men should behave toward women she is usurping the masculine privilege of preaching, specifically forbidden to women by Saint Paul.[53]

The Wife of Bath is thus an ambiguous character: from a modern viewpoint, she is both feminist, in her claims for women's authority via experience over the text-centered authority of men, and antifeminist, associating women with lust, deception, and troublesome speech.[54] Yet even if we celebrate the agency of her character, we must still acknowledge the role she plays in the development of a stereotypically vociferous and disorderly woman. Through her self-conscious long-windedness and gossipy, irreverent tone, the Wife of Bath goes further than Noah's Wife in both proclaiming and performing women's insubordinate speech.

Across the fifteenth century and beyond, poets, playwrights, and balladeers drew further upon the stereotype of the female gossip exemplified by Noah's Wife and the Wife of Bath. In a group of poems known as the "gossips' poems" or "alewife poems," women sit together to share news, secrets, and slander.[55] In the fifteenth-century vernacular song known as "The Gossips," for instance, women gather in a tavern to eat, drink, talk, and spend their husbands' money. Although the narrator reports that he or she dare not reveal "half the substance" of the women's conversation, the audience witnesses the fictional gossips praising their own company, delighting in eating and drinking, and offering each other moral support against beatings by husbands. Songs and poems that purport, like "The Gossips," to represent women's conversations reveal fears about the subversive content of female speech.[56] Like the Wife of Bath, women depicted in such works often discuss ways of ruling their husbands. In a prose work translated into English at the beginning of the sixteenth century, for instance, six old wives force a scribe to record the "gospels of distaves," a parody of the biblical gospels. The old wives' gospels consist, in part, of advice on how women might control their husbands.[57] Similarly, two early sixteenth-century poems by the Scottish poet William Dunbar describe conversations in which women discuss ways to alleviate the stresses of marriage and gain mastery over their mates. In "The Tua Cummeris," two gossips sit drinking wine and chattering on the first day of Lent. One woman advises the other to relieve her irritation at the hardship of fasting for Lent by venting her wrath on her husband. In "The Tretis of the Tua Mariit Wemen and the Wedo," gossips complain about their husbands and fantasize about how their lives would be different if they could choose their husbands again.[58] Women's company is thus dangerous, breeding insubordination against male authority.

Perhaps the most revealing of anxieties underlying gossips' poems is the subject matter of the late fifteenth-century "Talk of Ten Wives on Their Husbands' Ware," in which women meet in an alehouse and discuss their husbands' sexual equipment and prowess. Husbands' penises are compared in size and appearance to snails, beans, maggots, and small fingers, while two women complain about their husbands' inability to become erect. The all-female nature of the gathering is emphasized in the first verse of the poem, which tells the audience that the conversation related took place when "ten wives sat at the ale," and reiterates that there was "no man among them."[59] Like other poems in the gossips' genre, the "Talk of Ten Wives on Their Husbands' Ware" portrays women's speech as disruptive not only in its quantity but also because of the subversive subject matter of speech in an all-female environment. When one of the Middlewich jurors—Richard Hycokson, perhaps, or Henry le Vernon—heard such poems, he might well have thought of groups of women he saw in the tavern of Thomas del Mulne in Middlewich. He might have worried about the content of conversations between his wife and her friends as they sat drinking ale and trading stories and have reflected to himself that groups of female friends were likely to talk about things that ought not be mentioned. Speech among communities of women was potentially subversive.

The stereotype of the loud and disruptive woman—exemplified by Noah's Wife, the Wife of Bath, and the women of the gossips' poems—was not confined to secular poems and plays, nor to literature that ridiculed women. Women also spoke in defiant and powerful ways in some texts that received the stamp of approval from religious authorities, especially the legends of virgin martyrs. As Karen Winstead has pointed out, virgin martyrs evolved from fragile and submissive maidens in the early thirteenth century to defiant, powerful, and even disorderly characters by the fifteenth century.[60] In both literary and artistic representations, martyrs challenged male authority in the service of their faith. Marriage—and men in general—were portrayed negatively, and some artistic representations of martyrs depicted them wielding distaffs (the traditional emblem of female authority) as if they were swords. Likewise, the speech of late medieval virgin martyrs became especially sharp-tongued, even, Winstead has suggested, shrewish. When Chaucer depicts Saint Cecilia in the "Second Nun's Tale" of the *Canterbury Tales*, for instance, he has her speak words that might well have landed an ordinary woman in court as a scold: Cecilia calls her tormentor Almachius a "foolish officer and a vain justice," mocks his authority, and announces that his power is no more than "a bladder full of wind."[61] Similarly, Osbern Bokenham's mid-fifteenth-century legendary of thirteen women saints depicts female speech powerfully. When her breasts and tongue are cut off at the orders of a Roman judge, for instance, Saint Christine spits out part of her tongue into the judge's face so hard that he is partly blinded. Miraculously, she can still talk and points out to him that she still has the power of speech, while he has lost sight in one eye. As Sheila Delany has pointed out, Christine's tongue becomes a weapon in a very literal sense; for most of her fellow martyrs, tongues serve as more figurative implements of injury. Saint Katherine, for example, is faced with fifty orators hired by the emperor Maxence to win her over in debate, yet she defeats them all with a persuasive sermon. Maxence, furious at Katherine's victory, fumes at his emasculated speakers: "Where is your boasting / That you made when you first arrived? Why do you stand still this way? Are you tongueless?"[62]

Their stories set at a safe historical distance, the virgin martyrs portrayed in texts of the thirteenth to fifteenth centuries may not have threatened patriarchal authority quite so directly as Noah's Wife, the Wife of Bath, and the gossips, but nor were they remote from the close association between women and powerful, disruptive speech. Late medieval articulations of virgin martyr legends, as Winstead has argued, complement the stereotypes of aggressive and disruptive women found in contemporary sermons, tracts, poems, and stories. Yet while virgin martyr legends participated in the misogynous discourse about the disruptive potential of women, they also undermined that discourse by associating the "dangerous" trait of insubordination with women whom the church had branded as good and appropriate female role models. Their resistance to male authority justified in terms of their Christian faith, virgin martyrs might even be interpreted as authorizing dissent from behavior expected of women in a patriarchal society.

Indeed, as literary critics have pointed out, contemporary interpretations of even the most outrageously garrulous of women characters may not have been uniformly negative.[63] While we lack definitive information about how real medieval women and men like the townsfolk of Middlewich interpreted representational stereotypes, it seems possible that they might have experienced such characters in ambivalent ways. When Noah's Wife in the mystery plays, for instance, tells women in the audience that they should nag bad husbands and that she wishes she were a widow, she might be read as validating aspects of women's behavior and desires. Yet at the same time, her own behavior is made out to be ridiculous, an absurdity possibly enhanced by the fact that her role was played by a man in drag. Similarly, the verbal exuberance and confidence of the Wife of Bath and the complicity of women in the gossips' poems might have been read as simultaneously empowering and trivializing women. As Karma Lochrie has argued, gossip was associated with "a kind of insurrectionary discourse on the part of women as a marginalized medieval community, one that existed alongside—but also in resistance to—a variety of institutionalized, written discourses."[64] For medieval women, the separate spaces made by gossip could be liberating at the same time as they were a source of ridicule. Nor were such ambivalent interpretations necessarily confined to matters of gender: because medieval society was so hierarchical, Winstead has suggested, subversion of the gender order on the part of virgin martyrs might have doubled for subversion of other kinds of hierarchies. The clergy, she has proposed, might have used tales of virgin martyrs as vehicles for affirming celibacy over marriage or for representing the purity of the church compared with the evil of secular government. Thus the pervasive association of women characters with disruptive speech was not necessarily a thoroughly negative one. Rather, medieval people like those of Middlewich very likely read (or listened) both with and against the texts, producing for themselves individual and even contradictory interpretations of what it *meant* that women were so closely associated with excessive and usurpationary words. And very likely, the interpretation of the juror Richard Hycokson was different from the interpretation of Henry le Vernon, and different again from that of Matilda, Henry's wife.

Late medieval literature and art thus connected women with disruptive speech on multiple levels. As a category, women were linked with troublesome speech in advice literature directed at women and men and in fictional personifications of garrulous women. In late medieval poems, ballads, plays, sermons, and artwork, women were represented as speaking in ways problematic both in quantity and in content. However these representations were interpreted, the cultural coding of women as garrulous and of garrulity as feminine was firmly entrenched in late medieval culture. When Shakespeare came to create Kate in *The Taming of the Shrew*, and early modern pamphleteers and balladeers described characters like "Dame Slaunder" and "this Monster call'd A Scold," they tapped into a rich tradition much developed in the late Middle Ages.[65]

Women and Good Speech

Yet in spite of the overwhelmingly negative constructions of women's voices, there were specific, closely circumscribed settings and situations in which these same voices were validated and even respected. Sharon Farmer has drawn attention to medieval churchmen's occasional testimony to pious wives' influence over impious husbands. Thomas of

Chobham's early thirteenth-century *Manual for Confessors*, for instance, suggested that priests should encourage wives to "be preachers unto their husbands, because no priest is able to soften the heart of a man the way his wife can." If a wife failed to take on responsibility for persuasion, Thomas argued, that sin could be imputed to her. So wives ought to speak alluringly to their husbands, even "in the bedroom, in the midst of their embraces," to encourage reform of sins.[66] Thomas's comments were seldom developed fully, since most male commentators quickly overlooked the ways in which women could influence their husbands for the better and concentrated on reinforcing wives' reproductive capacities and their ability to be spiritual supporters, rather than guides. Christine de Pisan, however, returned to the theme in the late fourteenth century in her *Livres des trois vertus*, suggesting that women of all classes should take some responsibility for their husbands' spiritual well-being. Princesses, she advised, should admonish their husbands kindly and correct their errors, while wives of artisans and peasants should ensure that their husbands behaved in moral ways at work.[67] The very existence of a discourse about the validity of wives' pious speech suggests that women's relationship to speech was not *altogether* illegitimate. It is interesting to note, however, the very precise situations in which words were sanctioned: they had to be delivered by wives (not by daughters or sisters or other women); they had to be delivered in a manner that enabled husbandly authority to be maintained (sweetly, kindly, and/or during sex; in a domestic setting rather than a public one); and they had to be concerned with particular topics (first and foremost, moral reform).

Religious authors also used the Virgin Mary to validate women's speech in the familial context. Although Mary was celebrated for her taciturnity, poets and dramatists throughout the late Middle Ages put words into her mouth to try and dissuade people from sin. One of Mary's particular concerns in plays and poems of the genre of "Planctus Mariæ" or "lamentations of Mary" was to protect Christ's body.[68] For example, in "A Lamentation of Our Lady on Swearing," discussed further in Chapter 4, Mary grieves about the pains inflicted on her son by those who curse and blaspheme. In an uncharacteristically vehement tone, she promises that she will remember their sins on Judgment Day:

At doomsday, it is fully true,
You cursed swearers will cry and say:
"Ah, help now, the mother of Jesu!"
When I from them shall turn away;
For unless you leave your cursed lore
Of swearing oaths, to which you are accustomed,
You shall be damned for ever more,
And from all heavenly bliss refused.[69]

Mary was thus simultaneously praised for her silence, and applauded as the spokesperson for her son, condemning those who caused him pain. In the same way, ordinary women were both encouraged to remain quiet, yet permitted some small degree of authority on matters familial and religious.

Opportunities for domestic and familial speech are perhaps the exceptions that prove the rule. Whereas wives were encouraged to speak gently, privately, and on appropriate topics, speech outside these very circumscribed bounds was open to suspicion. Indeed, of all misogynist discourses, associations between women and illicit speech have proven some of the most enduring. The social and legal category of scold was imported into colonial New England (and at least one North American historical site currently boasts a "gossip" among its cast of "recreated" characters from the 1830s).[70] Not every medieval association has survived to the same degree as that between women and illicit speech. As Ruth Karras has explained, for example, the sin of lust was regarded in the Middle Ages as a particularly feminine failing.[71] While women are blamed sometimes still for arousing desires in men, modern Western culture departs from the medieval tradition in its assumption that men's sexual drive is stronger than that of women. Connections between women and disorderly speech, however, have proven more durable, and the fourteenth and fifteenth centuries played a vital role in connecting the category of women with that of disorderly speech. Much of this cultural knowledge was forged in the minds of ordinary people, like the Middlewich jurors of the fourteenth and fifteenth centuries, who noted the increasingly emphatic connections between women and disorderly speech in the poems, plays, sermons, sayings, and art that they read, heard, and saw every day.

Chapter 3

Women's Voices and the Law

Imagine this scene in a small medieval town. It is dusk on a late summer's day. Townsfolk hired to help with the harvest on nearby manors are trudging back home. Craftsmen and their wives have stopped work and closed up their stalls in the marketplace. People are lingering outdoors: in front of the church, beside the river, or outside the tavern. Illustrators of medieval manuscripts would have us think that such bucolic scenes typified the lives of ordinary people in the late Middle Ages: they worked hard, played hard, and went to bed happy. And maybe some did. The court records, however, often tell a different story. This town was Middlewich (Cheshire), and the year was 1425. Sometime in late August or early September, an argument broke out on the large bridge, where the road to Kinderton crossed over the Wichbrook. The protagonists were Agnes, daughter of Robert le Spenser, and Thomas Batesson and his wife Margaret, and the issue seemed to concern payment over use of a pan for boiling salt. Thomas claimed that Agnes owed him a saltpan plus 2s., but Agnes vehemently disagreed. "Thief!" she cried, as she denied his claim. The matter did not end there. Margaret Batesson leapt to her husband's defense, and more harsh words were exchanged. "You," shouted Agnes, "are a strumpet!" Margaret's response on this occasion is not recorded, but we should not assume that she was demure: in another argument with Agnes two years previously she had shouted for all to hear that Agnes was a thief and a "pyklepurse" (pickpocket). Before the borough court could sort out the rights and wrongs of this shouting match at one of its three-weekly sessions, however, another argument broke out between Agnes le Spenser and Thomas Batesson, this time at the tavern owned by Thomas del Mulne and his wife Margery. Perhaps it was started by Thomas Batesson, unable to resist the chance to press his claim against Agnes. Or perhaps Agnes seized the opportunity to let the people of Middlewich know that Thomas's claim was unfair. Again, she called Thomas a thief, along with "other dishonest names." Agnes's words were to cost her dearly. When the court next met, it found that she was in the wrong over the saltpan. It also labeled her behavior in the arguments with Thomas and Margaret

Batesson as "scolding" [Agnes "*obiurgauit . . . et dispersonauit*" Thomas and Margaret] and it fined her 4d. on each of three scolding charges—against Thomas on the bridge, against Margaret, and against Thomas in the tavern.[1]

If the same series of events had taken place in Middlewich a century earlier, not much would have been different. Salt boiling would still have been the town's main industry, and the town residents would doubtless still have squabbled over possession of saltpans. Late August or early September would still have been harvest time, although Middlewich workers may have been less lucky in finding wage labor in the early fourteenth century, an era of overcrowding and unemployment. The borough court would still have had responsibility for ensuring peace and order in the town. But the way in which the dispute between Agnes and the Batessons made it into the court would almost certainly have been different. Surviving court records from the 1320s mention no scolds. They do, however, list several cases of contempt, and a number of hues and cries.[2] Perhaps Agnes's accusations against Thomas and Margaret would have been deemed an unjust hue. Perhaps, since she argued a legal matter outside the courtroom, she might have been charged with contempt. Perhaps Thomas and Margaret would have brought a private defamation suit against Agnes in the borough court. Or perhaps the whole fracas would have been dismissed as an incident that was unpleasant and irritating but not subject to legal action. Legal constructions of speech in general changed during the late fourteenth and fifteenth centuries, but constructions of women's speech changed dramatically. By September 4, 1425, when Agnes was convicted thrice over for scolding, local courts and church courts had begun to view women's speech as especially deviant and problematic. This shift manifested in three ways. First, women's access to the hue and cry (a convention that had empowered women and their voices) was shut down. Second, women were increasingly named as defendants in defamation suits, a process complicated by the fact that jurisdiction over defamation was shifting from secular to lower-level church courts. Third, in both church courts and local courts, women constituted the overwhelming majority of those accused of the new crime of scolding. The net result was a legal devaluation of women's speech, a devaluation both reflecting and contributing to increasingly negative constructions of women's voices in late medieval culture.

Hues and Cries

Women did not talk much in medieval courts. That is to say, women appeared before courts far less frequently than men and, when present, were involved in fewer cases. Women were significantly underrepresented among those suing and among those being sued. They were accused of crimes of violence and crimes against property with far less frequency than men. They almost never occupied positions of local authority such as those of ale tasters, bailiffs, jurors, or *inquisitores.* And they only very occasionally appeared as pledges (or guarantors) for others. In secular jurisdictions, only about one in every seven people appearing before the court was female; in ecclesiastical jurisdictions, the ratio was slightly higher, owing to the large number of cases dealing with marriage or illicit sex.[3] Part of the reason for women's lack of participation was doubtless due to the convention by which the legal identity of most women was subsumed into that of their male relatives (a convention known as *couverture*). Husbands and fathers administered property and typically answered for their wives and daughters in cases of debt or broken contracts. But women's lack of participation also stems from the fact that the local court was, as Judith M. Bennett has pointed out, a forum that primarily reflected contracts and relationships among men.[4]

Because of their overall underrepresentation in courts, the few occasions on which women *did* frequently appear stand out. In many manorial and borough jurisdictions, for instance, they paid their own fees for practicing particular occupations, such as brewing, baking, and sale of foodstuffs. Women were also subject to the leyrwite fine for premarital sex in some manorial courts, and they were accused of prostitution in some church and local jurisdictions.[5] As discussed below, women made up the majority of those charged with scolding and defamation after the mid-fourteenth century. But there was one other way in which women also held their own in the courts, and this dated from well before scolding became common: women appeared in manorial and borough courts as raisers of the hue and cry.

As discussed in Chapter 1, the institution of the hue and cry, common in local courts particularly before the plague, was one in which both men and women had the ability to summon community support in pursuit of a criminal. Most hues were raised in response to physical assaults, either on the hue-raiser or on a member of his or her family. Others were raised to protect against damage to one's property. When John the schoolmaster of Clare (Suffolk) killed Roger Thruston's dog in 1361, for example, Roger's wife raised a hue on John. The court upheld the hue as justified and fined John 6d.[6] By using the hue and cry, Roger's wife introduced a case into the local court without the expenses of a private suit or the need for support from constables or presentment juries. Women like Roger's wife made good use of this system, both to protect themselves and to protect family members and friends. Despite the fact that women accounted for only about one in every seven local court

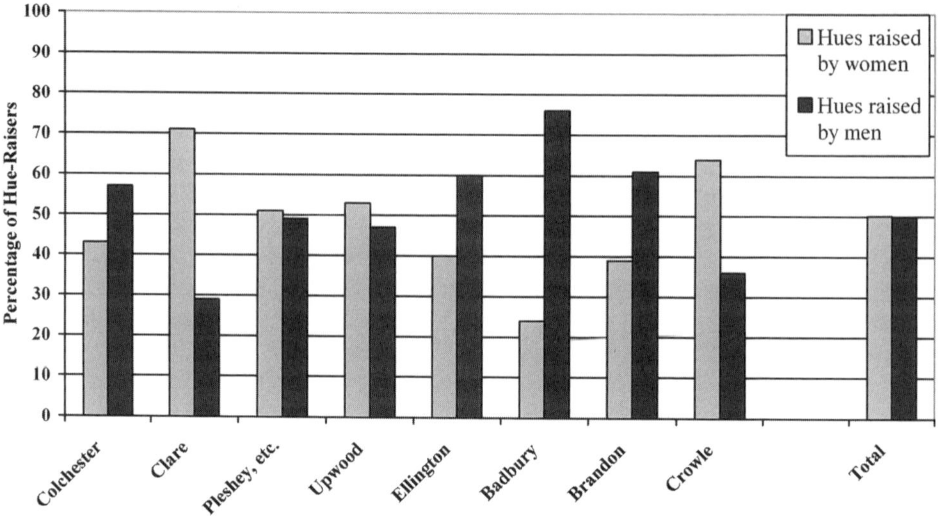

Figure 4. Hues Raised by Women and Men, 1280–1455. For Colchester, see *Court Rolls of the Borough of Colchester*, vol. 1, ed. and trans. Isaac Herbert Jeayes and W. Gurney Benham (Colchester: s.n., 1921); for Clare, TNA: PRO SC 2 203/45–70; for Pleshey, etc., TNA: PRO DL 30 64/809–69/853 (the Pleshey courts also include occasional courts from High Easter, Waltham, Mashbury, Chishall, Sawston, and Hoddesdon); for Upwood and Ellington, Sherri Olson, *A Chronicle of All That Happens: Voices from the Village Court in Medieval England* (Toronto: Pontifical Institute of Mediaeval Studies, 1996); for Badbury and Brandon, Miriam Müller, "Social Control and the Hue and Cry in Two Fourteenth-Century Villages," *Journal of Medieval History* 31 (2005): 29–53; for Crowle, LA CM 1/3–1/36.

appearances overall, they typically numbered about half of those named as raising hues. Figure 4 shows the participation of women and men in hue-raising in eight jurisdictions: the towns of Colchester (Essex) and Clare, the small Essex borough of Pleshey and associated manorial courts, the Huntingdonshire manors of Upwood and Ellington (the work of Sherri Olson), the Wiltshire manor of Badbury and the Suffolk manor of Brandon (the work of Miriam Müller), and the manor of Crowle (Lincolnshire).

As the graph demonstrates, between 24 and 71 percent of hues in these eight jurisdictions were raised by women. Among the hues of all eight jurisdictions combined (a total of 1195 hues), women raised 599, or 50.1 percent. Given the general medieval skepticism about the value of women's voices, we might expect that the courts, responsible for judging whether each hue was just or unjust, might be especially dubious about hues raised by women. This expectation, however, does not hold true. Among the first three jurisdictions combined (Colchester, Clare, and Pleshey), women's hues were judged unjust in 19 percent of cases, while 24 percent of men's hues were deemed unjust. In the manor of Crowle, women's and men's hues were found unjust in an almost identical proportion: 23.5 percent of men's compared with 25 percent of women's. Similar patterns were found for Ellington (where 15 percent of women's hues were found unjust compared with nearly 25 percent of men's), Upwood (15 percent of both women's and men's hues were found wanting), Badbury (where 18 percent of women's and 23 percent of men's hues were deemed unjust), and Brandon (where 19 percent of women's hues were found unjust compared with 23 percent of men's). If anything, therefore, women were typically judged *more* reliable than men in their use of the hue, meaning that the courts validated their voices.[7]

In light of the fact that women and men raised about the same number of hues, it is particularly interesting to note that men were much more likely than women to have hues raised on them. Figure 5 shows data on the targets of hues—those on whom the hues were raised—for the same eight jurisdictions, along with that of the Northamptonshire manor of Brigstock.

Here, the gender discrepancy is even clearer: between 70 and 94 percent of hues were called on men. Across the nine jurisdictions combined, men were named as the targets of hues in 1034 cases out of 1264 (a total of 82 percent). A similar pattern has been found by Anne and Edwin DeWindt for hues in the vill of Ramsey (Huntingdonshire): women raised 476 of 888 hues (54 percent) in the twelfth to sixteenth centuries but were targets in only 12 percent of the cases.[8] The whole system of hues and cries, therefore, was one that protected women and punished men in disproportionate numbers. Men were the net losers in the whole hue-raising dynamic: they were slightly less likely to call hues, but more likely to have their misdeeds revealed as a result of them.

The reasons for which women called the hue are also instructive because they allowed women to speak in their own defense and they enabled women to act publicly in support of others. Whereas both women and men called hues first and foremost when being personally attacked, women (more than men) also called hues to bring neighbors to the support of other victims of crime. Hues from the town of Clare demonstrate the frequency with which women's voices were raised in support of others. Among 173 just hues by women for which the cause is known, 130 (75 percent) resulted from an attack on the hue-caller herself.[9] The other 43 (25 percent) involved women calling hues to summon help for husbands, daughters, servants, fathers, masters, and others. Particularly frequent were hues raised by wives in support of their

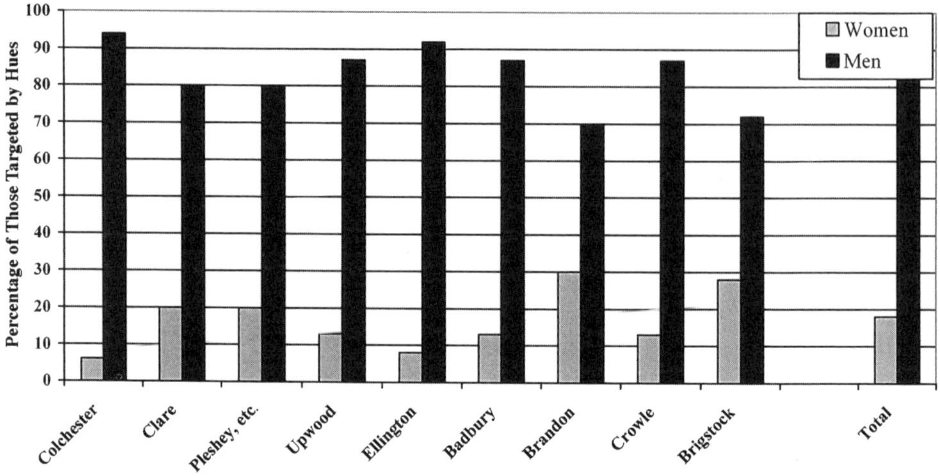

Figure 5. Targets of Hues, 1280–1455. The total numbers vary slightly from those of Figure 4 because full information about both hue-raiser and hue target is not always available. Sources: For Colchester, *Court Rolls of the Borough of Colchester*, vol. 1, ed. and trans. Isaac Herbert Jeayes and W. Gurney Benham (Colchester: s.n., 1921); for Clare, TNA: PRO SC 2 203/45–70; for Pleshey, etc., TNA: PRO DL 30 64/809–69/853 (the Pleshey courts also include occasional courts from High Easter, Waltham, Mashbury, Chishall, Sawston, and Hoddesdon); for Upwood and Ellington, Sherri Olson, *A Chronicle of All that Happens: Voices from the Village Court in Medieval England* (Toronto: Pontifical Institute of Mediaeval Studies, 1996); for Badbury and Brandon, Miriam Müller, "Social Control and the Hue and Cry in Two Fourteenth-Century Villages," *Journal of Medieval History* 31 (2005): 29–53; for Crowle, LA CM 1/3–1/36; for Brigstock, Judith M. Bennett, *Women in the Medieval English Countryside: Gender and Household in Brigstock before the Plague* (New York: Oxford University Press, 1987), 39.

husbands: 30 instances of uxorial hue-raising are recorded in surviving courts from Clare.[10] When Thomas Skot attacked Edward Lolleworth of Clare in 1389, for example, and Edward was injured to the point where he was bleeding, it was Edward's wife who prevented further pummeling by raising a hue and enlisting the support of her neighbors.[11] When men called hues, on the other hand, they tended to summon help for themselves, rather than for family members or others. Of 63 hues raised by men in Clare, 58 (92 percent) resulted from an attack on the hue-caller himself, 2 (3 percent) from an attack on someone else, and 3 (5 percent) from an attack on the hue-raiser's property. Miriam Müller has found similar patterns for the village of Brandon (Suffolk), in which ten wives raised the hue on behalf of their husbands, whereas no husbands raised the hue to summon help for their wives.[12]

By summoning others to a victim's aid, hue-raising provided a public forum for women to participate in disputes between families and to affirm networks of friendship or kinship. Many situations of violence in late medieval towns and villages stemmed from or were exacerbated by kinship ties: brothers would step into fights to support brothers, fathers would support sons, and nephews would fight for their uncles. Women certainly participated in this direct physical violence on occasion too, attacking those who assaulted their husbands, fathers, brothers, or sons, or starting their own fights. But more frequently, according to medieval court records, men fought with their fists while women fought with their voices. Women's public participation in family feuds is all the more significant because they had fewer opportunities than men to demonstrate their support of kinship networks. Judith M. Bennett has discussed the importance of personal pledging—the act of serving as guarantor to someone else appearing before the courts—to the maintenance of male kinship and friendship networks in late medieval England. Women very seldom served as pledges, but in calling hues on those who attacked members of their families, they similarly demonstrated their roles and their allegiances, albeit in a somewhat stereotypical way.[13]

For women, then, the hue and cry was an empowering institution. As Anne and Edwin DeWindt have pointed out, the hue and cry functioned as a passkey that enabled women to get their cases into court.[14] But this situation was not to last. As Chapter 1 explains, fewer hues came to the courts' attention by the last few decades of the fourteenth century, and more of these few were deemed unjust. Women and their voices were perhaps especially vulnerable in the transition away from hue-raising. Someone who called hues too often or without sufficient cause was like the proverbial boy who cried wolf, a nuisance within the community. Hue-raisers were increasingly regarded as akin to scolds, disrupting the community with disorderly voices. The case of Alice, wife of Richard Raules of Chedzoy (Somerset), who was charged as a "common hue-raiser and disturber of the peace of the lord King and of her neighbors" in 1372, provides one example. Alice was not cited explicitly as a scold, yet the offense of scolding was typically constructed in court records in just such a way: scolds were those who disturbed the peace and disturbed their neighbors. Two years after Alice was punished as a common hue-raiser, the first scolding presentment appeared in Chedzoy's court records, constructed along very similar lines to Alice's offense: Joan, wife of John Frend, was prosecuted as a common scold (*communis garrulatrix*) who disturbed the peace of the lord, and John and Joan were fined 12d.[15] In Chedzoy, the decline of *just* hue presentments and an expanding construction of *false* hue-raising seemed to anticipate the first prosecution of scolding.

Cases from elsewhere similarly suggest overlap between hue-raising and scolding and suggest that the potential for this slippage had been present from the very earliest scolding presentments, even before the decline of hues. When jurors in Colchester in 1312 investigated a hue and cry made by Juliana la Hunter on Osbert, servant of John Maymund, they found that no harm was done, but that Juliana was a scold.[16] By the early fifteenth century, the connections were more explicit. In the sheriff's tourn held at Northwich (Cheshire) in 1410, for instance, Robert of Ponnale and Thomas, Robert's son, were accused of raising an "enormous hue" without any cause on Hugh of Knottesford, calling him a thief and "many other vile names." Robert and Thomas were thus judged to be scolds (*rixatores*), responsible for sowing discord among their neighbors.[17] In the cases of Juliana, Robert, and Thomas, the raising of hues was considered akin to scolding; implicitly or explicitly, they were labeled *both* raisers of false hues *and* scolds.

Even when false hue-raising and scolding were not explicitly deemed parallel, scolds and raisers of false hues were seen as kin. Individuals prosecuted for scolding were often in trouble for false hue-raising at the same time or on a later occasion. The court rolls of Waltham (Essex) from 1390, for example, list that Christina atte Grene raised an unjust hue on John Cavenden. Immediately below, they record that the same Christina was a common disturber (of the peace) and a scold (*communis perturbatrix et garulatrix*), to the annoyance of her neighbors. Two years later, she was again in trouble for raising a hue and for being a common scold (*communis garulatrix*) among her neighbors.[18] Even if her repeated scolding and false hue-raising were entirely separate offenses, the people of Waltham likely drew connections between the two. Christina was one of the first in her village to be charged with scolding, and her prosecution sent a message to Waltham villagers about what constituted scold-like behavior. Scolding, they learned from the court, involved acting like Christina. If Christina's verbal improprieties included false hues, then perhaps, to Waltham villagers, scolding included elements of false hue-raising. Courts throughout late medieval England sent similar messages. Of five Nottingham scolds in 1395–96, two were simultaneously charged with raising a false hue, and in other places, many scolds were also to be found among false hue-raisers in previous or subsequent courts.[19] Scolding and the raising of false hues were still separate offenses, but the lines between them were becoming blurred. Until the late fourteenth century—before the decline of hues and cries and the blurring of boundaries between false hues and scolding—the institution of hue-raising served an empowering function for women. Raising of hues proved a means by which women's voices were validated twice over: once when villagers or townspeople pursued wrongdoers in response to the hues, and again when their hues were endorsed by the manorial and borough courts. A woman who called a hue drew the community's attention to her own situation or that of her friends or kin, using her voice as a powerful tool of summons. But with the decline of hue-raising as a means of communal policing from the late fourteenth century onward, women's legitimate opportunities to raise their voices seem to have been curtailed. The shift away from hue-raising as a means of community regulation was not designed or intended to curtail women's speech—as Chapter 1 explains, it was probably more closely associated with the rising authority of local elites—but it certainly functioned to silence women.

Defamation

At the same time as women lost access to the hue, they were increasingly charged with defamation. During the late Middle Ages, as outlined in Chapter 1, important shifts were taking place in the ways that courts adjudicated defamation cases. In the thirteenth and early fourteenth centuries, manorial courts frequently heard defamation allegations but, as the work of R. H. Helmholz has shown, they mysteriously disappeared from local jurisdictions during the fourteenth century and were reserved increasingly for ecclesiastical courts.[20] Despite some suggestions to the contrary, women were not significantly overrepresented among late thirteenth- and early fourteenth-century defamers. Rather, their especial association with defamation was cemented during the late fourteenth and early fifteenth centuries and persisted well into the early modern era.

Preplague defamation charges in manorial courts were almost always the result of private suits brought between two or more individuals. Typically, the plaintiff (or plaintiffs) would allege that the defendant (or defendants) had defamed him/her/them by use of particular words, resulting in monetary damages that the court might order to be reimbursed. The words of alleged abuse were so standard as to be almost formulaic: men (and sometimes women, too) were typically called "false" or "thieves" or "robbers," whereas women were most often the subjects of some kind of sexualized insult, such as "whore." Indeed, the heavily gendered nature of insults was one of the few elements of verbal abuse that remained constant throughout the thirteenth to seventeenth centuries: while conceptions of defamation changed and jurisdictional authorities shifted, the association between women and sexual morality and between men and economic morality persisted. Sometimes manorial court cases included legitimating details to help plaintiffs in claiming damages, and these give insight into the background of disputes. When William Plomer brought suit against Walter Kygges of Ingoldmells

(Lincolnshire) in 1303, for instance, he explained that Walter had called him "false man" and had claimed that William had taken one of Walter's hens and surreptitiously eaten it at the house of a neighbor. The jury, having established that William neither carried off nor ate Walter's hen, found Walter guilty of defamation.[21]

Women were certainly charged with defamation on occasion in preplague manorial courts, but in most places they were charged far less frequently than men. Indeed, women's participation in defamation suits was only a little higher than their participation in all civil matters in preplague local courts. In arguing that most preplague manorial jurisdictions did *not* regard women as especially frequent defamers, I differ from the argument of M. Patricia Hogan. Hogan has suggested—based on a study of five villages owned by Ramsey Abbey—that women *were* frequent defamers in late thirteenth- and early fourteenth-century manors, committing slander almost as frequently as men, and that defamation "suited the physique of women" as a weapon of the weak. In some villages, women may indeed have matched men among those charged with defamation. Hogan found in her study of Warboys (Huntingdonshire) that women were responsible for seven of thirteen slanders brought before the court between 1290 and 1353, and that women at Abbots Ripton (Huntingdonshire) committed three of six slanders in roughly the same period. Of Hogan's five villages taken as a whole, however, women were responsible for 39 percent or fewer of all defamations brought to the court's attention, and even this proportion is higher than the number of female defamers in most other local jurisdictions.

As Figure 6 shows, other jurisdictions besides the Ramsey villages were reluctant to prosecute women as defamers. In the Lincolnshire manors of Crowle and Ingoldmells, women were charged with three of fourteen and three of seventeen defamations respectively, and in Cuxham (Oxfordshire) men were responsible for all nine defamations brought before the court. Women featured as defamers slightly more often in the courts of Wakefield: one-third of fifty-seven defamation charges were brought against them. In total—if we add defamations from the Ramsey Abbey villages to those of Crowle, Cuxham, Ingoldmells, and Wakefield—women were charged as defamers in 47 of 154 cases (31 percent). This means that while women were brought before the court as defendants in defamation suits with slightly higher frequency than they appeared as defendants in other civil cases, they were not charged with defamation in vastly disproportionate numbers: Judith M. Bennett found that 24 percent of civil cases in Brigstock between 1287 and 1348 featured women as defendants. In other words, during this early period, in which defamation was largely a concern of the local courts, it was not associated *especially* closely with women. Women allegedly defamed

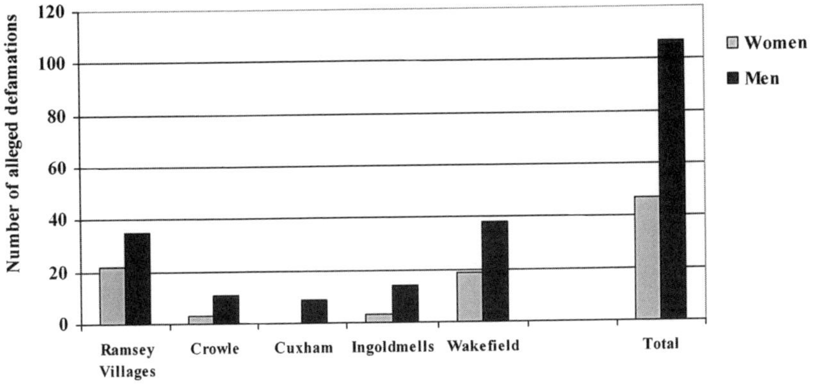

Figure 6. Defamation in Secular Jurisdictions, 1270–1379. The numbers here refer to allegations, not individuals. The outcomes of the cases are not taken into account. In other words, even if someone was found innocent of defamation, his/her case was nonetheless included in the count of defamers. Sources: for Ramsey Abbey Villages, M. Patricia Hogan, "The Slight to Honor: Slander and Wrongful Prosecution in Five English Medieval Villages," *Studies in Medieval and Renaissance History* 12 (1991): 3–42 (from Hogan's statistics, one can extrapolate that at least sixteen men and at most six women were charged with defamations at Broughton, but it is also possible that more men and fewer women were charged); for Crowle, LA CM 1/4–1/34; for Cuxham, *Manorial Records of Cuxham, Oxfordshire, c. 1200–1359,* ed. P. D. A. Harvey, Oxfordshire Record Society Series, vol. 50 (London: H. M. Stationery Office, 1976); for Ingoldmells, *Court Rolls of the Manor of Ingoldmells in the County of Lincoln,* ed. W. O. Massingberd (London: Spottiswoode, 1902); for Wakefield, *Court Rolls of the Manor of Wakefield,* vol. 1, *1274–1297,* ed. William Paley Baildon, Yorkshire Archaeological Society Records Series, vol. 29 (Leeds: Yorkshire Archaeological Society, 1900); *Court Rolls of the Manor of Wakefield,* vol. 2, *1297–1309,* ed. William Paley Baildon, Yorkshire Archaeological Society Records Series, vol. 36 (Leeds: Yorkshire Archaeological Society, 1906); *Court Rolls of the Manor of Wakefield,* vol. 3, *1313–1316 and 1286,* ed. John Lister, Yorkshire Archaeological Society Records Series, vol. 57 (Leeds: Yorkshire Archaeological Society, 1917); *Court Rolls of the Manor of Wakefield,* vol. 4, *1315–1317,* ed. John Lister, Yorkshire Archaeological Society Records Series, vol. 78 (Leeds: Yorkshire Archaeological Society, 1930); *Court Rolls of the Manor of Wakefield,* vol. 5, *1322–1331,* ed. J. W. Walker, Yorkshire Archaeological Society Records Series, vol. 109 (Leeds: Yorkshire Archaeological Society, 1944); *The Court Rolls of the Manor of Wakefield from October 1331 to September 1333,* ed. Sue Sheridan Walker, Wakefield Court Rolls Series of the Yorkshire Archaeological Society, vol. 3 (Leeds: Yorkshire Archaeological Society, 1982); *The Court Rolls of the Manor of Wakefield from October 1338 to September 1340,* ed. K. M. Troup, Wakefield Court Rolls Series of the Yorkshire Archaeological Society, vol. 12 (Leeds: Yorkshire Archaeological Society, 1999); *The Court Rolls of the Manor of Wakefield from September 1348 to September 1350,* ed. Helen M. Jewell, Wakefield Court Rolls Series of the Yorkshire Archaeological Society, 2nd series, vol. 2 (Leeds: Yorkshire Archaeological Society, 1981); *The Court Rolls of the Manor of Wakefield from October 1350 to September 1352,* ed. Moira Habberjam, Mary O'Regan, and Brian Hale, Wakefield Court Rolls Series of the Yorkshire Archaeological Society, vol. 6 (Leeds: Yorkshire Archaeological Society, 1987).

others less than half as often as men, the same frequency with which they damaged people's property or committed other petty crimes. The strength of the association between women and defamation was thus not forged in the preplague manorial context.

Rather, we must credit the church courts, which took over jurisdiction of defamation during the fourteenth century, with the feminization of defamation. Gaps in the records of lower-level church courts—forums such as episcopal visitations, archdeaconry courts, and consistory courts in which matters like defamation were likely to be heard—make the progress of this feminization much more difficult to trace. Few records survive for lower church court jurisdictions prior to 1400, and those that do seldom record defamation cases in significant numbers. By the fifteenth century, however, when lower church court records are more abundant and defamation cases abound, the pattern is clear: women were more frequently charged with defamation than men. In other words, the fragmentary survival of church court records obscures the process by which defamation became a largely female-associated crime, but it clearly happened.

While record survival is patchy, we can still get a few glimpses of the feminization of defamation. Of eleven alleged defamers in the diocese of Rochester between 1320 and 1348 (both ex officio cases brought to the consistory court and instance papers listed in the bishop's register), seven were women and four, men.[22] While this is a small sample indeed, women outnumbered men. On the other hand, men outnumbered women as alleged defamers among twenty-one cases pursued in the court of York between 1335 and 1399. Fifteen men and six women were named as defendants in defamation cases, and almost half of these (ten cases) involved men suing other men for defamation.[23] Women were similarly outnumbered in a 1397 visitation of the diocese of Hereford, in which nine men and four women were charged as defamers. In total, among these three fourteenth-century ecclesiastical jurisdictions, women accounted for seventeen (38 percent) of alleged defamers and men for twenty-eight (62 percent). In the fourteenth century, therefore, it seems that the strong association between women and defamation was yet to emerge in either secular or church courts.[24]

By the fifteenth century, however, the pattern was more distinct: women clearly outnumbered men as defamers in the ecclesiastical setting. L. R. Poos has examined cases involving 289 fifteenth-century defamers in the Deaneries of Wisbech (in the Diocese of Ely) and Middlesex and Barking (in the Diocese of London), as well as in the courts of the Prior and Convent of Durham peculiars.[25] He found that women were charged as defamers in 140 cases and men in 119, while the remaining 30 cases involved couples or other groups. In other words, of the 259 defamers for whom a gender can be securely attributed, 54 percent were women. Yet men were more likely than women to be identified as the victims of defamation: of 294 defamees, 116 were women, 152 were men, and 26 were members of couples or other groups. The large number of defamation cases examined by Poos underscores the reliability of his data. Nonetheless, other, smaller, samples would seem to support the trend he identifies: of 16 individuals charged with defamation in the register of John Chandler, dean of Salisbury, between 1404 and 1412, 8 were women and 8 men. The Salisbury data reflects also the gendered pattern of defamees identified by Poos: of those allegedly defamed, men numbered 10 and women 4.[26] By the fifteenth century, then, women composed at least half of all alleged defamers, whereas men composed more than half of those defamed. In other words, the net result of defamation charges in fifteenth-century church courts was to protect men and punish women, in much the same way that fourteenth-century hues and cries had protected women at the expense of men.

Connections between women and defamation in ecclesiastical courts proved enduring. Laura Gowing's study of defamation in early modern London found that 60 percent of 1258 defamation cases in the sixteenth and seventeenth centuries involved women as defendants. Interestingly, women also featured more significantly as plaintiffs by the seventeenth century: whereas 25 percent of defamation plaintiffs in the consistory court were female in 1572, 54 percent were female in 1633. Indeed, half of all cases in the sixteenth and seventeenth centuries involved women suing other women. The church courts had become a major locus for the defense and maintenance of female reputation, and their fifteenth-century function of protecting men at the expense of women had receded.[27]

The period between the mid-fourteenth and the sixteenth centuries thus mark an era of transition in which the crime of defamation became one that was increasingly associated with women. Whereas preplague manorial courts did not regard defamation as an especially female-associated crime, it soon garnered that reputation after it became the preserve of church courts. Patchy survival of fourteenth-century church court records makes it difficult to know whether the feminization of defamation arose around the same time as defamation cases crossed over from lay to ecclesiastical or whether it occurred once the switch was made. Evidence from York and Hereford suggests that fourteenth-century church courts may have seen more men than women charged with defamation, but this pattern had clearly changed by the fifteenth century when most defamation cases singled out women as defamers. Even though the feminization of defamation roughly coincides with the shift of defamation cases from lay to church courts, I suggest that this jurisdictional shift was not one of the major factors in causing the feminization. Rather, the increasing number of women charged with defamation correlates strongly with other changes in legal perceptions of women's voices. At the same time that women found themselves hauled up before church courts as defamers, they also found that their access to the hue and cry was restricted and—eventually—removed altogether. And during the same period—the last decades of the fourteenth century and first decades of the fifteenth century—they found themselves subject to a new charge in both local and church courts: the charge of scolding.

The Emergence of Scolding as a Legal Category

If changes in the system of hues and cries had begun to cast doubt on the value of women's voices, and the feminization of defamation suggested that women's speech was more likely than men's speech to be slanderous, then the rise of scolding presentments from the mid-fourteenth century sent an even clearer message that women were deviant speakers. Late thirteenth- and early fourteenth-century literary texts occasionally mentioned scolds, yet few preplague courts regarded scolding as an actionable crime rather than a moral failing. Like many crimes involving local order, scolding was never addressed in medieval statutes or acknowledged at a nationwide level, and it is impossible to pinpoint the exact date at which it was prosecuted for the very first time. The earliest cases of which I know come from Colchester in 1311, and a few other cases can be found for the first half of the fourteenth century, but it is not at all impossible that earlier presentments occurred.[28] What is more certain, however, is that scolding was not *widely* prosecuted until the second half of the fourteenth century and beginnings of the fifteenth century.

Trying to situate the first appearance of a particular crime in English local courts is an impossible task given the eccentricities of record survival, for there are both too many and too few sources. Because court rolls survive for hundreds of medieval manors and towns, it would take many lifetimes to search them all. At the same time, survival of records is erratic. While thousands of court rolls may survive for any single decade, few exist in a complete series. Records of individual court sessions are often missing or damaged. This is particularly the case immediately following the first wave of the Black Death, a period in which courts were sometimes postponed or sessions were not recorded due to the deaths of clerks or local officials. Given the impossibility of finding the truly earliest scolding presentment and identifying it as such, it is nonetheless helpful to have a general idea of when most courts adopted the category.

For the purposes of this study, I used two methods to search for early presentments: I sampled manorial and borough courts for selected years from the fourteenth century, and I read through as many early records as possible for jurisdictions that I knew to have prosecuted scolds later. Both methods have drawbacks, but the survival of records prevents absolute precision.[29] What they suggest is that scolds very seldom appeared in preplague courts, and that the situation of Colchester, where scolds were presented from the 1310s, was somewhat anomalous.

The rarity of preplague scolding cases is suggested not only by the very small number of cases found but also by the ways in which scolding (and other cases involving speech) were presented before the courts. In the small town of Pleshey, for instance, about twenty-three miles from Colchester as the crow flies, Little Juliana and Margery, wife of William of Berwyk, found themselves in trouble in 1344 for a crime that might have fallen under the category of scolding had the court regarded scolding as an actionable crime. The court heard that Little Juliana and Margery Berwyk were guilty of being nighttime gossips (*garulandi noctanter*) in the village, so that other villagers could not sleep, and they were fined a total of 6d. In Pleshey, problematic or disruptive speech was deemed punishable in 1344, but it had not yet acquired the label of scolding. Little Juliana and Margery might be regarded as protoscolds, individuals who might have been charged as scolds had the legal mentality and vocabulary for doing so existed among the people of Pleshey.[30] The first scolds to appear in surviving court records from Pleshey did not make their appearance until 1375.

The postplague novelty of scolding as a legal category in most jurisdictions is also suggested by the fact that when scolds *were* first presented among surviving court rolls, the ways in which their offenses were recorded were anything but uniform. Lacking an established tradition of correct procedures on how to record crimes, clerks translated the term "scold" as best they could, drawing from any one of a number of Latin terms to describe inappropriate speech. Often they chose different words and constructions at different times, even when the context suggested that a similar crime was being alleged. The court rolls of Bradford (Yorkshire) between 1355 and 1361, for instance, contain three different Latin words for the term "scold," plus several different constructions of the offense. Agnes de Baksholt was presented in 1355 for having hit Robert Dickson, and it was noted that she was a "*communis maledictrix gentes*," or (literally) "common speaker of evil about people." Two years later, Robert was fined as a "*communis litigator et communis obiurgator cum vicinis suis*," or "common scold with his neighbors." Both the terms "*litigator*" (or the feminine version "*litigatrix*") and "*obiurgator*" (or "*obiurgatrix*") translate as scold, and if any distinction existed between them in the fourteenth century, it has been impossible to discern it. In 1359, for instance, three Bradford women were presented as "*communes et notorii obiurgatrices,*" or "common and notorious scolds," and remanded to the next court session, in which they were described as "*communes litigatrices.*"[31] Jurors from the village of Allerton, under the jurisdiction of Bradford, presented Agnes de Wyndhill as a "*communis litigatrix,*" or "common scold" in 1361, and in the same year Bradford jurors presented Christina Jacdoghtre and Agnes Bastholpt as "*communes litigatrices cum vicinis suis,*" or "common scolds with their neighbors."[32] In other words, scolds presented in the Bradford courts between 1355 and 1361 might be described in Latin as "*maledictrices,*" "*obiurgatrices,*" "*litigatrices,*" or a combination of these terms.[33] They might be recorded as "common" offenders or as "common and notorious" offenders, and they might or might not be described as scolding with or among their neighbors. A similar variety of terms was recorded at Congleton (Cheshire) in 1369–70. Scolds were recorded as common "*rixatrices*" (or "*rixatores*") or "*litigatores*" (for some reason, both women and men in Congleton in these years were described with the masculine form of the noun).[34]

The absence of scolds yet presence of protoscolds in samples of preplague courts and the lack of uniformity in early scolding presentments, even within the same jurisdictions, suggest that prosecution of scolding was largely a postplague innovation. The emergence of scolding as a widespread legal category in the years following the Black Death was not accidental. Scolding was constructed as an offense against the unity of communities, and while towns and villages certainly articulated a communal identity before the plague, heightened inequalities and increased migration in the subsequent decades made the articulation of communal harmony all the more urgent. As argued in Chapter 1, increasing concern to regulate speech also reflected concerns about hierarchy, status, and authority in a period of social and economic disruption. The discourse on the "sins of the tongue" was easily adapted and applied to women, during the same era that their voices were devalued by the feminization of defamation and the removal of the hue and cry.

Scolding as a Female Crime

Both men and women were capable of committing "sins of the tongue," but the specific offense of scolding was always closely associated with women. Women predominated among those prosecuted as scolds, and many village and borough ordinances against scolding or quarrelsome speech made it clear that women were *expected* to be the main transgressors. An ordinance passed in the village of Wolveston (Durham) in 1379, for example, warned all women to desist from scolding and repudiating others in words and deeds, while their menfolk were warned against drawing knives or raising cudgels against their fellows. In the nearby village of East Merrington in the same year, all tenants were warned against knife and cudgel wielding and other crimes of violence, but women were again singled out in a warning to constrain their tongues and desist from evil speech and scolding.[35] Similarly, the court rolls of Yeadon (Yorkshire) in 1387 insisted that anyone who drew a knife or sword was liable to a penalty of 40d., whereas any woman who was "quarrelsome in words" faced a fine of 6d. When the ordinance was repeated seven years later, the fine for "any woman who is contentious with her neighbors" had been raised to 12d.[36] The association between women and words was not merely a manorial phenomenon. Borough ordinances from Ipswich (Suffolk), purportedly dating from the 1290s, specified the punishment of scolding women (employing the French term, "*communs tenceresses*"), and the compiler of the *Liber Albus* (rules for the governance of London) in 1419 either made or perpetuated comparable assumptions about the gendering of crimes. While "good folks" of each ward were said to be in the practice of indicting certain men as common whoremongers, adulterers, and bawds, they habitually convicted certain women as common courtesans (whores), adulteresses, bawds, and scolds.[37] The omission of scolding from the list of crimes attributable to men was no accident: in the articles that set out the rules for each London wardmote, scolding was again listed among a list of crimes for which women might be indicted, but was left out of the comparable list for men.[38] The 1486 Latin ordinances of the borough of Hereford used feminine nouns to refer to scolds, suggesting that women were perceived to be the main perpetrators of scolding in that town.[39] And in 1510, the borough of Northallerton (Yorkshire) decreed that "no woman, neither married nor otherwise shall commonly scold with her neighbours nor be rebellious at any time."[40] The very language of local ordinances thus shows that, from the time of its emergence as a legal category, scolding was reflexively a female-gendered crime.[41]

Court prosecutions fulfilled expectations about the gender of scolds suggested in ordinances. In most secular jurisdictions, women accounted for more than 90 percent of alleged scolds brought before the courts. The success with which scolding was associated with women is demonstrated by the fact that this proportion did not vary significantly over time, nor between smaller villages and larger towns. Figure 7 sets out the proportions of men and women accused of scolding in manorial courts, borough courts, and ecclesiastical courts.

As the graph shows, secular jurisdictions—regardless of size—were remarkably similar in the gender profiles of alleged scolds. Whether in

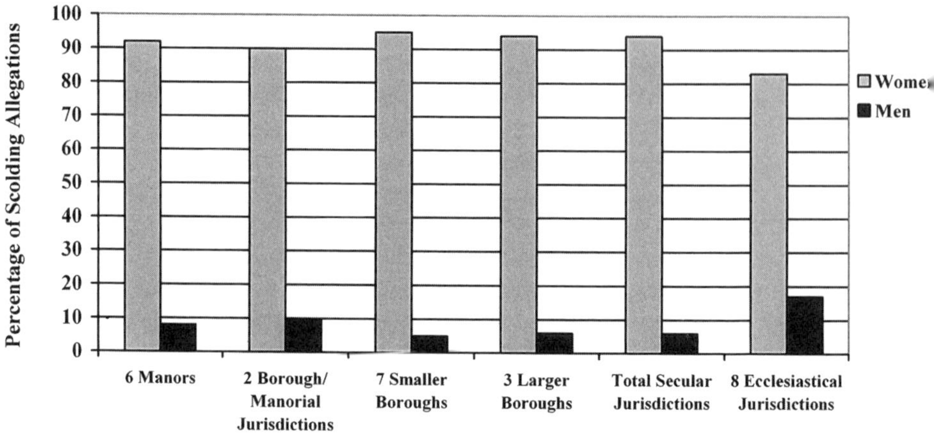

Figure 7. Scolding Prosecutions by Gender and Jurisdiction, 1311–1529. These numbers refer to scolding allegations, not individuals. Some individuals were charged more than once, and accusations against more than one individual in a single case have been counted separately. A husband and wife charged together as scolds, for instance, were counted twice. Sources for six manors: for Shotwick (Cheshire), TNA: PRO SC 2 156/13; for Widnes (Lancashire), TNA: PRO DL 30 1/20–5/70; for Chedzoy (Somerset), TNA: PRO SC 2 198/19, BL Additional Charters 15947–16102; for Yeadon (Yorkshire), *A Transcript of the Court Rolls of Yeadon 1361–1476: With the Early Rentals and Accounts of Esholt Priory, Charters, Deeds and Associated Material to 1500 A.D., Dissolution Rentals and Accounts*, ed. G. R. Price (Skipton: Maple-Bowes Publishers, 1984); for Tottenham (Middlesex), *Court Rolls of the Manor of Tottenham*, vol. 6, *2 Hen VIII–22 Hen VIII*, ed. F. W. Fenton (Tottenham: Tottenham Public Libraries, 1960), *Court Rolls of the Manor of Tottenham*, vol. 7, *23 Hen VIII–1 Edw VI*, ed. Ian George Murray (London: London Borough of Haringey, Libraries, Museum and Arts Service, 1975); for Battle (Sussex), HEH BA 546–655. Sources for two borough/ manorial jurisdictions: for Halton (Cheshire), with the manors of Runcorn & More, TNA: PRO DL 30 1/20–5/70; for Pleshey (Essex), with the manors of High Easter and Waltham, TNA: PRO DL 30 64/809–69/853. Sources for seven smaller boroughs: for Middlewich (Cheshire), TNA: PRO SC2 156/1–7; for Congleton (Cheshire), TNA: PRO DL 30 1/20–5/70; for Northwich (Cheshire), TNA: PRO SC 2 156/10–11; for Tamworth (Warwickshire/Staffordshire), "Court Rolls of Tamworth," trans. M. K. Dale (unpublished typescript, 1959); for Ramsey (Huntingdonshire), *The Court Rolls of Ramsey, Hepmangrove and Bury, 1268–1600*, ed. Edwin Brezette DeWindt (Toronto: Pontifical Institute of Mediaeval Studies, 1990); for Dunster (Somerset), SARS DDL 9/5, 10/2–3, 11/ 2, 12/1–4, 13/1; for Bridgwater (Somerset), *Bridgwater Borough Archives*, 3 vols., ed. Thomas Bruce Dilks, Somerset Record Society Publications, vols. 48, 53, 58 (London: Somerset Record Society, 1933–43). Source for three larger boroughs: for Nottingham, *Records of the Borough of Nottingham*, vols. 1–3, ed. W. H. Stevenson (London: B. Quaritch, 1882–85); for Colchester, *Court Rolls of the Borough of Colchester*, vols. 1–3, ed. and trans. Isaac Herbert Jeayes and W. Gurney Benham (Colchester: s.n., 1921–41); for Exeter, Maryanne Kowaleski, "Gossip, Gender, and the Economy: The Origins of Scolding Indictments in

manors, small towns, larger towns, or composite jurisdictions, women accounted for between 90 and 95 percent of alleged scolds. The proportions of women accused as scolds in manorial and borough courts also remained similar over time: they accounted for 94 percent of prosecutions between 1350 and 1399, 91 percent of prosecutions between 1400 and 1449, and 93 percent of prosecutions between 1450 and 1499. Other studies corroborate this strongly gendered pattern: Karen Jones and Michael Zell found that women accounted for thirty-four of thirty-seven (91.9 percent) accusations in the borough of Fordwich (Kent) between 1450 and 1570, and Marjorie McIntosh estimated that women made up between four-fifths and nine-tenths of scolding convictions in 175 fifteenth-century secular local courts.[42] These parallels underline the fact that scolding in secular courts was clearly and consistently a gendered crime.

Women were more likely than men to be charged as scolds in church courts too, but the discrepancy was not quite so large. Of 137 scolding cases from church courts between 1397 and 1519, only 114 (83 percent) were levied against women. Two factors might help explain this apparent discrepancy between ecclesiastical and secular courts. First, church courts were particularly sensitive to the behavior of clergy (who were, obviously, all male). In the episcopal visitation from Hereford, for instance, three members of the parish clergy were charged with scolding in the same words as were used to describe scolding among members of the laity. Ecclesiastical sensitivity to the behavior of clergymen might have distorted slightly the normal sex ratios among scolding charges. Second, charges of scolding in ecclesiastical courts seem sometimes to

---

Medieval England," forthcoming. Sources for eight ecclesiastical jurisdictions: for Hereford, "Visitation of Parishes by John Trefnant, Bishop of Hereford, 1397" (unpublished typescript from original in Hereford Cathedral Archives MS 1779); for Lincoln, *Visitations in the Diocese of Lincoln, 1517–1531*, vol. 1, ed. A. Hamilton Thompson, Lincoln Record Society Publications, vol. 33 (Hereford: Lincoln Record Society, 1940); for Salisbury, *The Register of John Waltham, Bishop of Salisbury 1388–1395*, ed. T. C. B. Timmins, Canterbury and York Society Publications, vol. 80 (Woodbridge: Boydell Press, 1994); *The Register of John Chandler, Dean of Salisbury 1404–1417*, ed. T. C. B. Timmins, Wiltshire Record Society Publications, vol. 39 (Devizes: Wiltshire Record Society, 1984); for Kent, *Kentish Visitations of Archbishop William Warham and His Deputies, 1511–12*, ed. K. L. Wood-Legh, Kent Records, vol. 24 (Maidstone: Kent Archaeological Society, 1984); for Wisbech deanery (Ely diocese), jurisdiction of prior and convent of Durham, Middlesex, and Barking deaneries (London diocese), L. R. Poos, "Sex, Lies, and the Church Courts of Pre-Reformation England," *Journal of Interdisciplinary History* 25 (1995): 585–607 (Poos did not include in his figures a further twelve cases involving couples or groups charged jointly).

have functioned as secondary charges for individuals presented primarily for other offenses. That is, in ecclesiastical courts, a scolding accusation sometimes operated as supplementary evidence of bad character, supporting an individual's culpability in a more dramatic crime. John Brown of St. Christopher's parish, London, for example, shocked fellow parishioners in 1520 by washing his hands in the holy water of the baptismal font at Easter. Although he was presented first as a "common defamer of his neighbors" (*communis diffamator vicinorum*), thus qualifying as a scold, before being charged for being "contemptuous" in his action at the font, the details of his case and punishment focused on the latter crime. For putting his hands in the font he was ordered to fast for forty days on bread and water alone and to recite three Hail Marys. But the scolding presentment, as if eclipsed by his spectacular impiety, was not mentioned in his punishment.[43] A scolding presentment could also serve as a secondary accusation made of women, as it was for Anna Miller, who was presented as a common scold (*communis diffamatrix vicinorum suorum*) in conjunction with a specific allegation that she had defamed Eleanor Dulyne.[44] But because men were more frequently presented before ecclesiastical courts overall, the use of scolding presentments to buttress other accusations might have resulted in relatively more male scolds. In any case, in ecclesiastical jurisdictions, like secular jurisdictions, women clearly predominated among those accused of scolding.

That the crime of scolding was gendered female is evident, however, in contexts outside the courtroom. Like manorial and borough ordinances, other discussions of scolding in the abstract also assumed that scolds were female. When scolding was mentioned in documents written in Latin, the noun for "scold" was typically feminine. The terms "*obiurgatrix*," "*litigatrix*," "*rixatrix*," "*contentrix*," "*garulatrix*," "*scolda*," and the like mean, by the suffixes "-ix" and "-a," not merely "scold" but "female scold." In the context of a court session, one might understand that the term used was gendered female when a woman was presented and (almost always) gendered male when a male was presented—hence "*garulatrix*" became "*garulator*" and "*litigatrix*" became "*litigator*."[45] But what is interesting is that the generic masculine form of the noun was seldom used when scolds were discussed in the abstract or en masse. Indeed, the first English-to-Latin dictionary specifically translated the term "scold" into the feminine nouns "*contentrix*" and "*litigatrix*."[46] The specifically feminine sense of the term was even more pronounced in another dictionary of the late fifteenth century which translated "scold" as "mulier, barda" (woman, stupid woman).[47]

From its earliest origins in the local and ecclesiastical courts of medieval England, therefore, scolding was a crime connected most closely with women. In a period in which women were charged with far fewer crimes than men overall, their overrepresentation in the scolding category is all the more significant. At the same time as women were losing access to the empowering institution of the hue and cry and beginning to be charged more often with defamation and scolding, attitudes toward female voices in general were inevitably shifting. By the time that Agnes, daughter of Robert le Spenser, hurled abuse at Thomas and Margaret Batesson in 1425, the people of the town of Middlewich had a vocabulary—indeed, a category—in which to place her and her words. Agnes was a scold, because a scold was a woman who raised her voice in public in a disruptive way. By 1425, the people of Middlewich had already prosecuted dozens of scolds, and they would prosecute dozens more over the decades that followed. To apply the label successfully in the future, they would draw on their own memories of what scolding entailed, defined partly by previous prosecutions such as that of Agnes.

Had the argument between Agnes le Spenser and Thomas and Margaret Batesson taken place in 1325, however, the people of Middlewich would almost certainly have thought about it differently than they did one hundred years later, because the intervening century had witnessed a sea change in the ways that women's voices were regarded in literature, in art, and in the courts. Agnes le Spenser, had she lived in 1325, would likely have appeared in court much less often than her brothers, pursuing fewer civil suits. But had she raised hues and cries against those who harmed her, they would have been taken seriously, and her voice would likely have been validated and legitimated by the court. She would have lived in an era when twice as many men as women were charged with defamation, and no particular legal suspicion attached itself to the words of women on the grounds of their sex. But Agnes was unfortunate to be born in a period in which the "sins of the tongue" had become thoroughly gendered, and the people of Middlewich thus knew that a woman who engaged in loud public disagreements might be punished for the same. The intertwined cultural and legal systems of late medieval English society worked together to reinforce the knowledge that the speech of women was both disruptive and illegitimate, and women like Agnes le Spenser were only too aware of the consequences.

Chapter 4

Men's Voices

Associations between women and disruptive speech had major implications for men as well as women. Because the category of women was so closely associated with illicit speech, men accused of speaking in problematic ways risked being labeled as womanly. In an age when masculinity might best be described, in the words of Vern Bullough, as "fragile," a man who was disruptive or excessive in speech risked his gender identity in a way that a woman did not.[1] Indeed, the term "old woman," sometimes applied to gossipy men in modern society, demonstrates the ways in which masculinity can still be undermined by an association with excessive speech. Yet men's relationship to speech in the Middle Ages was in some ways more complicated than that of women. Certain types of problematic male speech, for instance, escaped associations with effeminacy by being defined less as speech than as deeds or actions. Other types of problematic speech were prosecuted and condemned, but less emphasis was placed on their association with spoken words than on their association with rebellion and general insubordination. So although late medieval cultural connections between speech and women meant that illicit male speakers ran a risk of being considered womanly, it was a risk that some forms of speech and some speakers could transcend.

Men's Voices and the Risk of Effeminacy

When John Skelton sought to berate men for speaking ill in his 1529 poem "Against Venomous Tongues," he referenced speech's traditionally feminine connotations in a particularly emasculating turn of phase:

Sometime women were put in great blame,
Men said they could not their tongues atame;
But men take upon them now all the shame,
With scolding and slandering make their tongues lame.[2]

Others, too, condemned the limp appendage of which scolding men should feel ashamed and pointed out the association between disruptive speech and womanliness. "[H]e that cannot temper nor rule his own ire," explained a sermon of the mid-sixteenth century, "is but weak and feeble, and rather more like a woman or a child than a strong man."[3] Men who spoke angrily, in other words, were both effeminate and childish. Erasmus's early sixteenth-century treatise "On the Tongue" similarly coded problematic speech as "womanish" and unmasculine.[4] But these sixteenth-century associations between speech and effeminacy had late medieval antecedents. A fourteenth-century poem that lamented the degeneracy and unmanliness of contemporary knights, for instance, compared them explicitly to scolds, collapsing both class and gender into the charge:

> Thus is the order of knight turned upside-down,
> So that a knight can chide as well as any scold of a town.[5]

Scolding knights constituted one estate against whom the charge of effeminacy might be wielded.[6] Far more frequently charged as both womanly and garrulous, however, were the medieval clergy.[7] Theoretically celibate, the clergy attracted criticism both for their "scandalous lechery" and for being "too dainty in . . . appearance."[8] Some members of the church attracted particular concern: a fifteenth-century song, for instance, warned men to protect "your wife or your daughter . . . [o]r your son" against the lecherous advances of friars.[9] While these texts are part of broader antifraternal and anticlerical traditions, their ambivalent representations of clerical sexuality nonetheless point to concerns about the masculinity of members of the church. Feared as both voracious heterosexuals and predatory homosexuals, their manliness was decidedly dubious: indeed, some have even suggested that the medieval clergy represented a "third gender," neither fully male nor fully female.[10]

Ambivalence about the gender status of the clergy is also evident in the ways and frequency with which their voices were challenged. Priests, in particular, were hauled before ecclesiastical courts for gossiping about their parishioners' misdeeds. Just like women who, in the words of the Wife of Bath, "can hide no counsel," gossiping priests (armed with the secrets of the confessional) had the power to destroy reputations and expose people to ridicule.[11] In 1397, for example, the parishioners of Garway (Herefordshire) complained to the Bishop of Hereford that their priest, Thomas Folyot, frequented taverns "improperly and excessively to the great scandal of the clergy," and had publicly revealed the confession of Robert Scheppert, one of his parishioners. Parishioners elsewhere made similar complaints before the ecclesiastical courts: John, chaplain of the neighboring parish of St. Weonard (Herefordshire), was given to frequenting taverns and gossiping improperly; Stephen Froggesmere, rector of Bere Regis (Dorset) in 1405, publicized John Smyth's confession of theft; and John Springe, rector of Pettaugh (Suffolk) in 1499 was alleged to have "published abroad the confessions of his parishioners."[12] In addition to specific allegations of verbal indiscretion, gossiping priests occasionally found themselves charged with the "womanly" offense of scolding, in either church or lay courts. John Scarle of London, for instance, was charged in the mayor's court in 1421 for multiple offenses, including being a scold and a barrator, disclosing confessions, and committing blackmail, since he allegedly threatened to reveal the confessional secrets of his female parishioners unless they agreed to commit adultery with him.[13] Authors of moral treatises agreed that revelation of confessional secrets was a serious offense indeed: Robert Mannyng's fourteenth-century translation of a French poem included several added verses on priests' responsibility to safeguard confessions. Priests who betrayed confessional secrets, he explained, could expect to rot in hell. On earth their tongues were to be drawn out, while in hell they would be forced to chew on their tongues for all eternity.[14] Clearly some parishioners, such as those of Garway, St. Weonard's, Bere Regis, and Pettaugh, hoped for more immediate solutions by forcing indiscrete priests to answer for their misdeeds before their bishops, shaming them publicly by associating them with behaviors that late medieval society coded as feminine.

Medieval parishioners wanted priests to do more than keep secrets. It was also important that they stay remote from village politics and disputes in general. Unpopular priests in trouble for other offenses were often cited as "quarrelsome" or as "disturb[ing] the peace among [their] parishioners."[15] Complaints of quarrelsomeness among the clergy were often accompanied by allegations of drunkenness, and reports from some parishes certainly make it sound as though alcoholism was a problem among at least a few members of the clergy. Parishioners of Caundle Marsh in the Diocese of Salisbury in 1408 described their rector, Maurice, as drunk every day, continually frequenting taverns, neglecting services, and failing to visit the sick because of his drunkenness. They complained that he had pawned church property in the taverns and that he disparaged parishioners and made trouble between them.[16] Although cognizant of the church teaching that an imperfect priest could still perform the sacraments effectively in the eyes of God, medieval parishioners preferred their priests to be demure and restrained in their speech. They also expected clergy to occupy a quasi-parental role with regard to their parishioners. As gateways to God's grace, priests held authoritative positions, dispensing sacraments and handing out penances. They also possessed the power to report parishioners' misbehavior to church courts, and surviving church court records show not only that the clergy frequently reported lay misdeeds, but also that they could charge with defamation anyone who questioned this power.[17] Yet as well as possessing stern paternal authority, they were also expected to be nurturing and kind: the parishioners of Littlebourne (Kent) in 1511 were clearly bewildered and a little upset when they complained that their vicar "sometimes is malicious and looks on his neighbors with a grim and sour countenance whereas they think him, God knows, no hurt."[18] Priests were to be neither aggressive nor gossipy, neither malicious nor grim, neither overtly masculine nor effeminate, yet both paternal and maternal.

Yet priests were capable, too, of employing strategically the discourse about speech's effeminacy. Priests and *inquisitores* (laymen of relatively high social status) presented both scolds and those who gossiped in church before ecclesiastical courts. Yet whereas the Tutivillus exemplum and images (discussed in Chapter 2) made a forceful connection between women, words, and sin, men were much more likely than women to be hauled up before church courts for disturbing services by their chatter. Cases of impeding divine services were less frequent than cases of defamation or scolding, yet they were not altogether rare, especially by the mid-fifteenth century, as Figure 8 shows.

Among seventy allegations of talking in church and disturbing services in six dioceses, fifty-nine were laid against men, yet only eleven against women. Some men were charged repeatedly: Robert Pygge of the Wisbech parish of St. Peter, for instance, was cited in 1469 for failing to cease his gossiping, even after he had been admonished by the priest. Others, such as Bartholomew Edmund of Leverington, were cited on more than one occasion. Male chatterers were often presented in groups of up to three or four at once, suggesting that the intention was to make an example of a particularly loud or garrulous clique of friends.

The gap between representations and prosecutions of church-time chatterers is an interesting one. Did the association between church gossip and women make gossiping men more conspicuous? Did gossiping men pose more of a threat by setting a bad example for women? Were *inquisitores* better placed to detect male chatter due to the fact that all men (*inquisitores* included) sat on one side of the church and all women on the other?[19] To both priest and *inquisitores*, gossip during services must have represented a flaunting of authority, a disorderly form of insubordination that ran contrary to the increasingly popular discourse of order and good governance. The apparent contradiction between literary and artistic constructions of church gossip and those presented before the courts, however, demonstrates the very resilience of gender norms about speech. Whereas the proportion of men charged as church gossips did not change significantly over time, the stereotype of women

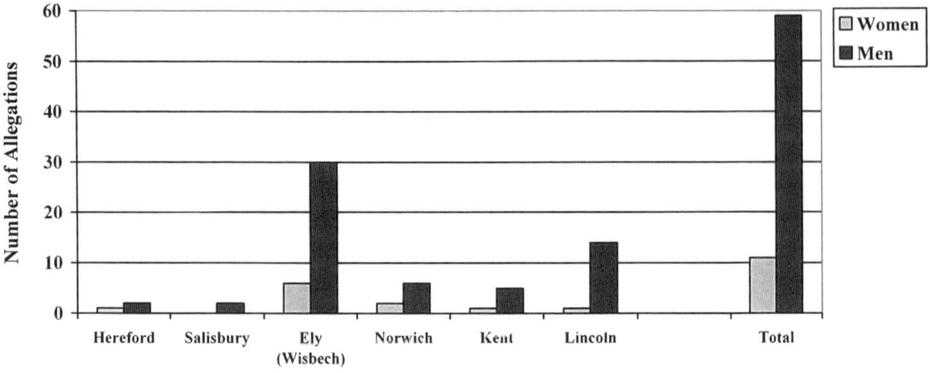

Figure 8. Church-time Chatter, 1397–1519. The numbers presented here refer to allegations, not individuals, so some individuals are counted more than once. Sources: for Hereford, "Visitation of Parishes by John Trefnant, Bishop of Hereford, 1397" (unpublished typescript from original in Hereford Cathedral Archives MS 1779); for Salisbury, *The Register of John Chandler, Dean of Salisbury 1404–1417,* ed. T. C. B. Timmins, Wiltshire Record Society Publications, vol. 39 (Devizes: Wiltshire Record Society, 1984); for Ely (Deanery of Wisbech), *Lower Ecclesiastical Jurisdiction in Late-Medieval England: The Courts of the Dean and Chapter of Lincoln, 1336–1349, and the Deanery of Wisbech, 1458–1484,* ed. L. R. Poos (Oxford: Oxford University Press, 2001); for Norwich, *The Register of John Morton, Archbishop of Canterbury 1486–1500,* vol. 3, *Norwich Sede Vacante, 1499,* ed. Christopher Harper-Bill, Canterbury and York Society Publications, vol. 89 (Woodbridge: Boydell Press, 2000); for Kent, *Kentish Visitations of Archbishop William Warham and His Deputies, 1511–12,* ed. K. L. Wood-Legh, Kent Records, vol. 24 (Maidstone: Kent Archaeological Society, 1984); for Lincoln, *Visitations in the Diocese of Lincoln, 1517–1531,* vol. 1, ed. A. Hamilton Thompson, Lincoln Record Society Publications, vol. 33 (Hereford: Lincoln Record Society, 1940).

as disturbers of church services persisted. Inevitably, therefore, men who were charged with gossip must have experienced some association with things effeminate. Indeed, some of the words used to describe their speech were akin to those used for scolding, one of the most feminine of crimes: Robert Pygge of Wisbech was described as a "*garulator in ecclesia*" while Bartholomew Edmund was cited "*pro garulatione in ecclesia.*" John Mayson junior of Emneth was allegedly a "*communis objurgator in ecclesia,*" whereas Robert Johnson of the same parish was accustomed to "*litigare in ecclesia et cimiterio* [churchyard]."[20] Each of these words (derived from the verbs *garrire, obiurgare,* and *litigare*) was also used in both local and ecclesiastical courts to describe scolds. So although the context of their chatter was carefully circumscribed, church gossips—mostly men—were almost scolds and were possibly intended to feel shamed by their association with a womanly crime. The discourse on the effeminacy of speech was one that could be employed strategically by both clergy and laity.

Swearwords as Deeds

Yet while medieval men—clergy and lay alike—risked being charged with womanly behavior if they gossiped or spoke angrily, certain types of speech transcended this association. In particular, the crimes of swearing and blasphemy—which tended to be identified primarily with men—escaped a close connection with effeminacy. Medieval profanities typically involved invoking parts of Christ's or God's body by swearing, for instance, "by God's flesh" or "by the bones of Christ." A common late medieval exemplum warned swearers that each time such an oath was uttered, the physical body of Christ in heaven was harmed. In a poem dated 1522, painted on the roof of the nave of All Saints Church, Almondbury (Yorkshire), Christ laments that "you unnatural man have in your mind / my bloody face, my wounds wide." He tells swearers that

> you do me more harm when you swear
> by members of my body
> than the Jews did that spilled my blood
> on the Mount of Calvary
> Therefore I pray that you lay your swearing aside.[21]

Because of the harms they inflicted on Christ with their oaths, habitual swearers were sometimes punished in kind with comparable pains, either on earth or in the afterlife. But just as the Tutivillus story was usually told with women as the culprits of gossiping in church, the swearing exemplum almost always featured men as the transgressors.[22]

Indeed, gender seems more central to the exemplum than social status. One tale, for example, told of a gentleman who went hunting on a Sunday (a sin in itself) but failed to catch anything. Miserable, he retreated to a tavern, and began to curse at his bad luck, muttering, "By God's blood, this day is unhappy!" Before too long, his nose began to bleed, which caused him to curse further, swearing by "God's passion," "God's wounds," "God's flesh," and "God's nails." Such blasphemy resulted in the gentleman hunter bleeding in great streams from his ears, eyes, wrists, joints of his hands, navel, and elsewhere. At the same time, his tongue, which was black as pitch, was shot out of his mouth in "a marvelous horrible loathsome and fearful manner." And thus the gentleman continued, bleeding and cursing, until he died, while those around him watched in horror.[23] Another tale, from the same source, involved the death of a young London apprentice who habitually cursed "by God's bones" and suffered an incurable "great marvelous sickness" that involved the flesh and skin of his arms, fingers, legs, feet, and toes dividing in half, as if cut with a knife, so that his bones were revealed.[24] Swearers could come from any social status. Commentators lamented that the commandment to refrain from taking God's name in vain was broken "among learned and ignorant, among young and old, among rich and poor, from a little young child that can hardly speak, to an old bearded man that age has nearly deprived of his right speech," yet they conspicuously failed to state that swearing took place among both women and men.[25] While medieval authors often said "men" when they meant "men and women," they reinforced the connection between males and swearing by consistently casting men as sample transgressors in their examples. And while authors of exempla generally chose men as sample sinners more often than women, other crimes involving speech (such as talking in church or slandering others) were typically illustrated by stories in which women served as transgressors.[26] Compared with the exemplum of Tutivillus and the women who gossiped in church, swearing was a reflexively male-identified crime. Furthermore, those who swore seemed to escape associations of effeminacy such as those attached to chiding knights and gossiping priests.

The male-associated nature of swearing was thrown into greater relief by stories and representations in which Mary, as mother of Christ, holds Christ's broken body or intercedes on his behalf to halt his suffering. John Mirk, for instance, repeated a common medieval tale in which a Roman justice, sent to a new land, brought with him the practice of swearing by God's passion, arms, sides, and bloody wounds. Soon, all the people of the land were cursing in a similar manner. But one day, a beautiful woman appeared before the justice, carrying her fair child who was all bloody and tortured. She confronted the justice, telling him that he and his men had dismembered her son, Jesus Christ, with their horrible oaths. As all the people watched, the earth opened up and swallowed the swearing justice. The people of the land quickly reformed their behavior and swore no more.[27] Mary also intercedes for her son in a poem in which she condemns the "cursed swearers" who have caused her son's body to be dismembered and promises that at Judgment Day she will turn away from swearers who beg her for mercy and ban them from heaven.[28] The poem continues with a series of sample curses from habitual swearers—tapsters, yeomen, dice players, archers, merchants, tennis players, and fighters—who regret their oaths in the final part of the poem as they suffer the pains of hell. While medieval people would almost certainly have interpreted the tapster as likely to be female, the other characters were probably assumed by the poem's audience to be male.

Like the Tutivillus exemplum, the story of the swearing men was also represented in visual media. Mary's lamentation on behalf of her cursed son was inscribed, with some slight variations, on a fifteenth-century stained-glass window from the parish church at Heydon (Norfolk), which represented twelve young men, each swearing by a particular part of Christ's body. This window is now lost (its inscriptions were recorded by antiquarians), and it is not certain whether Mary was actually depicted in the window or whether her words were simply recorded.[29] She does appear, however, in a contemporary wall painting from Broughton (Buckinghamshire) in which the body of the adult Christ lies across her lap (see Figure 9). Christ's body has been visibly damaged by the oaths of the surrounding men: his right foot and hand are missing and—in several places—his skin and flesh have been severed by swear-words. These profanities, we can assume, were uttered by the nine men surrounding Christ and his mother, seven of whom hold dismembered parts of his body, including a hand, a head, a heart, a foot, and bones. One man also holds a communion wafer, symbolizing the body of Christ.[30]

Christ and his mother also appear in another early fifteenth-century wall painting, this one from the church at Corby (Lincolnshire). The Corby painting, however, represents a different stage from the exemplum: each of the eight young men surrounding the Virgin and her son is accompanied by a devil who inflicts an appropriate punishment on the swearer's own body.[31] Although only two wall paintings depicting the swearing exemplum survive, we might note that their focus is significantly different from that of the Tutivillus representations. The men in the swearing wall paintings are no longer in the contexts in which they uttered their oaths but are instead turning toward Christ and his mother in acknowledgment of and regret for their misdeeds. Whereas Tutivillus and the women are represented at the collusive moment of their sin, still gossiping away as the demon eavesdrops, the swearing men are shown after their sin, displaying its physical, tangible consequences, either for themselves or for the body of Christ.

While women were occasionally connected with swearing, as exemplified by the Wife of Bath, who claimed that men could neither swear nor lie half so well as women, medieval tales, exempla, poems, and artistic representations overwhelmingly associated swearing and blasphemous speech with men.[32] Yet men who cursed somehow remained exempt from the charge of effeminacy leveled at complaining knights and indiscreet priests. The exemplum and representations showing the fate of the swearing men are both explicit and emphatic in their warnings about the evils of blasphemous speech, yet they do not claim such speech to be womanly. While poets and sermon authors were quick to imply womanliness in feeble knights or in men whose dress was thought to be too

Figure 9. Wall Painting of Swearing Men from Broughton (Buckinghamshire). Conway Library, Courtauld Institute of Art, United Kingdom.

modern or elaborate, they did not make similar charges against men who swore or blasphemed. How did medieval people reconcile the fact that troublesome speech in general was associated with women, while cursing and swearing in particular were associated with men? Part of the answer doubtless lies in the capacity of medieval culture, like modern culture, to incorporate contradictions and ambiguities. But part also, I suggest, lies in the ways in which swearing was constructed in late medieval England.

The exemplum of the men who swore by parts of Christ's body represents the crimes of the men less as speech than as *acts* or *deeds*. The oaths of the blasphemous men wreak physical, tangible results for Christ's body (and their own), in a way that women's gossip does not. Contemporary aphorisms and maxims suggest that an important distinction existed in late medieval and early modern England between words (typically gendered female) and deeds (associated primarily with men). "Words they are women, and deeds they are men," proclaimed a proverb first recorded in 1598 but probably dating from earlier.[33] By viewing the act of swearing as a deed, a physical attack on the body of Christ, the binaries of speech and deeds, women and men, could be maintained without disruption.

Male Speech as Deeds in the Courts

Speech could be constructed as a deed in the context of the courtroom too. In 1315, Geoffrey Shepherd of Redgrave (Suffolk) was puzzled to find himself sued for defamation by Richard the Chaplain. Geoffrey explained that he did not use any force in his conflict with Richard and protested being sued not for committing any act but instead for "wind." The "wind" to which Geoffrey referred was that of spoken words.[34] Like Geoffrey—and like exempla and visual representations—medieval courts also distinguished between words that were "wind" and words that implied deeds.[35] Unlike Geoffrey, however, they took "wind"-like speech, speech dangerous in and of itself, just as seriously as speech that implied or promised action. Moreover, the distinction between words-as-words and words-as-deeds was heavily gendered, especially from the late fourteenth century onward.

On some occasions, words that accompanied assaults were punished in the courts, but they were constructed in different ways from the closely associated crime of scolding. Men were far more likely than women to be charged with assault and other types of violence: they outnumbered women in allegations of violent crimes by a ratio of more than 5:1.[36] Presumably, men did not fight in silence, however verbal offenses that accompanied assaults are seldom mentioned in the court records. One exception can be seen in the court records of Battle (Sussex), in which men were often cited for committing assaults "*in verbis contumelios* [*sic*]" (with insulting or outrageous words), which may or may not have been accompanied by physical violence. Indeed, among surviving records between 1460 and 1470, men who made assaults with contumelious words numbered almost as many as scolds. Surviving courts from this decade list eight scolds—one man and seven women—whereas seven men are recorded as having made assaults with contumelious words (and many more for regular assaults). Yet the ways in which court records constructed scolding and assaults with contumelious words are revealing. Those committing assaults with contumelious words were presented as having committed specific actions, described with verbs, rather than as people occupying a particular identity, that of common scold, described with nouns. They also received slightly lower fines than scolds (3.29d. compared with 3.75d.), suggesting that the court regarded the offense of assaulting with contumelious words as less problematic than that of scolding.[37] In other jurisdictions, men who were disorderly in their speech were sometimes charged with general disruptiveness rather than with scolding per se. When John of Langham and Robert Porter of Leicester spoke "litigious words and threatening words" to Richard Gamson, bailiff of the lord Duke of Lancaster, on a market day in 1379, they were charged as disturbers of the peace rather than as scolds.[38] In the court records of Battle and Leicester, the distinction between doing and being, committing assaults with words and occupying the category of scold, was thus maintained quite explicitly.[39]

In addition to swearwords and "assaults with contumelious words," other types of problematic speech also managed to dodge the association with effeminacy. As Chapter 1 has explained, manorial and borough courts recorded particular concern from the late fourteenth century onward about the verbal abuse of community officials and inappropriate speech in the courtroom, and these offenses were committed especially by men.

As Figure 10 shows, those who allegedly abused bailiffs or constables or other local officials and those who muttered, gossiped, or created commotions in the courtroom were typically men. No women were named among the twenty-two charges of contempt and gossip in Methwold (Norfolk) between 1368 and 1406. A couple of women were charged at Crowle (Lincolnshire) for inappropriate speech in the courtroom (and a third was charged with general rebelliousness, not specifically directed against officials), but these are the exceptions to the rule. Verbal insubordination in the courtroom was largely a male crime.

Part of the explanation for men's preponderance among rebels and courtroom mutterers is doubtless that men were far more likely to be

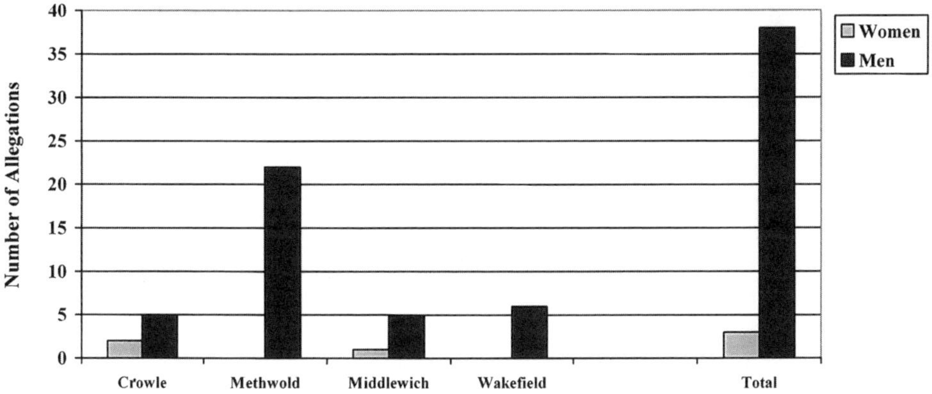

Figure 10. Abuse of Officials and Disruption in Court, 1332–1406. The numbers presented here refer to allegations, not individuals, so some individuals are counted more than once. These numbers do not include those cited for contempt of court unless the contempt was clearly verbal in nature. In some places, individuals could be cited for contempt if they arrived to court late or withdrew from the court before the session was completed. See, for example, *The Court Rolls of the Manor of Wakefield from September 1348 to September 1350*, ed. Helen M. Jewell, Wakefield Court Rolls Series of the Yorkshire Archaeological Society, 2nd series, vol. 2 (Leeds: Yorkshire Archaeological Society, 1981), 23, 100, 101, 124, 200. Sources: for Crowle (Lincolnshire), LA CM 1/22–1/42; for Methwold (Norfolk), TNA: PRO DL 30 104/1471–1480; for Middlewich (Cheshire), TNA: PRO SC 2 156/2; for Wakefield (Yorkshire), *The Court Rolls of the Manor of Wakefield from October 1331 to September 1333*, ed. Sue Sheridan Walker, Wakefield Court Rolls Series of the Yorkshire Archaeological Society, vol. 3 (Leeds: Yorkshire Archaeological Society, 1982); *The Court Rolls of the Manor of Wakefield from October 1338 to September 1340*, ed. K. M. Troup, Wakefield Court Rolls Series of the Yorkshire Archaeological Society, vol. 12 (Leeds: Yorkshire Archaeological Society, 1999); *The Court Rolls of the Manor of Wakefield from September 1348 to September 1350*, ed. Helen M. Jewell, Wakefield Court Rolls Series of the Yorkshire Archaeological Society, 2nd series, vol. 2 (Leeds: Yorkshire Archaeological Society, 1981).

actors in the courtroom context. Manorial courts required the attendance of the suitors—those who owed suit to the court—and these were generally the male heads of household. If a woman was engaged in conflict over debt or trespass, the case was typically brought by her husband or father (unless, she was a widow or—in the rare instance—she was trading as a *femme sole*). Yet men were also more likely to be charged as rebels for abusing officials outside the courtroom itself. They threatened rent collectors, cursed at constables, and bad-mouthed bailiffs. In some scenarios, one cannot help but wonder whether the same behavior coming from a woman might not have been described as scolding, rather than rebelliousness. In 1349, for instance, William, son of Philip Sagher, confessed in the court of Wakefield (Yorkshire) to having threatened John, son of Henry Forester, while John was performing his duty as ale taster. William was charged with contempt against the lord.[40] Women certainly were, occasionally, charged with rebellion against ale tasters—Sherri Olson cites examples from the Huntingdonshire manors of Upwood and Ellington in 1403 and 1425—but other women who protested the authority of local officials might have found themselves charged as scolds rather than rebels.[41] Karen Jones and Michael Zell have suggested that rebellion against local authority was a recurring theme in scolding prosecutions and that women tended to be more harshly punished for insubordination than men.[42] Similarly, Maryanne Kowaleski's work on the scolds of Exeter has highlighted the threat they posed to members of the local elite.[43] In other words, similar behaviors performed by men and by women might have been interpreted and labeled differently by the manorial or town officials on whom they were visited. Women, once again, were associated with an identity based around words, whereas men carried out rebellious deeds or deeds merely *accompanied* by injurious or contumelious words.

Male Scolds

Even on the rare occasions when men were charged as scolds, they might have been able to escape the association with things womanly. The low number of male scolds makes it difficult to generalize about their characteristics, but among the small sample three main patterns stand out. First, men accused of scolding were often charged alongside their wives. Of twenty men accused in manorial and borough courts between 1373 and 1464, for instance, six were accused of scolding together with their wives, and a further two were accused in groups alongside women who shared the same surname (and hence *may* have been wives, sisters, or some other female relation).[44] A typical example is that of Hugh Welesson of Middlewich. In 1434, Hugh and his wife Isabel were involved in an argument with Helen, wife of Peter Bradwall. Helen, the court heard, scolded (*obiurgauit*) both Isabel and Hugh, calling Isabel a "child murderer" and Hugh a "skallet [wretched] knave." Isabel and Hugh in turn scolded (*obiurgauerunt*) Helen, calling her a "lesyng blebberer" (lying bletherer). Helen was fined 6d. for each scolding (that is, a total of 12d.), and Hugh and Isabel were assigned a joint fine of 6d.[45] The record of the court proceedings reveals frustratingly little about the dynamics of this incident: How did it begin? Was Hugh perhaps drawn into the argument in an effort to support his wife? Was Isabel perhaps drawn in in an effort to support her husband? Nor do we know how Hugh felt about his scolding conviction—whether he felt deeply shamed, sorely aggrieved, or unconcerned. It is possible, however, that he and other men charged as scolds alongside their wives might have regarded their charges as *resulting* from their support of their wives. In other words, even though they were charged as scolds, they garnered such charges as the result of performing typically masculine and husbandly tasks. Although charged with a crime with strongly feminine associations, these associations might have been mitigated by their performance of stereotypically manly behaviors, those of providing support and protection for wives and other female family members.

Second, in examining male scolds we can also see that—if they had substantial social and economic resources—the "womanly" associations that accompanied scolding charges were not necessarily sufficient to remove them from positions of power. Male scolds (like female scolds) came from a range of social and occupational backgrounds, although members of local elites were perhaps overrepresented among the men. Of five male scolds from Middlewich, for example, three came from prominent local families, owned land and/or businesses, and regularly served in the relatively prestigious positions of juror or chamberlain. Moreover, scolding accusations did not necessarily spell an end to local prominence and public officeholding. In 1425, William Croucher was fined in the county court as a common "*litigator*" (scold) and "*baratemaker*" (troublemaker) among his neighbors in the town of Middlewich.[46] Yet William continued to be appointed as juror, town chamberlain, and churchwarden throughout the 1420s, 1430s, and early 1440s, positions to which no local woman was ever appointed. Men who could draw on social and economic resources were thus able to ride out scolding charges and associations of effeminacy without losing access to local power.

Third, men accused of scolding were often in trouble for multiple other offenses. John Scarle, for example, a parson of London, was simultaneously accused in a civil court in 1421 as a fornicator, a scold, a barrator, a discloser of confessions, and a wrongful practitioner of the profession of surgeon. Richard Maynhard of Bridgwater (Somerset) faced multiple charges across the 1370s and 1380s as a raiser of unjust hues and a regrator of fish. And William Croucher of Middlewich was almost constantly in trouble during the 1410s and 1420s in the borough court, sheriff's tourn, and county court for assault, looting, rape, theft, and participation in plans for murder. William's punishment for scolding followed a year in which he had appeared in the county court on no fewer than thirteen occasions, both alone and with accomplices.[47] Ruth Karras has proposed that when women were charged with scolding alongside multiple other crimes, prosecutors might have been trying to send the message that "[h]ere is a woman out of control."[48] Court records of male scolds suggest that, in the cases of at least some men, scolding convictions expressed the same sentiment as for women, whether or not they carried the same consequences. In such situations, scolding charges were typically only one of multiple ways in which local authorities attempted to discipline individuals regarded as unruly.

Men who appeared before the courts as alleged scolds may indeed have been regarded in their communities as womanly and emasculated. But the small sample of surviving cases in which men were charged suggests that some men may have been able to overcome such associations if prosecutions seemed to result from their support of family members, if they possessed substantial social and economic resources, or if their scolding presentments were overshadowed by other, more serious charges.

The relationship between men and speech in late medieval England was significantly more complicated than that between words and women. Because illicit speech was so emphatically coded a feminine failing, men who spoke too much or in inappropriate contexts risked the charge of effeminacy, of possessing "lame tongues," worn out by overuse. Yet despite the general connection between excessive or disruptive speech and effeminacy, certain types of illicit speech and certain male speakers managed to dodge such connotations. Crimes such as swearing, abusing community officials, and attacking others with contumelious or injurious words were often constructed—in both literary and artistic representations and in court records—as actions or deeds, as opposed to womanly words. The man who swore by "Christ's bones," muttered in the courtroom, or abused a bailiff was seen as committing a misdeed rather as misspeaking. Reflecting a long-standing cultural binary that connected women with words and men with deeds, the verbal crimes commonly committed by men were not represented as speech per se. Even on the few occasions when individual men were prosecuted for the female-associated crime of scolding, they may sometimes have been able to escape the connection with effeminacy by means of their social and economic resources or by constructing their alleged scolding as appropriate husbandly support of their wives. Men perhaps had more to lose than women by being disparaged as womanly, yet they also had more room to maneuver in avoiding such derision.

However, medieval men had still to negotiate one more twist to the complex gendering of speech norms: just as excessive speech was effeminizing, so too—on occasion—was excessive silence. When, as Priscilla Martin has pointed out, the Host in the *Canterbury Tales* tries to goad the Clerk into telling a story, he casts the Clerk's silence as unmanly:

You ride as shyly and quietly as does a maid
[W]ho were newly married, sitting at the table;
This day I have not heard a word from your tongue.[49]

The Clerk is emasculated by his failure to contribute verbally to the entertainment of the pilgrims. Just as garrulous men made their tongues lame with overuse, men who failed to use their tongues at all were seen as verbally impotent. Unwise silence, included in the twenty-four "sins of the tongue" enumerated and explained by Guillaume Peyraut in his thirteenth-century treatise, was akin to cowardice. As late medieval translations of Peyraut noted, priests who held their tongues, hesitating to intervene to prevent sins, put the souls of their parishioners in jeopardy and were as guilty as those who failed to blow their horns to warn of an enemy's attack.[50] Failure to speak could be just as unmanly as speaking too much.

Appropriate masculine speech in late medieval England thus occupied a middle ground between silence and garrulity; at either margin, men risked being seen as effeminate. While certain types of male speech were sheltered from an association with womanliness, the consequences for those who transgressed the boundaries could be humiliating. For late medieval English men, speech norms were both more fraught and more flexible than for their sisters and their wives.

Chapter 5
Communities and Scolding

On Tuesday July 23, 1426, almost the entire session of the borough court of Middlewich was given over to ten cases of scolding. First to be accused was Margery, wife of Thomas del Mulne. The town bailiff reported that Margery had scolded (*obiurgata fuit*) Isabel, widow of Thomas Dun, calling her a whore and "other dishonest words" and saying that Isabel's mother, father, and late husband were thieves. Isabel, also charged as a scold, responded by calling Margery a whore and saying that Margery's parents were thieves. Next came the cases of Alice Haynesson and Agnes Daa. Alice, it was alleged, called Agnes a "scallud hore [wretched or scurvy or miserable whore]," and Agnes, in response, claimed that Alice was a "cuttudhore [scantily dressed whore]." In the remaining cases, three more wives and one widow were accused of calling each other whores and/or thieves, while one female servant and one man were accused of scolding by "greatly defaming" their targets. Eight of the alleged scolds were found guilty, and the court collected from them a total of 8s.5d. in fines.[1]

The proceedings of Middlewich for July 23, 1426 are slightly unusual in the number of scolds presented in a single court session, yet they also demonstrate that the presentation of scolds was no rare or peculiar event: scolding prosecutions were so central to the maintenance of local order in Middlewich that a court session could be comprised of nothing but routine business and the punishment of scolds. Indeed, scolding and its prosecution played a much more important role in late medieval popular life than many have recognized. In early fifteenth-century Middlewich, at least one third of the population appeared in court connected to scolding in some way, whether as alleged scolds, targets of alleged scolding, or pledges (guarantors) for those charged. At Macclesfield, eighteen miles to the east, scolding cases made up one in every forty-five cases considered by the borough's court between 1349 and 1396.[2] Not only were scolding prosecutions relatively regular events, but scolds themselves were relatively ordinary individuals. Some historians have suggested that scolding charges were reserved for people regarded by contemporaries as seriously antisocial.[3] While a few convicted scolds were regularly in trouble for a wide range of offenses, the majority were fairly respectable or otherwise ordinary villagers and townspeople. Moreover, the significance of scolding spread well beyond the numbers of individuals accused in courts. Prosecution of scolds not only punished those whose speech was deemed disruptive or problematic: it also deterred other potentially disruptive speakers, and it served to empower those invested in the silence of others. The institution of scolding was not simply a way to stigmatize and censure those who were already regarded as marginal or odd. Rather, it was part of a much more complex social dynamic. Until now, I have focused broadly on the ways in which the voices of ordinary women and men were perceived and prosecuted in late medieval England. The next two chapters focus more specifically on the crime of scolding, examining first the role of local communities in defining and prosecuting scolds, and second the ways that individual scolds fit into these communities.

Scolding was centered first and foremost around local dynamics. Local jurors, constables, and bailiffs decided who was a scold and the decisions they made were influenced not only by the general discourses on the "sins of the tongue" and on women's susceptibility to such sins but also by the complex networks of personal loyalties and enmities in which they lived. The role of local individuals, some of whom were probably more invested than others in maintaining the legal category of "scold," led to considerable variation in the prosecution of scolding across time and place. Indeed even the way in which the term "scold" was defined and understood varied from one jurisdiction and one decade to another. Some jurisdictions never prosecuted scolds; others prosecuted them intermittently, seeming to forget about scolding for several years at a stretch; still others prosecuted scolds regularly for decades. Scolding prosecutions could play an important part in the peacekeeping regime of a given village or town, but the extent to which they did was determined largely by the choices of local officials and by those who exercised power and authority within the local dynamic.

Definitions of Scolding and Elements of the Crime

Scolding was never clearly defined; indeed, indeterminacy was critical to the construction of the offense in both legal and literary texts. From the late fourteenth century, authors and clerks assumed that their audiences were sufficiently familiar with the term "scold" (or its Latin equivalents) to require no further explanation. The term was used without further explanation in court records (both secular and ecclesiastical), poems, ballads, plays, and local ordinances. Although prosecuted in local and church courts from the mid-fourteenth century, scolding was never mentioned in medieval statute law. When proscribed in borough ordinances, it was not defined or exemplified. Indeed, some of the earliest direct attempts to define scolding appeared in dictionaries that translated English into Latin or French. A scold, according to the fifteenth-century monk and lexicographer Galfridus Anglicanus, was a contentious or litigious woman.[4] As a verb, "to scold" was often used in literary texts as a parallel to the verb "to chide," and "chiders" seem to have been roughly equivalent to "scolds."[5] Early modern legal commentators grouped scolds unproblematically alongside brawlers, eavesdroppers, defamers, slanderers, and other perpetrators of public nuisance.[6] William Sheppard, in the seventeenth century, explained that "[a] Scold in a legal sense is a troublesome and angry woman, who by her brawling and wrangling amongst her Neighbours, do break the publick Peace, and beget, cherish and increase publick Discord."[7] Medieval legal commentators were not nearly so helpful. Yet the lack of clear medieval definitions of scolding left ample scope for local jurisdictions to interpret the term as they saw fit. While frustrating to modern historians, the indeterminacy of late medieval scolding was an important part of its construction. Because scolding had such flexible meanings, it was easily adapted to multiple situations and served a diverse range of interests. Meanings were further complicated by the fact that definitions were certainly contested—both successfully and unsuccessfully—by those to whom the label was applied.

Some traces of geographical and temporal variation in the meaning of scolding are apparent in surviving court rolls. In the village of Halton (Cheshire), for instance, scolds were normally presented for particular specified offenses, and the Latin term for scolding was rendered as a verb. For example, when William le Hasty junior of Halton was presented in 1422 and fined 6d., it was because he "*litigauit cum*" Thomas Nothyngham. Agnes Bathe, at the same court, was similarly fined because she "*litigauit cum*" William Pole and called him a thief. But twenty-five miles to the southeast of Halton, in the town of Congleton, scolding was typically constructed less as a behavior than as an identity: a person *was* a scold, rather than *behaving* in a scoldlike way. Agnes, wife of John de Mynton, for instance, was one of three women presented before the court in 1422 and fined 12d. because she "*est communis litigatrix cum vicinis suis* [is a common scold among her neighbors]."[8] Like most local jurisdictions, the Congleton court used the word "scold" [*litigatrix*] as a noun, describing accused people as *common* scolds, rather than specifying instances of scolding. Whether this distinction between noun and verb was made by all members of the community or just by those who heard and recorded cases, the difference in construction demonstrates that the definition of scolding was open to variation across time and place, even among those who prosecuted it.

Indeed, the very way in which most people came to understand what was meant by the term "scold" was doubtless affected by the cases that they witnessed in the local courts. For example, in presenting Agnes, wife of John de Mynton, as a common scold, the bailiffs of Congleton's court were also saying something about what scolding entailed—that is, that scolding was being (in their eyes) like Agnes Mynton. In this way, the construction of scolding was affected by all kinds of information (much of it unrecoverable) about Agnes. For example, her age, her appearance, the way she interacted with others, her occupation, and her position in the community would each have sent out signals to others about what those who scolded looked like. Being a scold, then, was about more than just the act of excessive speech on any one occasion; it also entailed looking like a scold, occupying the social position of a scold, and possessing other characteristics that might make an individual prone to the charge of scolding, within the context of a local jurisdiction that claimed the power to punish speech it deemed problematic.

Indeterminacy was a critical part of the construction of scolding, yet people still had to do *something* in order to be accused of the crime. While they may indeed have been in the wrong place at the wrong time, and while they may have been particularly liable by virtue of their gender or social position, a person could not be charged as a scold if he/she was consistently amenable, silent, or withdrawn from community conflicts. The thing an individual had to do, the action he/she had to take, was to speak, and to speak in a way that could be perceived as disorderly and disruptive to the community at large. The label of scolding could only be applied successfully if three elements of the crime existed. First, one had to disagree with another individual or group of individuals. Disagreements could center on quite specific incidents, as when Alice de Pocstones of Nantwich (Cheshire) claimed in 1415 that Margery, daughter of Thomas le Harper, had stolen her handkerchief.[9] They might also reflect more longstanding tensions among individuals or families, situations in which any specific causes had been superseded by a more general enmity. Such tensions were apparent, for example, in conflicts between the Bole and Ryche families of Wellington (Somerset) in 1421. Alice Ryche was charged with scolding Joan, wife of John Bole, and stealing malt from his chamber. John Bole, in return, was accused of beating Alice Ryche and entering the garden of her husband John Ryche and stealing his property. In the Bole-Ryche dispute, Alice's alleged scolding was thus only one of multiple ways in which the families manifested their mutual dislike.[10] Second, in order to be charged as a scold, one had not only to disagree with another person or people but to voice one's disagreement. If Alice de Pocstones had kept her resentment about the missing handkerchief to herself or Alice Ryche had chosen to say nothing to Joan Bole in spite of the dispute between their families, they would not have been charged as scolds. But each chose to vocalize her dissent, and thus got into trouble. Finally, the *way* in which dissent was vocalized mattered in determining who was a scold. If Alice de Pocstones had used the courts to pursue her missing handkerchief, she may have risked charges of frivolous accusation but it is unlikely that she would have been charged as a scold per se. She might also have avoided scolding charges had she pursued her grievance in a less confrontational way or in a less public space. This third element—that disagreements needed to be voiced in a problematic way in order to fit the category of scolding—is the most difficult to pin down. Lack of detail in the court records makes it hard to determine what was so objectionable about the ways in which particular people spoke, but it would seem that courts were most concerned about disagreements voiced in public settings and disagreements that involved use of particularly inflammatory words.

Scolding usually took place in public spaces, in situations in which anyone could hear the verbal exchanges. In the few instances where the physical location of an alleged scolding was recorded, it is clear that it was space accessible to all. When the borough of Middlewich punished Agnes le Spenser on September 4, 1425, because she scolded (*obiurgauit*) Thomas Batesson on multiple occasions, the physical context helped distinguish the incidents from one another. Agnes allegedly scolded Thomas once at the large bridge, once in the inn owned by Thomas del Mulne, and once (in an unspecified place) along with his wife Margaret.[11] Both the large bridge and the inn of Thomas del Mulne were places accessible to others, places in which many people could hear Agnes's words. A similarly public space was invoked in the presentment of Alice, wife of Hugh Wytton in April 1425. Alice was prosecuted for having scolded (*obiurgata fuit*) Margery, wife of Richard Shene, in the church of Middlewich, disturbing church services and thus causing offense both to the king and to Christ. The place of Alice's alleged scolding constituted a double affront to public order, for the church was not only public space but sacred space as well. Accordingly, Alice was meted out the high fine of 16d. when she appeared before the court.[12]

The seasons in which scolds were prosecuted also attest to the public nature of scolding: in warmer months, people were more likely to spend time in the public space of the outdoors, and disputes between neighbors that might in winter have been confined within a house were more likely to take place in a public setting. Scolds were thus more likely to be presented before the courts in spring or summer than in autumn or winter. In Middlewich, scolds were twice as likely to be prosecuted in the warmer months of the year. While courts heard cases of fifty-three alleged scoldings between April and September, only half as many (twenty-six) appeared between October and March. A similar pattern emerged in the nearby jurisdictions of Halton, Widnes, and Congleton. Scolds were usually prosecuted in the thrice-yearly halmote courts, but the halmotes held during the summer months of July or August dealt with more than twice as many cases as those held during autumn or early spring.[13] Scolding almost always took place between members of different families and households, but one can imagine that, during the winter, the weather might sometimes have driven participants in an argument inside someone's house rather than enabling them to air their differences in the street or marketplace.[14] Part of what was so objectionable about the speech of alleged scolds, therefore, was often its public nature. As presentments sometimes stated, loud, public disagreements posed an "annoyance to all the neighbors" or a "disturbance to the common peace."

Inflammatory words also mattered. Much like today, medieval people seem to have regarded particular words as off-limits, words that, when hurled in insult, carried a particular power and weight beyond their literal meaning. The words used in cases of scolding are recorded only in a minority of cases; they seldom survive in cases where individuals were charged as "common" scolds, and many jurisdictions did not record inflammatory words at all. The words that do survive, however, are remarkably uniform. Much like defamers charged in church courts, scolds typically insulted men with the term "thief" and women with some variation on the term "whore." In fact, so formulaic were these insults that when Agnes, wife of Hugh de Wystanton of Shavington (Cheshire) was charged in 1410 for scolding Robert of Hennebury, it was also noted that she was a common scold (*communis litigatrix and obiurgatrix*), "calling men and women thieves and whores, that is to say all her neighbors." Similarly, in 1511, a church court heard that John Bocher of the parish of Wye (Kent) was "a great slanderer of his neighbors and calls them thieves and their wives whores."[15] Of fifty recorded insults from Middlewich between 1413 and 1443, twenty-three involved some variation on "thief," and a further twenty-three included terms such as "whore," "strumpet," or "harlot." Scolds from Halton, Widnes, Congleton, and associated manors were just as unimaginative: all thirty-seven inflammatory phrases recorded between 1357 and 1459 included some variation on "thief," "whore," or both.

Why was the term "thief" such a common pejorative? The centrality of commerce in the small market towns of late medieval England, the constant anxieties about regulation of trade, and the material vulnerability of medieval townsfolk and peasants perhaps help to explain why thieves were regarded with such abhorrence. Living in houses with walls so flimsy that they could be broken through and with yards easily accessible to the public, medieval people were somewhat at the mercy of their neighbors. Thieves were predators, people who broke the trust of the community and deserved to be shunned. To be *really* insulting, one might claim not only that a particular individual was a thief but that his/her relatives were too. When Hugh Welesson of Middlewich insulted William Batesson in February 1425, he said that William was a thief and so too was his father.[16] Formulaic though it might have been to insult his target's parents (and one can certainly think of modern corollaries), Hugh's insult suggested that the social status of thief was an hereditary status, passed from father to son. Similarly, when Isabel, widow of Thomas Dun, insulted Margery, wife of Thomas del Mulne, in 1426, she insisted that Margery's father and mother were thieves (and Margery reciprocated by saying that Isabel's mother, father, and late husband were thieves). Aspersions had already been cast on Margery's background in the previous year, when Agnes le Spenser said that Margery was a thief along with "all her kind."[17] To call someone a thief and to insist that their parents were thieves too made the status of thief seem like a congenital condition, in the same way that serfs who were born unfree carried unfree status for life and passed it on to their children.

Just as thieves represented the bottom stratum in a system of social esteem centered around economic morality, so those of loose sexual morals represented the antithesis of purity and continence in a world that placed great value on sexual order. Middlewich scolds, like those elsewhere, most often applied the term "whore" and its variations (such as "strumpet" or "stronge hore") to female targets (a total of twenty-three times). Occasionally their slurs, as recorded by court clerks, seemed to be tailored to the individuals they insulted. Alice Haynesson, for instance, had been presented several times for the generic insults of "thief" and "strumpet" prior to July 23, 1426; on that date, however, she was convicted of calling Agnes Daa a "scallud hore" and Agnes was presented for calling her a "cuttudhore" in response. Emmota le Chaloner also adapted an insult of sexual impropriety in 1434 when she called Alice, wife of Roger Wyche, a "wedded man's whore." Surviving court rolls from Middlewich do not record any instances of women being called "priest's whore," but the insult was well known elsewhere in Cheshire.[18] Defamation cases in church courts show that just as the status of thief was applied not only to individuals but also to their families, so too previous generations were sometimes accused of sexual immorality with such phrases as "priest's son," or "son of a whore."[19] For women, especially, the status of whore was about as low as one could get.[20]

"Thief" and "whore" and their synonyms accounted for the vast majority of inflammatory words recorded in scolding cases, but on rare occasions we get to see other words that, when uttered in the right (or wrong) contexts, were deemed especially disruptive. Some of these involved social status: the terms "serf" and "londleper" (vagabond), for instance, were discovered by L. R. Poos among insults hurled in defamation cases in fifteenth-century church courts. Similar slurs were used in Cheshire: the social status of Cecilia, daughter of Laurence de Aston, of the hundred of Wirral was maligned in 1412 when another woman called her a "churlesdoughter" (peasant's daughter).[21] And Helen de Bradwall, one of Middlewich's most notorious scolds, referred to Hugh Welesson in June 1434 as a "skallet [wretched] knave." Helen's choice of words was especially ironic since Hugh was a member of the local elite. In each such situation, social status was central to the affront, and the insults were presumably insulting precisely because they asserted that those maligned were of a lower social station than the insultees claimed to occupy.

In order to have the label of scold successfully applied, one thus had to speak in a way that was deemed obnoxious and disruptive to public order. When deciding what speech was obnoxious or disruptive, jurors and bailiffs seemed to pay particular attention to the places that words were spoken and the specific words that were used. Arguing with others in public places or using words like "thief" or "whore" were risky behaviors if one wanted to avoid the label of scold. Acknowledging the role that alleged scolds themselves played in their own conviction is not to suggest that they were unjustified in raising their voices, nor that they deserved their punishments. It is, rather, to point out that—short of utterly capricious prosecutions—a few elements of the crime had to be present in order for the charge to stick. An individual could not be prosecuted without some kind of speech act that could potentially be deemed disruptive. Within this broad definition, however, there was much scope for interpretation.

Jurisdictional Variation

If Helen de Bradwall had lived in the small town of Clare (Sussex) rather than the small town of Middlewich, chances are that she would not have been prosecuted for scolding. Insults like "skallet knave"—Helen's alleged slur of Hugh Welesson—were presumably uttered in Clare, yet surviving records do not make mention of any scolds. The surest way to have one's speech labeled as scolding, then, was to live in a jurisdiction that regularly prosecuted scolds, and not all jurisdictions did. One metaphor that might help us understand a jurisdiction's proclivity to prosecute scolds is to imagine it as a human population during the flu season. Like flu germs, the cultural discourse on female speech was inhaled by everyone, but only some jurisdictions were "infected." That is to say, the cultural category of scold did not always develop into the legal category of scold and—as with diseases—it was difficult to predict for certain which would be most susceptible.

Marjorie McIntosh has suggested that jurisdictions presenting scolding, eavesdropping, and nightwandering were more likely to be market centers than small villages, that they were slightly more common in the north and northwest than in the midlands and east central region, and that they were particularly likely to be located either along major rivers or roads or along the coast.[22] She also proposed that many places experiencing crimes of "disharmony"—such as scolding—were subject to rapid population growth from inward migration during the fifteenth century. As part of a broader project to chart changing patterns of misbehavior in late medieval and early modern England, McIntosh sampled a full year's records for between 128 and 184 jurisdictions in each twenty-year period between 1370 and 1599. Between 10 and 23 percent of jurisdictions in her sample prosecuted at least one scold in any given year throughout most of the fifteenth and early sixteenth centuries. The lowest percentages of jurisdictions prosecuting scolds were found in the 1370s to the 1410s, the 1480s to the 1490s, and the 1540s to the 1590s; the highest percentages were found in the 1420s to the 1470s and 1500s to the 1530s. McIntosh's arguments are interesting and suggestive, and it makes sense that places experiencing inward migration would be more likely to prosecute scolds, given concerns about speech and voices in an era of change.

Maryanne Kowaleski, in her examination of scolds in fourteenth-century Exeter, has also emphasized the importance of immigration in sparking scolding presentments. Kowaleski has argued that the immigration of young single women, able to command higher wages in an era of demographic decline, prompted resentment on the part of employers (who also served as jurors in the local courts). Indeed, empowered by economic independence and a later age of marriage, these women may also have behaved in more assertive ways, making themselves more vulnerable to charges of scolding.[23]

Drawing upon a different set of data, however, I would suggest that the most important factor determining which jurisdictions prosecuted scolds was neither demographic nor geographic but rather the presence of individuals who—for a variety of reasons—were personally invested in scold prosecution. Certainly these individuals, typically members of the local elite, might have been more likely to hear about scold prosecutions elsewhere if they lived in places that were well linked to communication networks. Demographic pressures might also have increased both misbehavior and the ways in which local officials viewed this misbehavior. But we should be cautious in ascribing patterns, I would suggest, given the irregular nature of record survival and the fact that prosecution of scolds could wax and wane significantly within a single jurisdiction over time. While McIntosh's information provides a useful snapshot of the possible contours of scolding over a long period of time, it is a somewhat fuzzy snapshot. Her method of sampling within a sample (one year within a twenty-year period for each jurisdiction) means that the proportion of jurisdictions presenting scolds is certainly underreported. Nonetheless, McIntosh's broad sample provides a useful, if imprecise, cross-section of the dynamic in scold-prosecuting jurisdictions. Kowaleski's data is extremely reliable for the town of Exeter, but it is not typical for the country as a whole: in comparison with scolds from elsewhere, Exeter scolds were poorer, and they came from families with little political clout. They also scolded men more often than women and they especially targeted men of higher socioeconomic status than themselves. My own data from secular jurisdictions in the fourteenth to early sixteenth centuries both confirms and complicates the picture laid out by McIntosh and Kowaleski. My sample is certainly narrower than McIntosh's, examining fewer jurisdictions, but it is also deeper, drawing on records of more than six hundred scolds. On the other hand, by investigating scolds in more than one locality, I am able to gain a broader picture than Kowaleski.

In most jurisdictions, levels of concern about scolding, as manifested in numbers of scolding presentments, were highly irregular, and these fluctuations did not correlate with any broad national pattern. Both "common scolds" and perpetrators of specific incidents of scolding were frequently presented in batches, often with several years in between in which no scolds appeared before the courts. Many local jurisdictions appear to have had periodic blitzes on scolding, rounding up large numbers of individuals who were perceived as creating a problem. Six Colchester women, for instance, were charged as scolds and disturbers of the peace in 1378. Four men and eleven women were similarly rounded up by local officials of Barkergate in the town of Nottingham in 1414 and accused of being common scolds (*communes litigatores* and *communes litigatrices*). And, as we have already seen, the prosecution of ten scolds consumed virtually the whole court session of Middlewich on July 23, 1426.[24] In each case, high numbers of scolds prosecuted in one jurisdiction do not seem to have been mirrored in high levels of prosecution elsewhere in the same immediate period: no regional or national pattern can be discerned.

By the late fourteenth century, the cultural category of "scold" was known throughout England, and presumably most jurors and court stewards were aware that some jurisdictions also saw the "scold" as a legal category. In some towns and boroughs, the attention of jurors and officials was directed by rules that specifically warned against scolding and even specified punishments, and it is possible that the earliest rules against scolding date back to the late thirteenth or early fourteenth centuries.[25] At Portsmouth in the late fourteenth or early fifteenth century, for example, those familiar with the town customs (the medieval term for rules) would know that "if there be any Chiders or Scolds they [should] be put in the Cucking stool and let . . . fall in to the Camber [River]." London's *Liber Albus* of 1419 deemed local aldermen responsible for expelling scolds from the city or punishing them by means of the cucking stool. In Worcester in 1467, responsibility for punishing "scolders, and chiders" lay with the bailiffs, according to the city ordinances. By the mid-sixteenth century, the mayor of Barnstaple (Devon) specifically included the routing of scolds in the oath he swore on coming into office. The "oath of Mr. Mayor" included a promise to repress "common scolsters and slanderers" as well as sowers of discord and those causing strife and debate among their neighbors.[26] Smaller jurisdictions did not usually compose lists of rules per se but entered new ordinances in the court rolls as they seemed necessary. In the late fourteenth century, manors like Yeadon (Yorkshire), and the Durham manors of Hesilden, Billingham, Wolveston, and East Merrington repeatedly passed ordinances against scolding or scoldlike behavior.[27]

The existence of rules against scolding does not, however, indicate that the rules were enforced consistently and thoroughly. In many cases, rules appeared after scolds had already been presented within the jurisdiction. The borough court of Colchester declared its jurisdiction over scolds from the late fourteenth century, and jurors from at least as early as the mid-fifteenth century were instructed to enquire about and present "common chiders and brawlers to the annoyance of their neighbors."[28] Yet Colchester courts had been prosecuting scolds intermittently from at least as early as the 1310s. It is possible that earlier lists of rules that included bans on scolding have not survived. But it is also possible that the laws followed—rather than prescribed—the practice. English villagers and townspeople were savvy about their legal rights, but vague statutes that required people to "keep the king's peace" could be interpreted broadly by court officials and jurors. The importance of local dynamics in interpreting who was a scold is evident in two main ways. First, the close involvement of particular individuals in prosecuting scolds suggests that local personalities could affect the definitions of scolding and the numbers of scolds prosecuted to a significant degree. Second, villages or towns in close geographical or administrative proximity sometimes followed roughly similar patterns in the numbers of scolds prosecuted, suggesting that local elites sometimes took cues from neighboring jurisdictions.

Sensitive Officials

Some of the intense concern manifested in blitzes of scolding presentments was very likely due to the interpretations and the sensitivity of local officials and other important individuals. In Middlewich in the mid-1420s, for instance, Thomas and William Batesson pursued multiple incidents of alleged scolding against themselves or their wives.[29] Between 1423 and 1425, Thomas was said to be the target of at least four scoldings, two of which were perpetuated by Agnes le Spenser, as discussed at the beginning of Chapter 3. Bailiffs also named William as the target of scolding on four occasions, and in addition he twice brought civil suits against alleged scolds (a rare occurrence). The wives of Thomas and William were also targets of scolding in these years: between 1423 and 1425, Margaret, wife of Thomas, was scolded twice and Katherine, wife of William, was scolded three times. Thomas and William Batesson were powerful men on the local scene, and they chose to use the legal category of scolding to protect their own reputations and further their own interests. Each had served as bailiff in earlier years, and Thomas was wealthy enough by the late 1420s to be one of three burgesses who rented the farm of Middlewich directly from the crown. Presentments of Middlewich scolds were generally brought by bailiffs, rather than by juries of presentment, but it is likely that important men like the Batessons could exercise a degree of influence in bringing cases to the bailiffs' attention. At least two of those who served as bailiff during the early 1420s were close associates of Thomas and William, men who had supported them in business or in court proceedings.[30] Furthermore, William clearly possessed the means (and inclination) to bring civil accusations of scolding before the court. By pursuing scolds, Thomas and William sought to protect their own reputations and perhaps to dissuade others from abusing them. Their sensitivity to scolding and willingness to ensure that scolds were punished added fifteen accusations to a total of thirty-five scolding cases in Middlewich between 1423 and 1425. That is to say, alleged scoldings of these two men and their wives accounted for 43 percent of scolding cases brought before the court in a three-year period.[31] In a small town like Middlewich, a few individuals concerned about scolding could make a real difference.

Just as influential individuals could claim to have been targets of scolds, so too individuals in positions of local authority might have decided that the prosecution of scolding was an effective means for enforcing general communal harmony, a harmony in which they were heavily invested. Court stewards had particular power to encourage presentation of various types of crime, since they were responsible for the instructions (or charge) to jurors, who in turn listed all the offenses committed by local residents in the period since the last court. If a particular steward emphasized one type of crime more than others when he asked jurors about recent local misdemeanors, this emphasis might have shown up in the number of presentations. Because we lack records of these verbal interactions or emphases, we cannot be absolutely certain that any one individual was responsible, but the records of prosecutions are sometimes suggestive. In 1410, for instance, William de Stanley was appointed to the stewardship of Halton, Widnes, Congleton, and other Duchy of Lancaster manors. In court rolls that survive from the period immediately prior to Stanley's appointment—that is, court rolls from 1405, 1406, 1409 and 1410—scolds had been presented only at Halton and only on five occasions in eleven court sessions. In the court that followed Stanley's appointment, however, four scolds were presented at Halton, and Congleton courts, which had not recorded a scold in surviving records since 1401, presented one scold.[32] Unfortunately, court records from the following decade are either missing or in such bad condition as to be illegible, so it is impossible to tell whether or not this trend of increased prosecution continued in subsequent years of William de Stanley's tenure. The revival of scolding prosecutions might suggest, however, that Stanley perhaps reminded the jurors of Halton, Widnes, and Congleton that presentment of scolding—or perhaps crimes involving communal harmony in general—was part of their responsibility.

The erratic pattern of scolding presentments thus owed something to the interests of powerful local individuals like William and Thomas Batesson and William de Stanley. Just as the varying priorities of modern local governments and police forces play an important role in determining which crimes are targeted most closely, the varying concerns of local officials in late medieval England doubtless played a significant role in the prosecution of some crimes more than others. Surviving records enable tantalizingly few glimpses of the people behind the policies, but those few glimpses suggest that geographical and temporal variations in numbers of scolds presented may have been due to some degree to variations in the sensitivity of bailiffs, stewards, and other individuals of local influence, some of whom cared greatly about scolding and some of whom did not.

Geographic and Administrative Connections

A second local factor in determining the frequency of scolding presentments was proximity—both geographical and administrative—to other scold-prosecuting jurisdictions. The correlation between courts in close geographical and administrative connection can be illustrated by examining presentments from the courts of Halton, Congleton, and Widnes between 1360 and 1460. In the late fourteenth and early fifteenth centuries, each of these jurisdictions was under the control of the Duchy of Lancaster, and each was administered by the same court steward (for instance, each was administered by William de Stanley, described above, from 1410).[33] In each of the three series of records—Halton, Widnes, and Congleton—scolds appeared regularly in courts between 1357 and the 1430s. Across the period, seventy-two scolds were prosecuted in Halton (with the attached manors of Runcorn and More), eighteen in Widnes, and thirty-four in Congleton.[34] While the numbers of scolds presented varied by jurisdiction, the pattern of scold presentments in each rose and fell in a roughly similar pattern across the hundred years from 1360 to 1460.

In each jurisdiction, the number of scolds fell slightly from the 1360s to 1370s and was relatively low until the 1400s. The numbers rose again in the 1410s, were particularly high in the 1420s and 1430s, but had fallen by the 1440s. While four full years of court rolls survive from the 1450s for Halton and Congleton and three years survive for Widnes, no scolds were presented anywhere. Whether due to changes in emphasis on scolding on the part of Duchy of Lancaster administrators, fluctuations in a pervasive regional discourse about scolding, or some other factor, the courts of Halton, Widnes, and Congleton were relatively in tune with one another when it came to presenting scolds. The immediate geographical and/or administrative proximity of jurisdictions could thus play an important role in the varied pattern of local scolding presentments.

While scolding prosecutions may indeed have been encouraged, as McIntosh and Kowaleski have suggested, by factors such as migration, location along roads and waterways, and population growth, scolding was also a crime with very flexible boundaries. This flexibility made it possible for powerful members of any community, from the smallest to the largest, the most central to the most remote, to prosecute as scolds anyone whose speech was deemed to be at odds with local expectations. Some jurisdictions prosecuted a lot of scolds; others prosecuted few or none. Scolding was grounded first and foremost in the dynamic of the local community and in the concerns of those who exercised local authority. Although these local officials were almost all men, women could also play a role in the prosecution of scolds, petitioning bailiffs and jurors to apprehend those whom they found disruptive and annoying. The concerns of local officials (and their petitioners) varied considerably over time and place.

Indeed, the very survival of the label of scolding owes something to this flexibility. During the fourteenth century, the legal category of "scold" had evolved at the intersection between the discourse on women's illicit speech and the precedents and conventions of local jurisdictions. Once identified as a crime that could be prosecuted in local courts, however, it remained a legal category throughout the late medieval and early modern periods. Much of the reason for this survival was its adaptability to local definitions, local personalities, local disputes, and local dynamics.

Chapter 6

Who Was a Scold?

Alice Inchemerssh of Kingsland (Herefordshire), wife of Thomas London, found herself in serious trouble on June 7, 1397. The parishioners of Kingsland told the bishop of Hereford that she was both a scold (*communis diffamatrix vicinorum suorum*) and an adulterer. Alice was accused in the church's court of committing adultery with three men: Roger Mascald, Wilkoc Walker, and John Ledder. For her crimes, Alice was suspended from the church; presumably she was re-admitted after performing the appropriate penance.[1]

Fifteen years later and one hundred miles to the south, in the manor of Carhampton (Somerset) in 1412, Margery Bythewater and her daughter Lucy were charged as common scolds (*communes obiurgatrices*), petty thieves, and nightwalkers (those who wandered around at night without a lawful excuse). Margery and Lucy were probably quite poor: Margery paid only 6d. per year in rent for a cottage with a yard, and the fact that she was held accountable for her own rent tells us that she was probably either widowed or had never married. Similarly, Lucy—described as Margery's daughter rather than as someone's wife—was probably unmarried. Margery and Lucy were each fined 6d.[2]

At the same time as Margery and Lucy Bythewater were charged as scolds in Carhampton, Henry le Vernon was living a comfortable life in the town of Middlewich, together with his wife Matilda. Described in county court records as a yeoman, Henry owned several properties in the town and served multiple times as chamberlain and as bailiff in the early fifteenth century. Yet, toward the end of what was probably a long life, Henry found himself hauled up before the same borough court that he had so often served as a juror. On June 22, 1434, the court heard, Henry had been scolded by Helen, wife of Peter de Bradwall, and called "harlot and thief." "Harlot" was an unusual word for an alleged scold to choose, but Helen de Bradwall was remarkably inventive with her insults. Whereas most scolds used the standard epithets of "thief" for men and "whore" for women, Helen used such terms as "wretched knave," and even "murtherchyld" ("child-murderer"). In response to being called a harlot and a thief, Henry claimed that Helen was a "thief and an untrue liar." Neither the fact that he came from a well-established local family, nor that he had served the town in official positions was enough to prevent Henry from being fined 12d. for having scolded (*obiurgauit*) Helen.[3]

What did these people have in common? Alice Inchemerssh, Margery and Lucy Bythewater, and Henry le Vernon came from different places in different decades. They were charged in different jurisdictions: a church court, a manor court, and a borough court. They varied in marital status: Henry and Alice were married (although Alice's alleged adultery suggests that her marriage may not have fulfilled all her needs) whereas Margery and Lucy were likely unmarried. They also varied in social status: although Alice's socioeconomic background is unknown, Margery and Lucy were probably poor whereas Henry was relatively well-off. Even the ways in which they were accused of scolding varied: Alice, Margery, and Lucy were charged as common scolds, and Henry for the more specific offense of scolding Helen de Bradwall. The cases of Alice Inchemerssh, Margery and Lucy Bythewater, and Henry le Vernon illustrate the flexibility of the label "scold." The label could be applied successfully to women or men, people who were poor or relatively well-off, people who were unmarried, married, or widowed, and people from all regions of England.

As Chapters 2 and 3 demonstrate, the legal and cultural categories of "scold" were both linked firmly with women. Yet not every woman was accused in courts of scolding, and on rare occasions men—like Henry le Vernon—were charged. What, then, made some people more liable to the charge than others? Despite the extreme flexibility of the label, as discussed in Chapter 5, some individuals *were* more likely than others to be charged as scolds, due to their social and familial positions and to other crimes with which they were associated. Although it is impossible to discern any absolute pattern applicable in every scold-prosecuting jurisdiction, alleged scolds seem more likely to have been single or married than widowed. In some jurisdictions, they were more likely to be poor than well-off, although in other jurisdictions status mattered much less. Scolds were also more likely to have been involved in feuds between families or in other petty crimes than those who stayed completely out of trouble. We must remember, though, that alleged scolds might have few or none of these characteristics. Henry le Vernon, for example, was married, but he was also male, well-off, and very seldom in trouble for other offenses. Anyone could be charged as a scold, but some people were more likely to be charged than others.

Scolding and Marital Status

Medieval men were distinguished from one another primarily by social status and occupation, but the most salient piece of a medieval woman's identity, beyond that of her gender, was her marital status. While medieval people acknowledged differences among peasant women, townswomen, and women of the aristocratic classes, the category of "woman" was most commonly divided into virgins, wives, and widows. A young single woman of the peasantry or townsfolk was expected to marry (even though, as the work of P. J. P Goldberg, Maryanne Kowaleski, Judith M. Bennett, and others have shown, an increasing number of women in postplague England stayed single throughout their lives).[4] Women were thus classified primarily in terms of their marital relationships with men: premarried, married, and postmarried. Their relationship to legitimate speech—as constructed both in literature and art and in courts—also varied according to their marital status. Indeed, relationship to legitimate speech was one of several factors that helped *define* marital status for some commentators: a garrulous single woman was not a "true" virgin, according to some, no matter whether or not she had engaged in sexual activity, whereas an old woman, especially a widow, was expected to be gossipy and querulous.

In examining court records of women charged with scolding, our estimates of marital status are hampered by the ways in which medieval scribes recorded women's names. In many cases, women's marital status was indicated as part of their names: Agnes, daughter of Robert le Spenser; Helen, wife of Peter de Bradwall; Isabel, widow of Thomas Dun. But in other cases, women's names were stated without any such identifier. Margery Bythewater of Carhampton, for instance, may never have been married, despite the fact that she had a grown daughter. Or she may have been a married woman whose husband was—for some reason or another—unmentioned. Or she may have been widowed. Studies of scolds' marital status inevitably, therefore, include a large number of women whose marital status is unknown. Probably more of these women of unknown marital status were single than married—scribes were more likely to identify someone as a wife than as a daughter—but we lack the data to be certain. Table 2 shows scolding allegations against women, arranged according to the marital status of the alleged scold. Allegations from Middlewich are listed separately, since I know more about the marital status of these women from a broader sample of court records, land deeds, and other data. Also included are data from the studies of Karen Jones and Michael Zell on Fordwich and Maryanne Kowaleski on Exeter.

Table 2 underscores the need to tread carefully when examining marital status, since the status of so many women is unknown. Indeed, the numbers of single, married, and widowed women must be regarded as bare minimums, since each category would almost certainly increase if we knew the marital status of every scold. Even given the fuzziness of the data, however, two patterns emerge: first, wives accounted for a substan-

TABLE 2. ALLEGATIONS OF SCOLDING AGAINST WOMEN BY MARITAL STATUS

Jurisdiction	*Single*	*Married*	*Widowed*	*Unknown*	*Total*
Sixteen secular jurisdictions, 1311–1529: Shotwick, Widnes, Chedzoy, Yeadon, Tottenham, Battle, Halton and associated jurisdictions, Pleshey and associated jurisdictions, Congleton, Northwich, Tamworth, Ramsey, Dunster, Bridgwater, Nottingham, Colchester	18 (5%)	127 (38%)	2 (0.6%)	193 (58%)	332
Middlewich, 1361–62, 1367, 1413–43	20 (24%)	30 (35%)	4 (5%)	31 (36%)	85
Fordwich, 1451–1570	0 (0%)	16 (80%)	0 (0%)	4 (20%)	20
Exeter, 1368–90	26 (18%)	68 (47%)	10 (7%)	40 (28%)	144
Four ecclesiastical jurisdictions, 1397–1530: Hereford, Salisbury, Ely, Lincoln	2 (3%)	42 (58%)	1 (1%)	28 (39%)	72

Note: All women described as "daughter of . . ." are treated as single.

Sources: *Sixteen secular jurisdictions*: for Shotwick (Cheshire), TNA: PRO SC 2 156/13; for Widnes (Lancashire), TNA: PRO DL 30 1/20–5/70; for Chedzoy (Somerset), TNA: PRO SC 2 198/19, BL Additional Charters 15947–16102; for Yeadon (Yorkshire), *A Transcript of The Court Rolls of Yeadon 1361–1476: With the Early Rentals and Accounts of Esholt Priory, Charters, Deeds and Associated Material to 1500 A.D., Dissolution Rentals and Accounts*, ed. G. R. Price (Skipton: Maple-Bowes Publishers, 1984); for Tottenham (Middlesex), *Court Rolls of the Manor of Tottenham*, vol. 6, *2 Hen VIII–22 Hen VIII*, ed. F. W. Fenton (Tottenham: Tottenham Public Libraries, 1960); *Court Rolls of the Manor of Tottenham*, vol. 7, *23 Hen VIII–1 Edw VI*, ed. Ian George Murray (London: London Borough of Haringey, Libraries, Museum and Arts Service, 1975); for Battle (Sussex), HEH BA 546–655; for Halton (Cheshire), with the manors of Runcorn and More, TNA: PRO DL 30 1/20–5/70; for Pleshey (Essex), with the manors of High Easter and Waltham, TNA: PRO DL 30 64/809–69/853; for Congleton (Cheshire), TNA: PRO DL 30 1/20–5/70; for Northwich (Cheshire), TNA: PRO SC 2 156/10–11; for Tamworth (Warwickshire/Staffordshire), "Court Rolls of Tamworth," trans. M. K. Dale (unpublished typescript, 1959); for Ramsey (Huntingdonshire), *The Court Rolls of Ramsey, Hepmangrove and Bury, 1268–1600*, ed. Edwin Brezette DeWindt (Toronto: Pontifical Institute of Mediaeval Studies, 1990); for Dunster (Somerset), SARS DDL 9/5, 10/2–3, 11/2, 12/1–4, 13/1; for Bridgwater (Somerset), *Bridgwater Borough Archives*, 3 vols., ed. Thomas Bruce Dilks, Somerset Record Society Publications, vols. 48, 53, 58 (London: Somerset Record Society, 1933–43); for Nottingham, *Records of the Borough of Nottingham*, vols. 1–3, ed. W. H. Stevenson (London: B. Quaritch, 1882–85); for Colchester, *Court Rolls of the Borough of Colchester*, vol. 1–3, ed. and trans. Isaac Herbert Jeayes and W. Gurney Benham (Colchester: s.n., 1921–41). *Middlewich*: TNA: PRO SC2 156/1–7; CRO DSS 3991 Drawer 2/2, DVE 1/K/28–32, tial proportion of scolds. In every jurisdiction, at least 35 percent of scolding allegations were levied against married women. The highest proportion of scolding wives (at least 80 percent) appeared in the borough of Fordwich. Also noteworthy is the fact that at least 58 percent of scolding allegations against women in church courts were specifically directed at wives. This suggests either that church courts prosecuted wives disproportionately or—perhaps more likely—that church courts were more inclined to record women's marital status and are thus a better indicator of the marital status of scolds generally. Studies from later periods also suggest a preponderance of married scolds: Martin Ingram found that wives made up about three quarters of alleged scolds in the early seventeenth-century records of Nottingham and Henley-in-Arden (Warwickshire), and Linda Lees found that most alleged scolds in Nottinghamshire between 1603 and 1660 were married.[5] Second, single women also accounted for a substantial proportion of scolds in most places, certainly more than widows, but their numbers may have varied more significantly among jurisdictions. Even if the four scolds from Fordwich whose marital status is unknown were all, in fact, single, single women would still have numbered no more than 20 percent of Fordwich scolds. Yet in Middlewich, single women made up at least 24 percent of scolds but very likely more, owing to the large number of women whose status was unknown, and in Exeter they comprised at least 18 percent of scolds. Widows, however, seem seldom to have faced scolding charges in any jurisdiction, despite David Underdown's claim that they were particularly prone to charges of scolding in the early modern era.[6]

When jurors prosecuted single women as scolds, they may well have thought about contemporary moral treatises and popular ballads that

DVE 1/M3/61–82, DVE 1/M4/1–17, DVE 1/R/1–10; *A Middlewich Chartulary*, part 1, ed. Joan Varley, Chetham Society Publications, new series, vol. 105 (Manchester: Chetham Society and the Liverpool School of Local History and Records, 1941); *A Middlewich Chartulary*, part 2, ed. Joan Varley and James Tait, Chetham Society Publications, new series, vol. 108 (Manchester: Chetham Society and the Liverpool School of Local History and Records, 1944). *Fordwich*: Karen Jones and Michael Zell, "Bad Conversation? Gender and Social Control in a Kentish Borough, c. 1450–c. 1570," *Continuity and Change* 13 (1998): 11–31. *Exeter*: Maryanne Kowaleski, "Gossip, Gender, and the Economy: The Origins of Scolding Indictments in Medieval England," forthcoming. *Four ecclesiastical jurisdictions*: for Hereford, "Visitation of Parishes by John Trefnant, Bishop of Hereford, 1397" (unpublished typescript from original in Hereford Cathedral Archives MS 1779); for Salisbury, *The Register of John Waltham, Bishop of Salisbury 1388–1395*, ed. T. C. B. Timmins, Canterbury and York Society Publications, vol. 80 (Woodbridge: Boydell Press, 1994); *The Register of John Chandler, Dean of Salisbury 1404–1417*, ed., T. C. B. Timmins, Wiltshire Record Society Publications, vol. 39 (Devizes: Wiltshire Record Society, 1984); for Ely (Deanery of Wisbech) and Lincoln, *Lower Ecclesiastical Jurisdiction in Late-Medieval England: The Courts of the Dean and Chapter of Lincoln, 1336–1349, and the Deanery of Wisbech, 1458–1484*, ed. L. R. Poos (Oxford: Oxford University Press, 2001).

linked the sexual chastity of unmarried women with their verbal chastity. During the fourteenth and fifteenth centuries, the very definition of virginity was often cast as chastity in speech as well as deeds, with some commentators even arguing that refraining from sexual intercourse was not sufficient qualification for the status of "true" virginity. An exemplum in the long poem *Handlyng Synne*, and in John Mirk's fifteenth-century homilies for lay people, for instance, included the story of a nun who went to hell "for nothing else / But that she always spoke wickedness / Among her fellows loudly." After her death, she was buried beside an altar, but two demons with burning swords soon arrived to beat the nun about the mouth. This exemplum used the figure of a chaste nun—the earthly model of holy virginity—to demonstrate the terrible power of evil speech. "For though her deeds were chaste," readers were warned, "Her words were all vile and waste."[7] The bottom half of the nun's body—which had preserved its virginity—was dispatched to heaven, while the top half descended to hell. The exemplum of the half-burned nun demonstrates the close connection between women's sexual and verbal misdeeds in late medieval pious writings. The half-damned body of the nun suggests that the mouth was to the top of the body as the sexual organs were to the bottom half; true and complete maidenly chastity required restraint from both sexual and verbal intercourse. "[A] maiden," said John Mirk in another sermon, "is of little worth who cannot suffer any oppression nor any diseases, without complaining; and is a clatterer, a jangler, a flyter, a curser, a swearer, and a scold of her mouth. This does not defend maidenhood, but rather casts it down. Therefore a maiden must be of few words, and look that she speak with honesty and respect to her person, for it is an old English saw: 'A maiden should be seen, but not heard.'"[8]

Similarly, treatises insisted that pure speech was an essential component of the category of "true" virginity. One fifteenth-century treatise on maidenhood, for instance, identified three degrees of maidens. First were those who had not committed any evil deeds, but were disposed to foul speech and evil touching. These maidens were guilty of sin because, by their evil speech and touch, they caused others to desire them. The second group kept both bodies and hearts pure but would have preferred to be married. Because they were wedded in their souls, they earned no rewards of maidenhood. But the final group—pure maidens—was undefiled in word, deed, and desire and hence deserved to be spouses of Christ. Similar connections were drawn in another short fifteenth-century treatise that sought to promote maidenhood. Young women were urged to avoid foul language and chattering. They were to refrain from swearing, chiding, and wearing fine clothes, since these vices promoted lechery.[9] Virginity was thus about more than just sex: it included close attention to the chastity of the tongue. As John Audeley urged young women:

In word, in deed, in will, in thought,
Your maidenhood befoul you not,
Lest to blame that you be brought
And lose your status, your honesty.[10]

Both loose tongues and loose morals could, according to contemporary associations, end in shame and disaster for young women. Yet for all that they were warned against evil speech, unmarried women were seldom stereotyped as gossips or nags in the same way as wives and widows were. Transgression of verbal norms cast doubt on maidens' morality, but verbal sins were ultimately less constitutive of identity than sexual sins. An unmarried woman who had sex became a whore; an unmarried woman who talked too much risked being viewed as a whore.

Connections between literary representations and court presentments are always hypothetical and speculative. Neither cultural representations nor court accusations reflect unmediated reality, but it is possible that some of the same anxieties about the verbal chastity of young unmarried women evident in literature were also manifest in the numbers of single women accused of scolding. Among records of the Middlewich courts from the 1410s to 1440s, nine women identified as servants or daughters (and who were thus almost certainly unmarried) appeared before the courts. Single women in Middlewich seemed to scold more often than wives: between them, they accounted for 21 scolding charges (an average of 2.3 each) compared with 1.4 charges each on the part of married women. *Why* did the people of Middlewich prosecute their servants and daughters as scolds, and prosecute them several times over? Without direct testimony from town officials, we can only speculate. Perhaps, mindful of the link between illicit words and illicit sex, bailiffs and others decided to intercede in the behavior of young women before chastity and marriage prospects were threatened. Perhaps they saw young unmarried women as a focus of concern because they were less directly under men's control than were wives. While ostensibly the responsibility of their fathers or masters, young unmarried women often lived away from their parents' homes and thus enjoyed the first tastes of relative freedom over their (limited) free time. And while unmarried women as a group were asset-poor, they nonetheless exercised more autonomous control than wives over whatever wages or resources they earned. A concern to control the verbal behavior of this group might therefore have reflected a more generalized anxiety about women outside the control of men. Certainly this is the argument that Kowaleski makes for Exeter, where, as she explains, a large pool of independent single women, in trouble for "disorderly" offenses such as prostitution and trespass as well as scolding, very likely generated anxiety among bailiffs and other officeholders of the town.[11]

Despite concerns about their virginity—both sexual and verbal—unmarried women were less closely connected with disruptive speech than were wives. Wives' uncontrollable tongues were a commonplace of late medieval English literature. As discussed in Chapter 2, ballads, proverbs, plays, and advice literature traded frequently on stereotypes of the garrulous wife and her henpecked husband. Ballads and aphorisms sometimes associated women as a category with excessive speech but, when marital status was specified, garrulous women in general often meant gossiping or scolding *wives* in particular. A Continental myth well known in fourteenth- and fifteenth-century England, for example, told the story of two monsters: Bigorne and Chichefache. Bigorne, or Fillgut, was "full fat and round," owing to his plenteous diet of henpecked husbands. Bigorne's counterpart, Chichefache, or Skinny Face, however, was "hungry, meager, slender, and lean" because she ate only "women who are meek," and these were very hard to find. Indeed, according to John Lydgate, whose early fifteenth-century poem on the pair is the first-known English reference to the monsters, Chichefache had only ever had one meal. Chaucer makes a reference to Chichefache in the "Clerk's Tale," in which "noble wives, full of high prudence" are warned with tongue-in-cheek to "Let no humility nail your tongue," lest they be swallowed by Chichefache.[12] The misogynous joke of the two monsters, which took wives' nagging and garrulity as a starting point, was also the subject of artistic representations. Lydgate's poem was apparently written to accompany painted cloths depicting the two monsters eating their respective foods in the home of a "worthy citizen of London," and late fifteenth-century wall paintings depicting the theme still survive in the French Castle of Villeneuve-Lembron, Puy-de-Dôme.[13] Bigorne (unaccompanied by Chichefache) is also thought to be the subject of misericords in Carlisle, Gloucester, and St. David's Cathedrals, a benchend at Cawston (Norfolk), and a roof boss in Southwark Cathedral. In each, a monster is depicted with the flailing legs of a man appearing from its mouth.[14]

While medieval literature continually lamented wives' nagging of their mates, wives were not prosecuted for scolding their husbands. Wives were legally subject to the wills of their husbands and, while a husband might claim that his wife's verbal misbehavior was legitimate grounds for desertion, he would certainly be seen as a cuckold if his wife were charged in court with scolding him.[15] Rather, scolding wives were most often prosecuted in courts for scolding other married women. Of the nineteen occasions on which wives in Middlewich scolded other women, eleven of the targets were other wives, three were unmarried women, two were widows, and three were women of unknown marital status. In fact, just like wives who raised hues in support of family members, wives were particularly likely to be charged with scolding for their participation in feuds or disputes that involved other members of their families. In Middlewich in 1434, for instance, when Helen, wife of Peter de Bradwall, allegedly called Isabel, wife of Hugh Welesson, a "murther-chyld," or "child-murderer," she participated in a long-standing and complex conflict involving members of the Batesson and Bradwall families on the one hand, and members of the Welesson family on the other. Tensions manifested in the form of physical assaults, pursuit of debts, and accusations of scolding.[16] Certainly wives sometimes participated in the out-and-out violence that often accompanied feuds between families, but the more typical scene—as represented by court prosecutions—was one in which husbands fought one another with their fists while their wives fought with their voices. In the era in which hue-raising was still regarded as a legitimate and regular means of communal control, women called hues to assist their husbands in situations of violence. After the decline of hue-raising in the late fourteenth century, however, they continued to raise their voices, not only to represent their own concerns, but also in the interests of their husbands and families.

Widows, on the other hand, were very seldom charged with scolding, despite the bad press they received in contemporary art, literature, and popular culture. The legal position of medieval English widows was theoretically more advantageous than that of unmarried women or wives, since widows controlled their own dowries, were responsible for their own debts, could use town or manor courts to pursue those who owed them money, and were often named as executors of their husbands' wills, taking care of property until children were old enough to inherit. The status of widow also carried a degree of social and religious esteem. Following patristic traditions, widows in religious texts were regarded as more spiritual than wives. The removal of their husbands allowed widows a "second virginity," and closer access to God, uncompromised by spousal demands. But while widows seemed better off in some ways, they were also often among the most economically vulnerable and the most morally suspect. Widows were overrepresented among the poor, in both town and countryside. Even in guilds, where they were often able to continue their husbands' workshops and memberships, their rights were fragile—they could not vote or hold office and their privileges were curtailed if they remarried.[17] In the witch craze of the sixteenth and seventeenth centuries, this economic vulnerability and dependence on the goodwill of their neighbors was to play a role in widows' liability to be charged with witchcraft.[18] In the late Middle Ages, widows were not yet accused as witches, but they were often represented as lustful and wanton, lacking in sexual morality and verbal propriety.

For even while religious authors told widows that they ranked second—above wives but below virgins—in the eyes of God, they also were also aware of popular stereotypes that cast widows and elderly women as gossips. Anchoresses were warned against listening to "garrulous old gossips" and "old wom[en]" who would feed their ears with gossip and scandal.[19] The association between gossip and old women, particularly widows, was also a feature of popular art and literature. In this regard, popular constructions of widowhood overlapped considerably with those of wives. Best known, perhaps, is Chaucer's Wife of Bath, widowed five times over, who performs the character of the irrepressible gossip and reflects on her career as a nagging wife in the prologue to her tale. The Wife of Bath is thus both a widow and a wife, and her character certainly owes something to earlier representations of female rebellion and garrulity in such figures as Noah's Wife. Constructions of widows differed from those of wives, however, in two main ways. First, the speech of widows, like that of young women, was very directly linked to their sexuality. While wives' voices were certainly connected with their sexual appetites in popular constructions, explicit associations between sexuality and verbosity especially characterized representations of widows. William Dunbar's lengthy poem of the late fifteenth or early sixteenth century, "The Tretis of the Tua Mariit Wemen and the Wedo," depicts the widow as unashamedly lascivious, insincere, and shrewlike by her own admission. Her tales of how she hated and cheated upon her two former husbands are considerably longer and more vehement than those of either of her companions, both of whom are still married.[20] Second, widows' voices differed from those of wives in that they were generally constructed as more dangerous, particularly when exercised in the company of younger women. Wives' voices were annoying; widows' were not only annoying but they could also lead others astray. Poems and prose depicting gossips, popular in the fourteenth and fifteenth centuries, almost invariably included widows among their chief protagonists.[21] Dunbar's widow, for instance, initiates the conversation about men and how to fool them and encourages the wives to follow her example. A similar role is played by Dame Isengryne in the "Gospelles of Distaves," which tells of a group of women who regularly sit together to spin and gossip. Dame Isengryne, five times widowed, but now sixty-five years old and married to her sixth husband, begins proceedings. While "a fair wife in her time," Dame Isengryne is now "greatly withered; her eyes were hollow, and her eyelids somewhat reversed and red, always watering." Drawing on her great age and great experience, the Dame enlightens the assembled women on the subject of men's unfaithfulness and complains to her neighbors about her husband.[22]

Artistic representations also suggest derision of old women's speech. Women's heads are depicted on late medieval misericords, stone pillar capitals, and corbels with their gorgets over their mouths.[23] By the fourteenth century, gorgets (garments that covered the neck and sometimes extended as far as the bottom of the chin) were typically worn by widows and nuns. Regular gorgets ended below the mouth, but in these artistic representations, women's mouths are completely covered, and in some cases, such on as a misericord from Winchester Cathedral, the gorget extends as far as the tip of the woman's nose. Although the precise meaning of these images is unknown, they seem part of an iconographic tradition that alluded to the illegitimacy of widows' speech. The obscuring of widows' mouths perhaps functioned as a visual joke. To medieval English people, who delighted in the nonsensical and in physical humor, the images possibly said, "Look—here is an old woman who cannot speak! What a contradiction in terms!" The context of several such representations makes it clear that the image of the gagged woman was intended to be humorous. On one of the Winchester misericords, for instance, a gagged woman appears on the left supporter. To her right—in the center and on the right supporter—are two smirking men, caricatured in their jollity.[24] Typically placed among other comic caricatures and carvings, the meanings of these representations have yet to be explored in full by art historians, yet they almost certainly alluded in some way to the problematic relationship between elderly or widowed women and speech.

The overwhelmingly negative and garrulous representations of widows in late medieval and early modern literature might lead one to expect that widows would be particularly liable to accusations of scolding. Such was the assumption made by David Underdown, in the first modern academic article on scolding, published in 1986. But as scholars have noted since, court prosecutions of widows for scolding were relatively rare. Martin Ingram found only a few widows among sixteenth- and seventeenth-century scolds, and Jones and Zell came across none at all among their sample of scolds from Fordwich. Only about 7 percent of scolds in late fourteenth-century Exeter, Maryanne Kowaleski found, can be identified definitively as widows, although it is possible that a few more were among those whose marital status was not stated.[25] A similarly low proportion of widows were accused of scolding in Middlewich. Only four women explicitly identified as widows appear in surviving court records of scolds, and two of these women were able successfully to plead innocence. At least three of the four widows were members of Middlewich's local elite, coming from families with both economic resources and political clout. Certainly they do not fit the stereotype of the poverty-stricken poor widow who would later be singled out as a witch.

Widowhood was thus the marital status in which artistic and literary constructions of women's voices were furthest from those of the courts, and the disparity is puzzling. Perhaps widows took heed of the prescriptive and popular literature and were indeed submissive and respectful. Perhaps age and experience taught them how to effect their purposes without running the risk of being labeled scolds. Perhaps the people of late medieval England found literary and artistic representations of widows' speech sufficient outlets for manifesting their anxiety over widows' voices and did not need to reinforce the stereotype by means of the courts. Or perhaps, in an era of underpopulation, widows did not yet seem the drain on community resources that they would become by the early modern period, the era of witchcraft accusations.

Women's relationships to legitimate speech thus varied considerably over the course of their lifetimes. A woman who followed the life course constructed as typical—who managed to preserve her virginity until marriage, who married, and who outlived her husband—would have found that her speech was regarded in different ways during different periods of her life. As a young woman, her speech might have been constructed as a verbal manifestation of her sexual status, so that if she talked too much, she would have run the risk of being thought unchaste. As a wife, she would have encountered concern about the ways in which she spoke to her husband. Yet she would also be more vulnerable to charges of scolding in the community at large, sometimes in arguments of her own making and sometimes in disputes involving her family. Once her husband died, she risked being seen as a garrulous old woman without discretion, yet court prosecutions suggest that she was less likely to engage in loud public arguments that might be construed as scolding. Indeed, just as women's speech varied according to their marital status, so too the constructions of what it meant to be an unmarried woman, a wife, or a widow in late medieval England were constituted in part by ideas about legitimate speech. Part of what it meant to be a virgin, as so many medieval commentators argued, was that one was supposed to be verbally chaste in addition to being sexually innocent. Part of what it meant to be a wife was that one was expected to nag a resistant husband. And part of what widowhood implied was engagement in gossipy—if not confrontative—speech. Speech, like sex, defined, bounded, and helped constitute women's relationship to men. And the very pervasiveness of the discourse that linked women with deviant speech meant that speech norms could readily be adapted and adjusted to each marital category.

Scolding and Socioeconomic Status

Just as scolds were drawn from each marital status, they also came from a range of socioeconomic statuses below that of the aristocracy and gentry. In some communities, poor women were most likely to be charged with scolding, but in other places burgesses and members of the local elite were just as susceptible. Similarly, scolds could come from families that were new to the region or they could come from long-established families. In some places they were more likely to be charged with scolding those higher than themselves in social status, whereas in other places the relative status of scold and target mattered less.

Behavior labeled scolding was behavior that claimed, through the act of speech, a power to label and chastise others. It was fundamentally, therefore, concerned with status. By taking on the roles of labeler and castigator, alleged scolds threatened to usurp the positions of others accorded such functions. In Middlewich in 1414, for instance, when Alice, servant of John le Baylly, said that Tybota, servant of John de Morton, was a thief and a whore, she exercised and articulated public judgment on Tybota's behavior and character, a power that local officials preferred to reserve for themselves.[26] Further, in the moment of asserting the power to label and chastise, Alice performed the active role of speaker, forcing upon others—especially the targets of scolding—the more passive role of audience. She thus claimed both the attention of those within earshot and the power to link Tybota with the negative identities of thief and whore. Alice's judgment of Tybota was deemed illegitimate precisely because she did not occupy any sanctioned positions that might have given her words credibility and authority within specific contexts. Had she been the town bailiff, she might have accused Tybota of theft in the borough court. Had she been a priest or one of the *inquisitores*, she might have accused Tybota of sexual impropriety before an ecclesiastical court or episcopal visitation. Had she been among men appointed as jurors, she might have had the opportunity to exercise such an opinion in the county court. In 1417, for example, thirty-two people from Middlewich and the surrounding area were charged with having broken into the house of Ralph Madok of Bostock and having conspired to kill him. Among them was Agnes Cause of Middlewich, described by the jurors as a "strumpet."[27] Presumably the jurors who presented Agnes and her thirty-one accomplices were not accused as scolds for the act of identifying her in terms of her perceived sexual and/or moral behavior. In fact, Agnes may or may not have been a woman of loose sexual morals—elsewhere she was identified as a "servantwomon"—but the jurors of the county court had sufficient authority in this situation to describe Agnes as a strumpet without risking condemnation as scolds.

Because both scolding and witchcraft were crimes that were associated especially with women, some historians have drawn explicit connections between those charged with each offense and have assumed that scolds, like witches, were not only old but also economically marginal. David Underdown, for instance, wrote that "[w]omen who were poor, social outcasts, widows or otherwise lacking in the protection of a family, or newcomers to their communities were the most common offenders." Sixteenth- and seventeenth-century scolding, he claimed, was "overwhelmingly . . . committed by women of low status against equals or superiors."[28] Underdown's arguments were challenged by Ingram, who argued that there was little to distinguish scolds from their neighbors in terms of social status, and by Jones and Zell, who found that Underdown's arguments could not be substantiated by their data from Fordwich. Ingram and Jones and Zell agree that scolds in the early modern era, at least, mostly came from the "lower middling ranks" or from members of the local elite, wives of jurors and local officials.[29] Although Underdown, Ingram, and Jones and Zell have dealt primarily with the early modern period, rather than the late medieval era, their findings suggest that the socioeconomic backgrounds of scolds could vary. Different jurisdictions fitted the label "scold" onto slightly different groups of women.

Medieval jurisdictions varied also in the socioeconomic status of their accused scolds. The most comprehensive data on the socioeconomic status of medieval scolds comes from Maryanne Kowaleski's as yet unpublished study of scolding in Exeter. Kowaleski examined 116 scolds (150 incidents of scolding) between 1368 and 1390, comparing alleged scolds with the population at large from her very complete series of economic and political data for the town. Exeter scolds, Kowaleski found, were generally poorer and less politically powerful than the overall population. Only a very few scolds came from families who were part of the local oligarchy or belonged to the freedom of the city, and just over one-fifth came from families that provided jurors. Rather, the majority of scolds (about two-thirds) were drawn from families with virtually no political clout, families that provided Exeter with neither officeholders nor jury members. Exeter scolds were also very likely poorer than most of the population. In murage tax assessments from 1377, the households of scolds were charged, on average, 3d. less than other households in Exeter. Those accused of scolding more than once, Kowaleski found, were generally of even lower political and economic status than scolds presented on only one occasion. Kowaleski also compared the socioeconomic status of alleged scolds with those whom they scolded, 58 percent of whom were men. Targets of scolding, she discovered, ranked significantly higher in socioeconomic status than either scolds or the population at large. Of seventy-two alleged targets, just over one quarter belonged to the town oligarchy, and a further 40 percent came from families who provided jurors or minor officeholders. Particularly interesting is Kowaleski's observation that almost half of the alleged targets of scolding (or their husbands) served as jurors or other officeholders in the year immediately prior or subsequent to the scolding presentment. Kowaleski's findings indicate that status was a crucial component in determining who was charged with scolding in late fourteenth-century Exeter.[30]

Status was less important, however, elsewhere. Less information survives on the socioeconomic background of Middlewich scolds, but the data that does exist suggests that people of higher social status were just as liable to be charged with scolding as laborers and the poor.[31] Ten of Middlewich's fifty-one scolds between 1413 and 1443 were among ninety-six men and women who can be identified as members of the local elite. A further ten belonged to the burgess category (which contained a total of 262 members). Five scolds can be identified as belonging to the ranks of laborers and the poor, and the remaining twenty-six are of uncertain social status. Identifiers of socioeconomic status are more likely to exist for members of higher socioeconomic groups, so it is probable that most of the twenty-six scolds of uncertain status were in fact laborers or members of the poor (combined, laborers, the poor, and people of uncertain status accounted for 386 people whose names can be found in surviving records). In other words, a member of the local elite in Middlewich had about a 10 percent chance of being accused of scolding, a member of a burgess family had about a 4 percent chance of being accused, and a member of the laboring classes or the poor or a person of unknown social status had about a 9 percent chance of being accused. The high number of people for whom no socioeconomic status can reliably be identified should make us proceed cautiously, yet the numbers are still significant: even if all the Middlewich scolds of uncertain status were poor, the fact that so many members of the local elite were charged with scolding suggests that status was far less important in determining who was a scold in fifteenth-century Middlewich than it was in fourteenth-century Exeter. After all, even respectable figures like Henry le Vernon, who served as the town's chamberlain and owned several properties, might find themselves charged as scolds.

Middlewich scolds not only included members of the local elite, but they also included people from long-established local families. Of the fifty-one alleged scolds, at least thirty (or their husbands or fathers) had previously appeared in the local court, and nineteen of these had first appeared six or more years before they were presented for scolding. Indeed some, like Henry le Vernon, had lived in the borough for more than thirty years before being charged as a scold. For a further twenty-one scolds, the scolding presentment was the first time they appeared in surviving records, but at least ten of these individuals (or their husbands or fathers) appeared in records for several years thereafter, which suggests either that they had always lived there or that they were presented as scolds soon after settling as long-term residents.[32] These figures suggest that the majority of scolds were not transients but instead were members of established families.

Middlewich scolds also differed from Exeter scolds with regard to the targets of their scolding: indeed, scolds and their alleged targets were much alike. For a start, the clear majority of targets were women, and this would seem to be the typical pattern for other places besides Exeter, too. Of seventy-four scolding allegations in which the target was specified, fifty-six targeted women alone, thirteen targeted men alone, three targeted a married couple, one targeted two men and a woman, and one targeted two women. Of a total of eighty targets, therefore, women accounted for 78 percent and men for only 22 percent. This pattern was borne out elsewhere: of seven incidents of scolding presented in Nottingham in 1459, six involved women scolding other women, and one involved a married couple who used abusive words against the town's mayor "and other trustworthy folk."[33] Middlewich scolds were similar to their targets in socioeconomic status as well as gender. As perpetrators of a crime that usurped authority, one might expect that scolds would tend to direct their illicit words against those of higher socioeconomic status. In Middlewich, however, most alleged scolds were charged with scolding individuals of the same status. Of the seventy-seven incidents of scolding recorded in Middlewich courts, socioeconomic data is available for both scold and target at the time of the alleged scolding in only twenty-three cases. Of these, fifteen took place between individuals of the same social ranks, four involved an individual of lower rank scolding a person of higher rank, and four involved a higher-rank scold attacking a lower-rank target. Because scolding was so often a reciprocal offense—in which one individual scolded another and was scolded in return—most scolding prosecuted in Middlewich courts took place between equals or balanced itself out across status lines. Henry le Vernon, for instance, a long-established member of the local elite, allegedly engaged in an exchange of scolding with Helen, wife of Peter de Bradwall, a burgess who did not belong to the elite group, and both were hauled up before the court as scolds.

The Middlewich data, combined with previous scholarship on scolding, suggests that the relationship between socioeconomic status and the label of scold could vary widely across time and place. In fourteenth-century Exeter, status was very important in determining who was most likely to be accused of scolding, with members of the lowest-ranking groups prosecuted disproportionately. In fifteenth-century Middlewich, status was considerably less central to the construction of the offense. Individuals who had served as town chamberlain were prosecuted alongside tranters; respectable elderly widows were prosecuted alongside servants. In Macclesfield (Cheshire) in the late fourteenth century, the pattern was different again: wives who were charged with scolding apparently tended to come from middle-ranking burgess families (including families of officeholders) and *not* from among the local elite.[34] Local communities exercised considerable autonomy in their constructions of scolding, enabling them to interpret the term "scold" in ways that fit the needs of those with the power to apply the label. In Exeter, Kowaleski has suggested, the overrepresentation of poorer single women as scolds might reflect a concern about the numbers of young female migrants into late medieval towns. In Middlewich, which experienced considerably less immigration, the more diffuse pattern of scolds' socioeconomic backgrounds perhaps reflects a wider range of local issues, including conflicts between families belonging to the local elite. In Macclesfield, the issues at stake in the maintenance of local order and government were doubtless different again. Status mattered a lot more in some places and periods than in others.

Scolding and Other Crimes

Individuals were more prone to scolding accusations if they were associated with certain other types of crime. As noted in Chapter 3, those who raised false hues were particularly liable to be charged with scolding; indeed, jurors and bailiffs may well have seen false hue-raising and scolding as variations of the same crime. Women who were charged with crimes of violence, with offenses against sexual propriety, and with nightwalking or eavesdropping were especially likely to be labeled as scolds too.

Despite the medieval associations between women and words, men and deeds, female scolds were often charged with assault. Of the ten women most often responsible for committing physical violence in Macclesfield, six were also presented as scolds.[35] Twenty of Middlewich's 51 scolds were charged at some point in surviving records with "making an affray of the peace," a term that usually translates as committing assault. Indeed, seventeen out of Middlewich's 46 women scolds (37 percent) were charged with affrays, compared with only 23 of the 221 women (10 percent) who did not appear as scolds in court records between 1413 and 1443. In some cases, however, the scolding seems to have been a component of the affray, perhaps even akin to an affray. Alice, servant of Robert le Potter, for instance, scolded (*obiurgauit*) Agnes de Waryhull in 1423 with "dishonest words against the peace of the lord king and in an affray." In the case of Katherine Frere of Boxley (Kent), assault and scolding were also closely linked: Katherine was charged in a church court as a "common brawler and a chider and a slanderer of her neighbors" who had recently struck her own mother.[36] Kowaleski also found that 13 percent of scolding accusations in Exeter were directly associated with a physical assault.[37] Other alleged scolds, however, were charged with assaults that were obviously quite discrete from their scolding presentments: Agnes Daa of Middlewich, for instance, was charged in 1425 with beating Joan Roper with a wooden beam. She was also sued by William Dillcworth in the same year for various assaults committed on members of his household while she had been in service with him.[38] Women who were in trouble for scolding, therefore, were frequently women who had come to the attention of local authorities for more physical types of disorderly behavior.

Scolds were also overrepresented among those charged with prostitution or other offenses related to illicit sexuality. The case of Alice Inchemerssh of Kingsland, described at the beginning of this chapter, was not unusual. Church courts took particular responsibility for prosecuting adultery, and Alice, along with Wilkoc Walker, one of her alleged paramours, was charged as both an adulterer and a scold. As Ruth Mazo Karras pointed out in her study of prostitution, 45 of the 161 women charged as whores in London's church courts between 1489 and 1492 were simultaneously charged as scolds. Secular jurisdictions associated scolding and illicit sex too: Agnes Couke was banished from the small town of Dunster (Somerset) in 1435 because she was a prostitute "by day and night" as well as a scold (*communis garrulatrix*).[39] In Exeter, at least 15 percent of scolds were accused of sexual offenses, including prostitution and brothel-keeping.[40] Town ordinances often grouped scolding and whoredom together in lists of punishable offenses, and regulations for the Southwark brothels specifically instructed jurors to look out for scolds among the prostitutes.[41] As Karras argues, the close connection between scolding and whoredom reinforced fears about independent women, women outside the control of men.

When women were prosecuted for wandering around after dark, it is possible that authorities sought to prevent their opportunities to engage in illicit sex. Nightwalking was most often with a crime of men, but some jurisdictions prosecuted women too, and scolds seem to have been liable: Margery and Lucy Bythewater of Carhampton, described at the beginning of this chapter, were simultaneously scolds and nightwalkers. Three years later and two miles down the road, in the small town of Dunster in 1415, three women and one man charged with scolding were also charged as nightwalkers. Nightwalking, with its connotations of stealth and secrecy, raised the possibility that people were committing immoral or illegal deeds, acts that could not be seen and could not, therefore, be inspected and regulated by community officials. Closely allied with nightwalking was the crime of eavesdropping, and eavesdroppers were often prosecuted as scolds too. The case of Eleanor de Werberton, presented at the sheriff's tourn in Wylaston (Cheshire) in 1404, is not unusual: Eleanor was accused as a common scold (*communis litigatrix*) who wandered around at night, listening under the eaves and windows of her neighbors' houses to the conversations happening within. She used this information, the court alleged, to defame her neighbors and create discord among them.[42] Walter Goodhewer of Colchester and his wife Sabina were accused of a similar crime in 1373, as was Joan, wife of John atte Stone of Battle (Sussex), in 1465.[43] Like scolds, nightwalkers and eavesdroppers dealt in illicit information.

Alleged scolds, therefore, were especially likely to attract censure for other types of crime, whether verbal, physical, or sexual. Some individuals charged with scolding, a lack of verbal self-control, may have found that other elements of their behavior were scrutinized more closely. The petty theft and nightwalking of Margery and Lucy Bythewater might have escaped notice—or at least censure—had it not been for their scolding. On the other hand, accusations of sexual, physical, or verbal misconduct seemed to increase the likelihood that a scolding charge would follow. The parishioners of Kingsland, for instance, may not have bothered to report Alice Inchemerssh for scolding, had she not already been scheduled to appear on three counts of adultery. The imprecise definition of scolding made it a particularly useful label to apply to anyone who seemed generally disruptive or problematic, to people who had crossed the threshold in the eyes of local authorities from merely being irritating to being disruptive and threatening to local peace and order.

Alice Inchemerssh, Margery and Lucy Bythewater, and Henry le Vernon came from different places, different times, and different jurisdictions. They occupied different socioeconomic categories and different marital statuses and had different rap sheets in terms of other petty crimes. Yet each was convicted of scolding and each paid a penalty. Although scolds were more likely to be single or married than widowed, more likely to be in trouble for other crimes, and certainly more likely to be female than male, the vague contours of the crime meant that almost anyone could be charged. These vague contours also meant that different jurisdictions could construct the crime in response to local conditions and desires. Yet their constructions were not uncontested. Factions within the ranks of local officials, such as the Batesson-Bradwall alliance in Middlewich, could turn the label of scold on members of their own socioeconomic group. Caught in the crossfire were people like Henry le Vernon. Neither his membership in a well-established local family, nor his service as bailiff, juror, and chamberlain, nor his ownership of several properties was enough to prevent him from being gored by the same discursive sword that he, as a member of the local leadership, had helped to forge. The plight of Henry le Vernon, fined 10d. and presumably subject to considerable humiliation, reminds us that almost anyone could be charged as a scold.

Conclusion

Consequences of the Feminization of Deviant Speech

In 1387, Helen, wife of Hugh Plombere of Bridgwater (Somerset), was sentenced to the pillory. Helen had been convicted as a scold (*communis garulatrix*) and disturber of the peace, and her prescribed punishment suggests that she was a repeat offender. In theory at least, scolds convicted in manorial or borough courts faced the same punishment as alewives and bakers who cheated their customers: they were fined for their first three offenses, and subject to the "cucking stool" thereafter. A "cucking stool," also known as a "ducking stool," "tumbrel," or "thewe," consisted of a chair attached to the end of a beam, which could be suspended above a pond, river, or waterlogged pit.[1] The offender was strapped into the chair, which was lowered into the water and raised again. The experience was uncomfortable, probably frightening, and certainly humiliating. Although the Bridgwater records literally state that Helen was headed for the pillory—a wooden framework in which one's hands and head would be locked—the clerk very likely used the term to refer to the cucking stool, sometimes called "the pillory for women." Bridgwater possessed such a contraption—at least, it had had one eight years earlier, in 1379, when Alice, wife of Philip Berecorne was ordered to undergo "the tumbrel" because of her repeated scolding convictions. Helen was more fortunate, however, than Alice: her friends appealed to the court to commute her punishment to a cash fine. Rather than see Helen suffer the indignity of the cucking stool, they paid the considerable sum of 3s.4d., an amount equal to about two or three weeks' wages for an unskilled laborer of the period. Helen was lucky to have such loyal friends, although her experience was not unique: a Colchester mother and daughter ordered to undergo "the thewe" in 1334 were also able to exchange their punishment for a fine of 2s. as a result of their friends' intervention.[2] As much a community spectacle as hangings or public whippings, the cucking stool was an instrument of shame, and balladeers would later make up songs about the humbling of a furious woman, the "cucking of a scold."

This chapter examines the consequences of women's increased association with problematic speech. For Helen Plombere, Alice Berecorne, and other women convicted of scolding, the consequences were immediate and concrete: they paid fines or suffered physical punishments, avoided the eyes of their neighbors for a few days, and got on with their lives. Perhaps they guarded their tongues more carefully in future, but perhaps—as high rates of recidivism in towns like Middlewich and Exeter might suggest—they did not. The consequences of scolding and the more general connection between women and illicit speech went well beyond the punishment of scolds, however: it affected the ways in which all women's voices were perceived and, hence, it affected both women's power and men's power. Yet the construction of women's voices as gossipy and argumentative was not always a thoroughly disempowering construction. Troublesome voices were not welcomed—indeed, they were sometimes feared—and this fear brought a degree of authority to the voices of some women. Even women like the Wife of Bath, whose unruly speech makes her seem so ridiculous, used their voices to exercise power over their husbands, their companions, and their audiences. The very ambivalence of women's connection with unruly speech, I argue, was what necessitated the reiteration of that connection.

Consequences for Individuals: The Punishment of Scolds

As a means of punishment, the cucking stool perhaps dated as far back as the eleventh century. While initially reserved for cheating bakers and brewsters, it seems to have been associated with troublesome speech in some regions from the late thirteenth century. In the Welsh courts of Ruthin in 1296, a man who defamed a woman with "contumelious words," was initially sentenced to the "thewe," although his punishment was later remitted to a fine.[3] A list of borough ordinances from Ipswich (Suffolk), purportedly dating from the 1290s, warns that scolding women might face the "theu."[4] Rituals surrounding public ducking, the punishment that Helen Plombere so narrowly escaped, varied slightly from place to place. In Portsmouth, in the late fourteenth or early fifteenth centuries, scolds were ducked in the Camber river, and in Leominster (Herefordshire), scolds were still being ducked in one of the town's rivers in the early nineteenth century, except when the water level was too low. The popularity of cucking stools as a mode of punishment is evidenced by mentions in court records, in town accounts (in which expenses for their construction and maintenance were recorded), and in contemporary artistic and literary representations. Towns such as Saffron Walden (Essex) and Macclesfield (Cheshire), both of which prosecuted scolds from the late fourteenth century, used their cucking stools as local referents, identifying streets by names like "Kuckyngstolende" or "Cuckstoolpit-hill."[5]

In places without convenient or reliable access to rivers, ponds, or waterlogged pits, scolds might sit in the cucking stool for a specified period of time. Alice Shether of London, for example, was sentenced in 1375 to an hour in the thew. If Alice's punishment was like that of other London scolds, she might also have been required to hold a distaff dressed with flax, while minstrels drew attention to her punishment.[6] Another variation on the theme was found in Northallerton (Yorkshire), where scolds were required to wear a crown as they sat in the tumbrel.[7] In some jurisdictions, the convicted scold may have been wheeled to the cucking stool in a handcart, which seems to have been part of the shaming ritual itself: certainly adulterers, adulteresses, and common courtesans in early fifteenth-century London were supposed to be accompanied by processions with minstrels. Late medieval misericords sometimes depict an obstreperous woman holding a distaff being pushed in a barrow, which may represent her en route to punishment for scolding.[8] Scolds in Leicester in 1467 were required to sit on a cucking stool outside their houses for as long as the mayor decreed, and then carried on the cucking stool to the four gates of the town.[9] While towns and manors were anxious to ensure that they had cucking stools at the ready to punish offenders, they were also concerned that the equipment be safe. The oath sworn by the mayor of Northampton in the late fifteenth or early sixteenth centuries required him to enquire "if the pillory and the tumbrel be strong or well repaired or not [so that] if any man or woman be deemed thereto that he or she shall neither lose life nor limb but go up safe and come down safe without any perishing of body."[10] Punishments, even of the most humiliating kind, needed to be free from danger. Just as jurisdictions presented scolds in slightly different ways, so too they varied in the modes of their punishment in accordance with local traditions and conditions.

But while cucking stools were theoretically owned and maintained by every manor and town, many jurisdictions failed to satisfy this requirement in the fourteenth and early fifteenth centuries and regularly commuted the punishment to a cash fine. Emmota le Chaloner of Middlewich, for instance, was presented for scolding on at least five occasions between 1433 and 1434, yet on each occasion she was fined, not ducked, without any recorded intervention by friends. Despite the fact that antiquarians have located a suitable spot for ducking in Middlewich and even described what a scold ducking in the town might have looked like, there is no evidence that the town ever actually possessed a cucking stool.[11]

Fines, the most typical punishments for scolding, generally ranged from as little as 2d. to as much as 40d., depending on the jurisdiction, the seriousness of the alleged scolding, the extent of community tolerance, and—to some extent—the convicted scold's ability to pay. Like other fines, the rates for scolding were set by court-appointed affeerors who might or might not choose to levy heavy fines on those who were persistent offenders or those who could best afford them. Even within a single jurisdiction, the disparity in the wealth of offenders could result in a broad range of fines. Among eight fines levied on scolds in Middlewich on July 23, 1426, one was charged 6d., two were charged 8d., three paid 12d., one 20d., and one 24d.[12] The lowest fine was reserved for a servant, whereas the highest fine was levied on a widow of high social status and economic means. Neither had previously appeared as a scold in surviving records. In Middlewich, fines levied on married scolds tended to be higher than those on single women: the average fine for a scolding wife between 1413 and 1443 was 7.95d., compared with an average of 5.13d. paid by servant-women and daughters. Having access to a household budget, married women could find the money for higher fines, but they may also have had to cope with spouses who considered fines for scolding prosecutions a waste of conjugal resources.

By the late fifteenth and early sixteenth centuries, convicted scolds occasionally faced other punishments. In Dunster (Somerset), for instance, two women convicted of scolding were expelled from the town in 1472. Sometimes scolds were given a chance to redeem themselves prior to expulsion: "Norfolke the cake maker's wife" was convicted as a "common scold and a slanderer of her neighbors" in Tottenham in 1535. She was fined 4d., and ordered to "amend her demeanor" before Michaelmas Day. If she did not, she would be banished from the town and required to pay 20s. if she was found there illegally.[13] From the late sixteenth century, punishments for scolds became even more brutal with the introduction of "scolds' bridles" or "branks," nasty metal cagelike devices that encompassed the head and locked the mouth shut. Sometimes these incorporated a piece of barbed metal that went into the mouth itself, to pierce the tongue at the slightest wriggle.[14] Scolds' bridles were used in North America too: the African slave Olaudah Equiano witnessed a female slave in Virginia being punished with such a contraption in the late eighteenth century.[15]

Church courts also punished scolds, but their punishments operated on a different system. Those who failed to gather enough pledges or who admitted their guilt were sometimes forgiven if they promised to remedy their behavior. Others were punished by public floggings or by some act of public contrition, such as participation in a procession, fast, or pilgrimage. In some jurisdictions, penitential punishments were occasionally commuted to cash payments, much as Helen Plombere's prescribed ducking in the borough court of Bridgwater had been.[16] Isabel, wife of John Austyn of Emneth, was punished by the Deanery of Wisbech in 1479 or 1480 for her scolding. Although she initially claimed innocence, she soon changed her mind. Perhaps her neighbors, tired of being called "whores, strumpets, [and] fyssenagges [unchaste women]" did not agree to act as compurgators. Isabel was required to follow the procession in church for the next two Sundays in the manner of a penitent, wearing a veil around her head, a kirtle (gown), and bare feet. She was to carry a wax taper priced at 1d., which she would later offer before the image of St. Edmund. After fulfilling her penance, Isabel swore that she would govern her tongue carefully in future and that if she were to scold again she would pay 6s.8d. As Isabel's case shows, church court punishments could be every bit as humiliating as a ducking in a cucking stool.[17] Some church courts required convicted scolds to seek the forgiveness of their neighbors, an exercise in humility that must have been difficult for even the most repentant to perform.[18]

In addition to official punishments meted out by the courts, those convicted of scolding faced social consequences. In many jurisdictions, they were presented before the courts as "common scolds," people occupying the identity or label of scold, rather than people who strayed once or twice from norms of appropriate speech. Scolding, in late medieval English culture, was important enough to be used as a noun, an identity. Not every aspect of late medieval behavior warranted the status of identity: those who committed assault, for instance, did not carry the title of assaulter, nor were they prosecuted as common assaulters. Scolding was a behavior that permeated identities, a behavior that could become a label, part of the knowledge that a community associated with an individual.

What did it mean for an individual when he or she was labeled a scold? For a woman, it very likely confirmed that her voice ought not to be taken seriously. Helen, wife of Hugh Plombere, the woman who escaped the cucking stool thanks to the intercession of her friends, may have found it more difficult to be heard when she had genuine grievances. As his name suggests, Hugh Plombere was indeed a tradesman, a roofer who laid lead on roofs to make them waterproof. Helen very likely, therefore, worked in some small-scale business, perhaps as an alewife or a baker, in order to boost the household income. When she haggled with a customer over the price of ale or when she bought fish in the marketplace for the family's supper, did the people of Bridgwater remember that she was a scold? When she and her husband argued, did he remind her that her voice had been deemed illicit? Men elsewhere certainly did: when Henry Cok of Trottiscliffe (Kent) and his wife were brought before the bishop of Rochester in 1347 for living separately from one another, Henry said that his wife behaved very badly toward him, using insulting words. Whether or not Henry's wife had ever been formally charged with scolding, Henry's claim—and the bishop's subsequent order that she desist from scoldlike behavior—shows that husbands could and did use the identity of illicit speaker against their wives.[19] Cultural connections between scolding and other illicit behaviors and identities also affected the ways in which scolds were regarded in their communities. Regulations against scolding were often coupled with regulations against prostitution or other sexual offenses, nightwalking, eavesdropping, general disturbance of the peace, and harboring of criminals. Women with uncontrollable voices, in contemporary literature, ballads, plays, artwork, and other media were connected with sexual immorality, violence, and even keeping company with the devil. The guilt by association that adhered to a woman accused of scolding could thus be a heavy burden indeed.

Broader Consequences: Women's Voices and Women's Power

The discourse that connected women with illicit speech affected more than just those accused of scolding, however. While penalties for scolding certainly affected the lives of convicted scolds in dramatic ways, the fear of falling under the nebulous label of "scold" and being dealt such punishments constrained, to a greater or lesser extent, the voices of many villagers and townspeople of late medieval England. In particular, scolding prosecutions and constructions of troublesome female speech sent a message about women's voices in the public arena. Although contemporary literature had plenty to say about nagging wives, most speech deemed inappropriate took place in the public sphere and involved people outside the immediate family. Women overshadowed by the devil gossiped in the public context of the church. Women trading stories and secrets about how to gain mastery over husbands or the size of husbands' sexual apparatus did so in the public context of the tavern. And scolds who engaged in loud arguments did so in the marketplace or on the bridge or in some other public forum. Their crime consisted not only of disturbing the public peace, but of publicizing information or slander that ought to have been shared privately or not at all. Indeed, their crime was partly that of inserting their female voices into a masculine public domain.

Medieval men could and did speak publicly in several contexts. They attended the courts, both secular and ecclesiastical, to air their differences, serve as pledges for one another, and pass judgment on miscreants. They served as community officials, as bailiffs collecting rents and fees and apprehending criminals, as ale tasters checking the quality of ale, and as churchwardens overseeing the day-to-day running of the parish. They acted as priests, speaking publicly the words of the mass and the advice of the sermon. They performed in mystery plays, enacting stories that inevitably ended with the triumph of good over evil. Not all men had all of these rights and opportunities, but women had few or none. Particularly after the fourteenth-century decline of hue-raising as a community institution, women's opportunities for licit, sanctioned, public speech were limited indeed. The message sent by scolding prosecutions and by cultural constructions of female voices was clear: a woman should not speak loudly in a public domain. She could certainly speak as necessary to carry out economic transactions or exchange news, but she should not raise her voice or command a large audience. If she defied such rules, she might find herself subject to the ever-flexible label of "scold." Constructions of women's speech and the consequences for a woman who fit the stereotype of scold thus helped ensure that women's status did not change markedly over the fourteenth and fifteenth centuries. Attitudes toward speech were a crucial component of the "patriarchal equilibrium," helping to counterbalance any demographic advantages that might otherwise have resulted in a "golden age."

Why Illicit Speech Was Feminized

What was at stake in the emphatic discourse that associated women with illicit speech in late medieval England? What was it about representations of transgressive female speech that medieval people found permissible, and even (we can assume by virtue of their frequent repetition) desirable? The multifaceted obsession with women's speech, manifest in court prosecutions, borough and manorial ordinances, wall paintings, misericords, sermons, ballads, plays, poems, aphorisms, and other media, served a broad variety of functions, and we should be reluctant to accept a monocausal explanation.

First, those who emphasized the disorderly, insubordinate nature of women and their speech may have been motivated, in part, by the power that accompanies acts of labeling, classification, and condemnation. As Michel Foucault has explained, power often operates by drawing out, naming, categorizing, and lingering over that which it seeks to control. Foucault focuses particularly on the nineteenth-century medical profession's "perverse" fascination with homosexuality, in which homosexuals as a "species" were closely analyzed and classified, even as they were condemned.[20] Perhaps those who commissioned misericords, composed ballads about gossiping women, or charged scolds also, at some level, took perverse pleasure in classifying and naming female deviance. Similarly, as sociologists remind us, both institutions and individuals increase their power by seeking out crimes to label and punish. A member of the local elite like Thomas Batesson of Middlewich sent a clear message about his own power as he brought cases against alleged scolds and persuaded bailiffs to do the same. In applying the label of "scold," he not only brought economic and social opprobrium on those who had offended him, but he also claimed for himself the power to determine what should be classified as a scoldlike behavior.

Simultaneously, images of the assertive, vocal woman might have served as an outlet or "safety valve" for masculine anxiety, just as the inversion of hierarchies at Carnival time helped to release class and religious tensions. For a day or two prior to Lent, peasants might take the role of lords, boys might dress as bishops and preach mock-sermons, and people might dress up animals in human clothing. Representations of powerful women, therefore, might suggest something about the tensions between the sexes, namely that these were sufficiently powerful to necessitate ritual release. Thus, while misericords and other popular art and literature might, at one level, have represented a celebration of disorder, at another level they perhaps leaked some of the neuroses of a patriarchal society, condensed into easily recognizable symbols. In a premodern era that constantly battled nature in the forms of the weather and the landscape, images on misericords of animals (nature) dominating humans might have seemed like potent images indeed, and representations of powerful women—both verbally and physically powerful—may similarly have tapped into a whole range of anxieties about the permanence of patriarchy in a time of social change. Yet even among these world-upside-down images, there were very real limits. We do not see scenes that would threaten social stability at more fundamental levels: no poems or carvings celebrate, for example, two women having sex or villages starving as a result of crop failure. Marginal art and popular literature could indeed be transgressive, but there were limits to the transgression. For medieval men, the image of an insubordinate woman reflected an imaginable anxiety, and concerns about their own cuckolding might perhaps have been vented by prosecuting scolds in the courts or lampooning them in ballads or wall paintings.

A third explanation for cultural investment in women's unruly speech is that it may have enabled men to distance themselves from the same association. After the Black Death, nobles sought to castigate rebellious peasants by condemning their audacious, insubordinate voices. But as the demographic and economic consequences of the plague took effect, groups of the more successful peasants—those able to buy up the land of plague victims and shrug off the bonds of serfdom—began to distinguish themselves from the rabble at large. Social regulation and concern about good governance increased, as individuals saw the chance to make their way from the peasantry to the yeomanry by means of local offices. Through the exercise of power, local elites distinguished themselves from the insubordinate masses. The power to label and castigate unruly speakers was thus passed on from the church to the nobility to members of the local elite, who prosecuted men for an array of offenses against good governance—playing at dice, hedgebreaking, living as vagabonds, and committing affrays—and women for scolding. As churchwardens and community leaders, these same members of the local elite commissioned wall paintings and wood carvings to reinforce their concerns. Individuals, both men and women, could also use scolding charges as a way to distinguish and distance themselves from their neighbors. To return to the example of Thomas Batesson, his accusations against others for scolding implied that his own speech was somehow legitimate and more restrained. Individual women, too, made their own "patriarchal bargains" as they charged other women with defamation or complained to jurors that their neighbors should be charged as common scolds.[21]

Of course, representations of women as unruly, disorderly speakers may not always have functioned to curtail women's power. While it is hard to read agency into the fate of a woman prosecuted as a scold, some women may have interpreted representations of disorderly and defiant female speech in literature and art as affirming. As Natalie Zemon Davis and Joy Wiltenburg have shown with regard to early modern representations of the "woman on top," the meanings of such ritualized inversions could be multivalent. Topsy-turvy and carnivalesque representations could indeed reinforce hierarchies by providing a safety valve for patriarchal tensions. Yet they could simultaneously serve as a force of change, promoting resistance to gender hierarchies.[22] For female readers (or listeners), the figure of the disorderly woman may well have served an empowering role. So while a member of the local elite such as Thomas Batesson of Middlewich might have sided with Noah as he watched a mystery play, his wife Margaret might instead have been cheering on Noah's Wife. Even some scolding accusations led to situations in which women found support, as demonstrated by the case of Helen, wife of Hugh Plombere, who escaped the cucking stool due to the intervention of her friends. At the very least, we know that her friends considered the punishment too harsh and that they did not want to distance themselves from her. Perhaps, however, their support might also be construed as implicit endorsement of her character and maybe even her behavior. While certainly damaging to women in many ways, therefore, the discourse on women's verbal impropriety could simultaneously be empowering.

Women and men doubtless participated in the discourse about women's illicit speech for a wide variety of reasons. Yet although medieval culture emphatically connected women's voices with disorder and trouble, the connection was never absolute or permanent. Despite the fact that the vast majority of accused scolds were women and despite the demonization of women's speech in multiple media, the discourse associating women with inappropriate speech remained fragile, ambiguous, and needing to be proven over and over. Scolding and literary and artistic representations made women's speech seem troublesome, but individual women could transcend this association, and the association could be extended to apply to men.

Although the connection between women and illicit speech has needed constant reinforcement, it has proven durable. Truisms about women and gossip are still repeated today. Even the category of "scold" proved remarkably long-lived, accompanying settlers to Puritan New England and surviving in some parts of England until the nineteenth century.[23] "Brabbling" women were punished by means of fines or the cucking stool in eighteenth-century Virginia.[24] The cucking stool owned by the town of Leominster (Herefordshire) was apparently last used in 1808 or 1809 to duck a "very disorderly old woman," and residents of the town of Beverley (Yorkshire) in 1829 were able to recollect use of the cucking stool to duck scolds within their own lifetimes. As late as 1824, the town of Congleton (Cheshire) punished a scolding woman by making her wear a scold's bridle.[25] The category of scold survived in large part, I suggest, because of its flexibility. While certain people were more likely than others to bring scolding cases before the courts, the label proved sufficiently amenable to local and temporal variations to make it highly adaptable. Some local officials took particular exception to incidents of scolding and brought multiple cases against alleged scolds, while others seemed less concerned. Some jurisdictions prosecuted scolding as a behavior, while others used the label "scold" as an identity. And in some instances, it is clear that scolding accusations played a role in long-standing feuds among families, feuds manifested in physical and legal as well as verbal conflicts. Scolding survived as a cultural category precisely because it could be adapted to challenge the verbal power of almost anyone, from Alice, wife of Philip Berecorne, repeatedly punished for scolding in Bridgwater in the 1370s, to Henry le Vernon, respectable ex-chamberlain of Middlewich in 1434.

Yet despite the remarkable flexibility of scolding as a cultural category, certain elements of its construction remained consistent across the centuries. In particular, scolding continued to involve concerns about authority and about women. Anxieties about social status and the maintenance of traditional hierarchies played an important role in expanding the preplague discourse on "sins of the tongue" into a postplague concern to limit speech at the local level. Whereas concern about speech in the thirteenth and early fourteenth centuries focused around the maintenance of religious and royal power, the social and economic disruption of demographic disaster prompted more intense anxieties about the immediate, localized threats of peasants' and townspeople's unruly voices and actions. The crime of the scold was, in part, one of usurping local authority, infringing upon the judicial role reserved for men of high local status. Furthermore, the words used in alleged instances of scolding tapped into social, economic, sexual, and moral hierarchies. Even while alleged scolds came from a range of socioeconomic backgrounds, issues of status, order, authority, and hierarchy remained central to the construction of scolding as an offense.

Yet ultimately the construction of scolding adhered more closely to hierarchies of gender than those of social status. Scolding and similar behaviors—gossiping, nagging, and general verbal insubordination—remained emphatically associated with women. Records of scolding punishments from the postmedieval era attest to the continued importance of gender in the construction of scolding. Whether prosecuted in fourteenth-century Colchester, fifteenth-century Middlewich, seventeenth-century Massachusetts, or nineteenth-century Leominster, scolds were most likely to be female and women were most likely to be regarded as disorderly speakers. Simultaneously, literary and artistic representations of women's speech reflected and reinforced the discourse that problematic speech was an especially feminine failing. In forging the close connection between women and disorderly speech that persists even to the present, much of the cultural work was done by the people of late medieval England. Attitudes toward women's speech helped maintain the patriarchal equilibrium of late medieval England, and they bequeathed to the early modern period a tool to help maintain it in the future.

Notes

Unless otherwise noted, translations from Middle English and Latin into Modern English are my own.

Abbreviations

BL	British Library, London
CRO	Cheshire Record Office
EETS	Early English Text Society publications
HEH	Henry E. Huntington Library, San Marino, California
LA	Lincolnshire Archives
SARS	Somerset Archive and Record Service
Statutes	*Statutes of the Realm: Printed by Command of His Majesty King George the Third . . . from Original Records and Authentic Manuscripts.* 11 vols. Reprint of 1810–28 ed. London: Dawsons, 1963.
TNA: PRO	The National Archives: Public Record Office, London

Introduction

1. "The Castle of Perseverance," in *The Macro Plays*, ed. Frederick J. Furnivall and Alfred W. Pollard, EETS, extra series, vol. 91 (London: Kegan Paul, Trench, Trübner, 1904), 156, lines 2649–52.

2. Chris Wickham, "Gossip and Resistance Among the Medieval Peasantry," *Past and Present* 160 (1998): 3–24, at 16–17.

3. Scholarship dealing with the relationship between orality and literacy constitutes an entire field of its own, and it is not a field that I deal with here in any depth. For a stimulating argument for the centrality of texts to all medieval life, see Brian Stock, *The Implications of Literacy: Written Language and Models of Interpretation in the Eleventh and Twelfth Centuries* (Princeton, N.J.: Princeton University Press, 1983). Other useful discussions of the orality-literacy connection can be found in the work of Walter Ong (especially *Orality and Literacy: The Technologizing of the Word* [London: Methuen, 1982]) and Jack Goody (especially *The Interface Between the Written and the Oral* [Cambridge: Cambridge University Press, 1987]).

4. Rosamond Faith, "The 'Great Rumour' of 1377 and Peasant Ideology," in *The English Rising of 1381*, ed. R. H. Hilton and T. H. Aston (Cambridge: Cambridge University Press, 1984), 43–73. Peasants and townspeople in the uprisings of 1381 were similarly conscious of the power of documents when they stormed the abbey of St. Alban in search of a (probably nonexistent) charter that they

believed to proclaim their freedom, and when they burned court rolls on which manorial officers recorded oppressive fines and fees.

5. The metaphor of the tongue as sword appears in an anonymous fifteenth-century poem, "Against Traducers," printed in *Religious Lyrics of the Fifteenth Century*, ed. Carleton Brown (Oxford: Clarendon Press, 1939), 278, line 15. See also John Skelton's poem, "Against Venomous Tongues," in which he asserts that "Malicious tongues, though they have no bones, / Are sharper than swords, sturdier than stones." In *The Complete Poems of John Skelton, Laureate*, 4th ed., ed. Philip Henderson (London: J. M. Dent, 1959), 245–49, lines 59–60. Paul Sheneman discusses other variations on the theme in "The Tongue as a Sword: Psalms 56 and 63 and the Pardoner," *Chaucer Review* 27 (1993): 396–400.

6. Pierre Bourdieu, *Language and Symbolic Power* (Cambridge, Mass.: Harvard University Press, 1991), 39.

7. Michel Foucault, in particular, sees discourses as having agency within themselves. Texts have a life (and agency) of their own once they are created, a situation that Foucault refers to as the "death of the author." This view is expanded in *The Archaeology of Knowledge* (London: Tavistock Publications, 1972).

8. Christopher Dyer, "Power and Conflict in the Village," reprinted in his *Everyday Life in Medieval England*, 2nd ed. (London: Hambledon and London, 2000), 1–12.

9. Anne Reiber DeWindt, "Local Government in a Small Town: A Medieval Leet Jury and Its Constituents," *Albion* 23 (1991): 627–54.

10. For instance, this verse apparently formed the text for a sermon by the rebel John Ball: Thomas Walsingham, *Historia Anglicana*, vol. 2, *A.D. 1381–1422*, ed. H. T. Riley, Rolls Series, vol. 28, part 1 (London: Longman, Green, Longman, Roberts & Green, 1864), 32.

11. Marjorie Keniston McIntosh, "Finding Language for Misconduct: Jurors in Fifteenth-Century Local Courts," in *Bodies and Disciplines: Intersections of Literature and History in Fifteenth-Century England*, ed. Barbara A. Hanawalt and David Wallace (Minneapolis: University of Minnesota Press, 1996), 87–122.

12. TNA: PRO SC 2 156/3–7; A. M. Tonkinson, *Macclesfield in the Later Fourteenth Century: Communities of Town and Forest*, Chetham Society Publications, 3rd series, vol. 42 (Manchester: Chetham Society, 1999), 52.

13. James E. Thorold Rogers, *Six Centuries of Work and Wages: The History of English Labour*, 7th ed. (New York: Swan Sonnerschein, 1903), passim.

14. James E. Thorold Rogers, *A History of Agriculture and Prices in England*, vol. 1, *1259–1400* (Oxford: Clarendon Press, 1866), 281; Rogers, *Six Centuries of Work and Wages*, 77, 329; Lord William Henry Beveridge, "Westminster Wages in the Manorial Era," *Economic History Review*, 2nd series, 8 (1955–56): 18–35, at p. 34; R. H. Hilton, *The English Peasantry in the Later Middle Ages: The Ford Lectures for 1973 and Related Studies* (Oxford: Clarendon Press, 1975), 102–3; Simon A. C. Penn, "Female Wage-Earners in Late Fourteenth-Century England," *Agricultural History Review* 35 (1987): 1–14; Sandy Bardsley, "Women's Work Reconsidered: Gender and Wage Differentiation in Late Medieval England," *Past and Present* 165 (1999): 3–29. See also John Hatcher's response to my article at "Debate—Women's Work Reconsidered: Gender and Wage Differentiation in Late Medieval England," *Past and Present* 173 (2001): 191–98, and my reply to him at "Debate—Women's Work Reconsidered: Gender and Wage Differentiation in Late Medieval England—Reply," *Past and Present* 173 (2001): 199–202.

15. Caroline M. Barron, "The 'Golden Age' of Women in Medieval London,"

Reading Medieval Studies 15 (1989): 33–58; "Introduction: The Widow's World in Later Medieval London," in *Medieval London Widows, 1300–1500*, ed. Caroline M. Barron and Anne F. Sutton (London: Hambledon Press, 1994), xiii–xxxiv.

16. Simon Penn makes tentative suggestions in this direction ("Female Wage-Earners in Late Fourteenth-Century England"), echoed by Richard Smith ("Human Resources," in *The Countryside of Medieval England*, ed. Grenville Astill and Annie Grant [Oxford: B. Blackwell, 1988], 204–17, at p. 211) but Goldberg significantly enlarges upon them. See especially his *Women, Work, and Life-Cycle in a Medieval Economy: Women in York and Yorkshire c. 1300–1520* (Oxford: Clarendon Press, 1992).

17. Maryanne Kowaleski, "Gossip, Gender, and the Economy: The Origins of Scolding Indictments in Medieval England," forthcoming. I am very grateful to Professor Kowaleski for giving me a copy of her paper and allowing me to cite it.

18. As, for instance, in the preamble to the 1351 Statute of Labourers (*Statutes*, vol. 1, 311). For a particularly bitter condemnation of postplague laborers, see John Gower, *The Voice of One Crying*, book 5, chapters 9–10, in *The Major Latin Works of John Gower: The Voice of One Crying and the Tripartite Chronicle*, ed. Eric W. Stockton (Seattle: University of Washington Press, 1962). For the complaint about remarrying widows, see the continuation of Ralph Higdon's *Polychronicon*, excerpted and translated in *The Black Death*, ed. Rosemary Horrox (Manchester: Manchester University Press, 1994), 85. Another chronicler recorded that the immediate postplague shortage of workers caused women and children to be used to drive ploughs and carts, a labor reserved for men under normal conditions, but this was not construed as a critique of women (see the *Eulogium Historiarum sive Temporis*, compiled at Malmesbury Abbey [Wiltshire] in the 1350s, excerpted and translated in *The Black Death*, ed. Horrox, 64).

19. For discussion of variations on this phrase, see Margaret Aston, "Corpus Christi and Corpus Regni: Heresy and the Peasants' Revolt," *Past and Present* 143 (1994): 3–48. Barbara A. Hanawalt also notes the gendered ramifications of the rhyme in "Peasant Women's Contribution to the Home Economy in Late Medieval England," in *Women and Work in Preindustrial Europe*, ed. Barbara A. Hanawalt (Bloomington: Indiana University Press, 1986), 3–19, at p. 7.

20. See especially Judith M. Bennett, "Confronting Continuity," *Journal of Women's History* 9 (1997): 73–94.

21. Judith M. Bennett, *Ale, Beer, and Brewsters in England: Women's Work in a Changing World, 1300–1600* (New York: Oxford University Press, 1996).

22. See, for instance, *Fama: The Politics of Talk and Reputation in Medieval Europe*, ed. Thelma Fenster and Daniel Lord Smail (Ithaca, N.Y.: Cornell University Press, 2003); *Speaking in the Medieval World*, ed. Jean E. Godsall-Myers (Leiden: Brill, 2003); *The Hands of the Tongue: Essays on Deviant Speech*, ed. Edwin D. Craun (Kalamazoo, Mich.: Medieval Institute Publications, forthcoming).

23. Edwin D. Craun, *Lies, Slander, and Obscenity in Medieval English Literature: Pastoral Rhetoric and the Deviant Speaker* (Cambridge: Cambridge University Press, 1997). For discussion of slander, defamation, and gossip in the works of Shakespeare, see Kenneth Gross, *Shakespeare's Noise* (Chicago: University of Chicago Press, 2001).

24. L. R. Poos, "Sex, Lies, and the Church Courts of Pre-Reformation England," *Journal of Interdisciplinary History* 25 (1995): 585–607; Laura Gowing, *Domestic Dangers: Women, Words and Sex in Early Modern London* (Oxford: Clarendon Press, 1996); Steve Hindle, "The Shaming of Margaret Knowsley: Gossip,

Gender and the Experience of Authority in Early Modern England," *Continuity and Change* 9 (1994): 391–419; Karma Lochrie, *Covert Operations: The Medieval Uses of Secrecy* (Philadelphia: University of Pennsylvania Press, 1999); Joy Wiltenburg, *Disorderly Women and Female Power in the Street Literature of Early Modern England and Germany* (Charlottesville: University Press of Virginia, 1992).

25. Bernard Capp, *When Gossips Meet: Women, Family, and Neighbourhood in Early Modern England* (Oxford: Oxford University Press, 2003); Pamela Allen Brown, *Better a Shrew than a Sheep: Women, Drama, and the Culture of Jest in Early Modern England* (Ithaca, N.Y.: Cornell University Press, 2003).

26. See, for example, T. N. Brushfield, "On Obsolete Punishments, With Particular Reference to Those of Cheshire. Part II: The Cucking Stool and Allied Punishments," *Journal of the Architectural, Archaeological and Historic Society, for the County, City and Neighbourhood of Chester,* 1st series, 2 (1861): 203–34; William Andrews, "Punishing Scolding Women," in *Bygone Cheshire,* ed. William Andrews (Chester: Phillipson and Golder, 1895), 242–50; and John Webster Spargo, *Juridical Folklore in England Illustrated by the Cucking-Stool* (Durham, N.C.: Duke University Press, 1944). In addition to articles devoted solely to scolding, local historians frequently discussed local evidence of scolding and its punishments. See, for instance, William Borlase, *The Natural History of Cornwall* (Oxford: Printed for private circulation, 1758), 303; George Poulson, *Beverlac; Or, The Antiquities and History of the Town of Beverley,* vol. 1 (London: G. Scaum, 1829), 221; William Beaumont, *A History of the Castle of Halton and the Priory or Abbey of Norton* (Warrington: P. Pearse, 1873), 98.

27. David E. Underdown, "The Taming of the Scold: The Enforcement of Patriarchal Authority in Early Modern England," in *Order and Disorder in Early Modern England,* ed. A. Fletcher and J. Stevenson (Cambridge: Cambridge University Press, 1985), 116–36; Martin Ingram, "'Scolding Women Cucked or Washed': A Crisis in Gender Relations in Early Modern England?" in *Women, Crime and the Courts,* ed. Jenny Kermode and Garthine Walker (London: University College of London Press, 1994), 48–80; Marjorie Keniston McIntosh, *Controlling Misbehavior in England, 1370–1600* (Cambridge: Cambridge University Press, 1998); Karen Jones and Michael Zell, "Bad Conversation? Gender and Social Control in a Kentish Borough, c. 1450–c. 1570," *Continuity and Change* 13 (1998): 11–31; Kowaleski, "Gossip, Gender, and the Economy."

28. For discussion of the frequency, attendance obligations, and meeting places of manorial courts, see H. S. Bennett, *Life on the English Manor: A Study of Peasant Conditions 1150–1400* (Cambridge: Cambridge University Press, 1937), 200–204. Middlewich's moothall is mentioned in account records (on occasions when money had to be put aside for its repair). It was also known as the "hall of pleas." See TNA: PRO SC 2 156/4; SC 6 793/2.

29. Civil accusations were occasionally levied alongside bailiff's prosecutions in instances of scolding or assault and enabled the alleged target to receive monetary damages. Seven examples of civil scolding/defamation charges survive from Middlewich. The verdict is not recorded in one case, but of the other six cases, the civil suit was successful on only one occasion. See Chapters 1 and 3 for further discussion of civil defamation suits.

30. See, for example, F. J. C. Hearnshaw, *Leet Jurisdiction in England: Especially as Illustrated by the Records of the Court Leet of Southampton* (Southampton: Cox & Sharland, 1908), 43–64; John S. Beckerman, "The Articles of Presentment of a Court Leet and Court Baron, in English, c. 1400," *Bulletin of the Institute of Historical Research* 48 (1974): 230–34.

31. For further discussion of charges to jurors, see particularly McIntosh, *Controlling Misbehavior,* 36–38.

32. Mark Bailey does a good job of unraveling the varieties of manorial and leet courts in his introduction and translation to manorial records, *The English Manor, c. 1200–c. 1500* (Manchester: Manchester University Press, 2002), 167–92.

33. SARS DDL 9/5, 10/2–3, 11/2, 12/1–4, 13/1. For a brief discussion of Dunster's courts, see H. C. Maxwell Lyte, *A History of Dunster and of the Families of Mohun and Luttrell* (London: St. Catherine's Press, 1909), 302–12.

34. DeWindt, "Local Government in a Small Town," 629.

35. TNA: PRO DL 30 4/54.

36. I am simplifying a more complex jurisdictional picture here. Those interested to find out more about the various systems of king's courts should see Anthony Musson, *Public Order and Law Enforcement: The Local Administration of Criminal Justice in England, 1294–1350* (Woodbridge: Boydell Press, 1996), Robert Palmer, *The County Courts of Medieval England, 1150–1350* (Princeton, N.J.: Princeton University Press, 1982), and Anthony Musson and W. M. Ormrod, *The Evolution of English Justice: Law, Politics and Society in the Fourteenth Century* (Basingstoke: Macmillan Press, 1999).

37. TNA: PRO CHES 25/10, m. 23r.

38. For an overview of lower-level ecclesiastical jurisdictions, see the substantial introduction to *Lower Ecclesiastical Jurisdiction in Late-Medieval England: The Courts of the Dean and Chapter of Lincoln, 1336–1349, and the Deanery of Wisbech, 1458–1484,* ed. L. R. Poos (Oxford: Oxford University Press, 2001).

39. *Lower Ecclesiastical Jurisdiction,* ed. Poos, xlv–xlviii; R. H. Helmholz, "Crime, Compurgation and the Courts of the Medieval Church," *Law and History Review* 1 (1983): 1–26; *The Register of John Waltham, Bishop of Salisbury 1388–1395,* ed. T. C. B. Timmins, Canterbury and York Society Publications, vol. 80 (Woodbridge: Boydell Press, 1994), 211; *Kentish Visitations of Archbishop William Warham and His Deputies, 1511–12,* ed. K. L. Wood-Legh, Kent Records, vol. 24 (Maidstone: Kent Archaeological Society, 1984), 55.

40. *The Register of John Morton, Archbishop of Canterbury 1486–1500,* vol. 3, *Norwich Sede Vacante, 1499,* ed. Christopher Harper-Bill, Canterbury and York Society Publications, vol. 89 (Woodbridge: Boydell Press, 2000), 228–29. The original term for "reviler" used here is unclear, since Harper-Bill's calendar of these records is in modern English.

41. TNA: PRO SC 2 156/5, mm. 4v., 5r., 5v. Of this fine, 6d. may have due to her failure to attend court when first accused.

42. For discussion of how the interests of local courts and church courts could overlap and play out in defamation cases, see P. R. Schofield, "Peasants and the Manor Court: Gossip and Litigation in a Suffolk Village at the Close of the Thirteenth Century," *Past and Present* 159 (1998): 3–42.

43. My primary sources on Middlewich were the records of 196 borough court sessions between 1413 and 1443, the large majority of which (187 courts) survive in the Public Record Office of the National Archives in London (TNA: PRO SC 2 156/3–7). The remaining nine courts were partially transcribed by a seventeenth-century antiquarian; the originals have been lost (*A Middlewich Chartulary,* part 1, ed. Joan Varley, Chetham Society Publications, new series, vol. 105 [Manchester: Chetham Society and the Liverpool School of Local History and Records, 1941]; *A Middlewich Chartulary,* part 2, ed. Joan Varley and James Tait, Chetham Society Publications, new series, vol. 108 [Manchester: Chetham

Society and the Liverpool School of Local History and Records, 1944]). Lacking a charter, Middlewich's burghal status was somewhat ambiguous during the late Middle Ages. Even if Middlewich was not a borough in the strictest sense, it was largely controlled from the thirteenth century, if not earlier, by men who described themselves as burgesses. By the middle of the fourteenth century, the burgesses claimed collective ownership of the town's brine springs, and they forced nonburgesses to pay annual licensing fees for the right to make salt.

44. For more on Middlewich and roads, see H. J. Hewitt, *Mediaeval Cheshire: An Economic and Social History of Cheshire in the Reigns of the Three Edwards*, Chetham Society Publications, new series, vol. 88 (Manchester: Chetham Society, 1929); W. B. Crump, "Saltways from the Cheshire Wiches," *Transactions of the Lancashire and Cheshire Antiquarian Society* 54 (1940): 84–142; and Dorothy Sylvester and Geoffrey Nuty, *The Historical Atlas of Cheshire* (Chester: Cheshire Community Council, 1958), 55. The town's name—Middlewich—literally means that it was the middle of the three "wiches" or salt springs. For background information on Middlewich, the introduction to *A Middlewich Chartulary*, part 1, ed. Varley, is particularly useful. See also A. F. Earl, *Middlewich 900–1900* (Chester: Ravenscroft, 1990), and the introduction to *A Middlewich Chartulary*, part 2, ed. Varley and Tait. Hewitt's *Mediaeval Cheshire* is old but sound and devotes considerable space to the salt towns, and Dorothy J. Clayton's *The Administration of the County Palatine of Chester 1442–1485*, Chetham Society Publications, 3rd series, vol. 35 (Manchester: Chetham Society, 1990) contains much helpful information about Middlewich's place within the Palatinate of Chester.

45. D. Huw Owen, "Wales and the Marches," in *The Agrarian History of England and Wales*, vol. 3, *1348–1500*, ed. Edward Miller (Cambridge: Cambridge University Press, 1991), 92–106, at pp. 98–101; A. R. Bridbury, *England and the Salt Trade in the Later Middle Ages* (Oxford: Clarendon Press, 1955).

46. In fact, most surviving local court records from Cheshire include a significant number of scolding prosecutions. See, for example, those of Frodsham (TNA: PRO SC 2 155/83), Northwich (TNA: PRO SC 2 156/10–11), Shotwick (TNA: PRO SC 2 156/13), and Halton, Runcorn, More, and Congleton (TNA: PRO DL 30 1/22—5/70; SC 2 155/84). A. M. Tonkinson found that scolding prosecutions made up 2.2 percent of all court business in the Macclesfield borough court between 1349 and 1396 (*Macclesfield in the Later Fourteenth Century*, 52). By contrast, scolding cases were apparently rare in the portmote and pentice courts (run by the mayor and sheriffs respectively) in the city of Chester: see Jane Laughton, "Women in Court: Some Evidence from Fifteenth-Century Chester," in *England in the Fifteenth Century: Proceedings of the 1992 Harlaxton Symposium*, ed. Nicholas Rogers (Stamford: P. Watkins, 1994), 89–99 at p. 98.

47. Janet Coleman, *Medieval Readers and Writers, 1350–1400* (New York: Columbia University Press, 1981), 23.

48. Gowing, *Domestic Dangers*.

49. Felicity Riddy, "Mother Knows Best: Reading Social Change in a Courtesy Text," *Speculum* 71 (1996): 66–86.

50. Coleman, *Medieval Readers and Writers*, 58–156.

51. For instance, this was an issue in the Iconoclast Controversy of the Byzantine Church in the eighth and ninth centuries. Bernard of Clairvaux, in the twelfth century, was concerned that spending large amounts of money on church decoration was a form of idolatry, and Adam of Dore, an English Cistercian abbot of the thirteenth century, was similarly troubled by frivolity in church painting (M. R. James, "Pictor in Carmine," *Archaeologia* 94 [1951]: 141–66).

John Wyclif, the fourteenth-century heretic, also queried the use of some religious images (W. R. James, "Lollards and Images: The Defense of Religious Art in Later Medieval England," *Journal of the History of Ideas* 34 [1973]: 27–50).

52. Miriam Clare Gill, "Late Medieval English Wall Painting in England: Content and Context (c. 1330–c. 1530)" (Ph.D. diss., Courtauld Institute of Art, University of London, 2002), 83. I am very grateful to Dr. Gill for giving me a copy of her dissertation.

53. C. David Benson, "*Piers Plowman* and Parish Wall Paintings," *Yearbook of Langland Studies* 11 (1997): 1–38; Miriam Gill, "Preaching and Image: Sermons and Wall Paintings in Later Medieval England," in *Medieval Monastic Education*, ed. George Ferzoco and Carolyn Muessig (London: Continuum, 2000), 155–80.

54. David Park, "Wall Painting," in *Age of Chivalry: Art in Plantagenet England 1200–1400*, ed. Jonathan Alexander and Paul Binski (London: Royal Academy of Arts, with Weidenfeld and Nicolson, 1987), 125–30.

55. For representations of women on misericords, see Elaine C. Block, "Half Angel—Half Beast: Images of Women on Misericords," *Reinardus* 5 (1992): 17–34. For English misericords in general, see G. L. Remnant, *A Catalogue of Misericords in Great Britain* (Oxford: Clarendon Press, 1969) and Christa Grössinger, *The World Upside-Down: English Misericords* (London: Harvey Miller, 1997).

56. For brief discussions of gossiping women in wall paintings, stone and wood carvings, and stained-glass windows, for instance, see E. W. Tristram, *English Wall Painting of the Fourteenth Century* (London: Routledge and Paul, 1955), 108–12; Richard Marks, *Stained Glass in England During the Middle Ages* (Toronto: University of Toronto Press, 1993), 80–81; and Veronica Sekules, "Women and Art in England in the Thirteenth and Fourteenth Centuries," in *Age of Chivalry*, ed. Alexander and Binski, 41–48 at p. 41. For discussion of the theme of cursing men, see Christopher Woodforde, "A Medieval Campaign Against Blasphemy," *Downside Review* 55 (1937): 1–6; Woodforde, *The Norwich School of Glass-Painting in the Fifteenth Century* (New York: Oxford University Press, 1950), 183–92. Miriam Gill has recently examined images of both gossiping women and swearing men in her articles "Female Piety and Impiety: Selected Images of Women and Their Reception in Wall Paintings in England after 1300," in *Gender and Holiness: Men, Women and Saints in Late Medieval Europe*, ed. Samantha J. E. Riches and Sarah Salih (London: Routledge, 2002), 101–20 and "From 'Urban Myth' to Monumental Image: English Warning to Swearers," in *The Hands of the Tongue*, ed. Craun. Gill also deals with some of these images in her dissertation, "Late Medieval English Wall Painting in England: Content and Context (c.1330–c.1530)."

57. Geoffrey Chaucer, *The Riverside Chaucer*, 3rd ed., ed. Larry D. Benson (Boston: Houghton Mifflin, 1987), 108, lines 227–28.

Chapter 1

1. Examples of hellmouths on bench-ends can be seen at Horning (Norfolk), Southwold (Suffolk), and Freckenham (Suffolk). Hellmouths were frequently incorporated into wall paintings that depicted the scene of the Last Judgment (and were thus known as dooms). Examples can be found in the Church of St. Thomas of Canterbury in Salisbury and the Guild Chapel in Stratford-upon-Avon. A wonderful stained glass window incorporating a hellmouth survives at Fairford (Gloucestershire). For discussion of hellmouths throughout northern

Europe, see Pamela Sheingorn, "'Who can open the doors of his face?': The Iconography of Hell Mouth," in *The Iconography of Hell*, ed. Clifford Davidson and Thomas H. Seilor (Kalamazoo, Mich.: Medieval Institute Publications, 1992), 1–19. For discussion of hellmouths in mystery plays, see Patricia Grace Dignan, "Hellmouth and Villains: The Role of the Uncontrolled Mouth in Four Middle English Mystery Cycles" (Ph.D. diss., University of Cincinnati, 1994).

2. The broad distribution of Peyraut's *Summa* has been noted by Bettina Lindorfer: Paris's Bibliothèque Nationale alone possesses about fifty thirteenth-century copies of the manuscript ("*Peccatum Linguae* and the Punishment of Speech Violations in the Middle Ages and Early Modern Times," in *Speaking in the Medieval World*, ed. Jean E. Godsall-Myers [Leiden: Brill, 2003], 23–42 at p. 27). As Lindorfer notes, these manuscripts vary in their degree of faithfulness to the original text.

3. Edwin D. Craun, *Lies, Slander, and Obscenity in Medieval English Literature: Pastoral Rhetoric and the Deviant Speaker* (Cambridge: Cambridge University Press, 1997).

4. *Statutes*, vol. 1, 35, 44.

5. Ibid., 35.

6. Ibid., 101–2; W. S. Holdsworth, *A History of English Law*, vol. 2, 3rd ed. (London: Methuen, 1922), 366.

7. *Statutes*, vol. 2, 9.

8. TNA: PRO CHES 25/12, m. 24r. Andrew's claim that Richard was a disrupter of the peace might seem relatively fair in light of Richard's frequent involvement in local troubles.

9. TNA: PRO CHES 25/12, m. 25r.

10. The process by which the royal courts won back jurisdiction over defamation from the spiritual courts is discussed by R. H. Helmholz in the introduction to *Select Cases on Defamation to 1600*, ed. R. H. Helmholz, Seldon Society Publications, vol. 101 (London: Seldon Society, 1985) and by J. H. Baker in the introduction to *The Reports of Sir John Spelman*, vol. 2, Seldon Society Publications, vol. 94 (London: Seldon Society, 1978), 236–48.

11. *Statutes*, vol. 1, 35. See also ibid., 44.

12. Ibid., 364; John Capgrave, *The Chronicle of England by John Capgrave*, ed. Francis Charles Hingeston, Rolls Series, vol. 1 (London: Longman, Brown, Green, Longmans and Roberts, 1858), 264.

13. In this paragraph and the following paragraph, I rely heavily on J. G. Bellamy, *The Law of Treason in England in the Later Middle Ages* (Cambridge: Cambridge University Press, 1970).

14. TNA: PRO CHES 25/10, mm. 1–4.

15. Dorothy J. Clayton, *The Administration of the County Palatine of Chester 1442–1485*, Chetham Society Publications, 3rd series, vol. 35 (Manchester: Chetham Society, 1990), 71.

16. For discussion of some late fourteenth- and early fifteenth-century cases of treason, see Judith Ferster, *Fictions of Advice: The Literature and Politics of Counsel in Late Medieval England* (Philadelphia: University of Pennsylvania Press, 1996), 32–35.

17. Immediately following the plague, grain prices rose because of the shortage of harvest workers. By the 1370s, they had begun to fall because production did not drop as sharply as population. See David Farmer, "Prices and Wages,

1350–1500," in *The Agrarian History of England and Wales*, vol. 3, *1348–1500*, ed. Edward Miller (Cambridge: Cambridge University Press, 1991), 431–525.

18. Rosamond Faith, "The 'Great Rumour' of 1377 and Peasant Ideology," in *The English Rising of 1381*, ed. R. H. Hilton and T. H. Aston (Cambridge: Cambridge University Press, 1984), 43–73.

19. Cited in ibid., 44. The full (translated) text can be found in *The Peasants' Revolt of 1381*, ed. R. B. Dobson (London: Macmillan, 1970), 76–78.

20. For a full discussion of the causes of the revolt and a blow-by-blow account of the events of 1381, see R. H. Hilton, *Bond Men Made Free: Medieval Peasant Movements and the English Uprising of 1381* (London: Temple Smith, 1973).

21. Bellamy, *Law of Treason*, 103–5.

22. Paul Strohm, *Hochon's Arrow: The Social Imagination of Fourteenth-Century Texts* (Princeton, N.J.: Princeton University Press, 1992), 42, n. 6.

23. Ralph Hanna III, "Pilate's Voice/Shirley's Case," *South Atlantic Quarterly* 91 (1992): 793–812, at pp. 800–801.

24. Margaret Aston, "Corpus Christi and Corpus Regni: Heresy and the Peasants' Revolt," *Past and Present* 143 (1994): 3–48, at p. 23.

25. See, for instance, *The Westminster Chronicle, 1381–1394*, ed. L. C. Hector and Barbara Harvey (Oxford: Clarendon Press, 1966), 2.

26. Marjorie Keniston McIntosh's *Controlling Misbehavior in England, 1370–1600* (Cambridge: Cambridge University Press, 1998) has done much to highlight the role of jurors, constables, and others of "middling status" who were responsible for local-level governance in the late medieval and early modern period. These local officials were able to exercise considerable autonomy and discretion in deciding which offenses ought to be prosecuted in lower-level courts, both secular and ecclesiastical. McIntosh notes especially the ways in which discourses about harmony, order, and poverty were co-opted by jurors in the local court setting (*Controlling Misbehavior*, 168–208). Others have gone further in emphasizing the ways in which membership in this local government served the specific interests of a group rising in social status during the fifteenth century. In the words of Barbara A. Hanawalt in her comment on McIntosh's book, "The price to be paid for greater community order . . . was the tyranny of a small group of village oligarchs" ("Good Governance in the Medieval and Early Modern Context," *Journal of British Studies* 37 [1998]: 246–57, at p. 257). Shannon McSheffrey highlights the ways in which service as a juror helped to define not only status but also gender: those who acted as jurors not only performed but also arbitrated respectable masculinity in late medieval London ("Jurors, Respectable Masculinity, and Christian Morality: A Comment on Marjorie McIntosh's *Controlling Misbehavior*," *Journal of British Studies* 37 [1998]: 269–78.

27. *Halmota Prioratus Dunelmensis: Containing Extracts from the Halmote Court or Manor Rolls of the Prior and Convent of Durham 1296–1384*, ed. W. H. D. Longstaffe and John Booth, Surtees Society Publications, vol. 82 (Durham: Surtees Society Publications, 1886), 153–54.

28. *English Gilds: The Original Ordinances of More than One Hundred Early English Gilds*, ed. Joshua Toulmin Smith and Lucy Toulmin Smith, EETS, vol. 40 (London: N. Trübner, 1870), 4, 104, 315; Gervase Rosser, "Going to the Fraternity Feast: Commensality and Social Relations in Late Medieval England," *Journal of British Studies* 33 (1994): 430–46, at p. 441.

29. McIntosh, *Controlling Misbehavior*, 34–35.

30. *A Book of London English 1384–1425*, ed. R. W. Chambers and Marjorie

Daunt (Oxford: Clarendon Press, 1931), 43; *English Gilds*, ed. Smith and Smith, 138.

31. *Calendar of Plea and Memoranda Rolls Preserved among the Archives of the Corporation of the City of London at the Guild-hall*, vol. 4, *1413–37*, ed. A. H. Thomas (Cambridge: Cambridge University Press, 1943), 127, 141, 155.

32. Marjorie McIntosh noticed a few presentments for barratry in fourteenth- and fifteenth-century local courts of smaller communities: *Controlling Misbehavior*, 60, n. 10.

33. Anne Reiber DeWindt, "Local Government in a Small Town: A Medieval Leet Jury and Its Constituents," *Albion* 23 (1991): 627–54, at p. 636; J. A. Raftis, *Warboys: Two Hundred Years in the Life of an English Mediaeval Village* (Toronto: Pontifical Institute of Mediaeval Studies, 1974), 221.

34. TNA: PRO DL 30 1/21.

35. TNA: PRO SC 2 156/2.

36. TNA: PRO SC 2 205/24.

37. *Beverley Town Documents*, ed. Arthur F. Leach, Seldon Society Publications, vol. 14 (London: B. Quaritch, 1900), 16.

38. TNA: PRO DL 30 104/1471.

39. LA CM 1/36.

40. TNA: PRO DL 30 104/1477; Anne DeWindt, "Local Government in a Small Town," 635.

41. "How to Hear Mass," in *The Minor Poems of the Vernon Manuscript (With a Few from the Digby Manuscripts 2 and 86)*, part 2, ed. Frederick J. Furnivall, EETS, vol. 117 (London: Kegan Paul, Trench, Trübner, 1901), 493–511, line 395.

42. For an example of a bishop instructing that those who gossip in church should be presented to his court during his forthcoming visitation, see *Kentish Visitations of Archbishop William Warham and His Deputies, 1511–12*, ed. K. L. Wood-Legh, Kent Records, vol. 24 (Maidstone: Kent Archaeological Society, 1984), 55.

43. Anne DeWindt, "Local Government in a Small Town," 635–37.

44. On this point, see, for instance, P. R. Schofield, "Peasants and the Manor Court: Gossip and Litigation in a Suffolk Village at the Close of the Thirteenth Century," *Past and Present* 159 (1998): 3–42, especially his citations at n. 43.

45. For occasions on which a village or town was amerced for their failure to respond to a hue, see, for example, three instances from Warboys (Huntingdonshire) in 1306, for which the town was fined 13s. 4d. (Edwin Brezette DeWindt, ed., *A Slice of Life: Selected Documents of Medieval English Peasant Experience* [Kalamazoo, Mich.: Medieval Institute Publications, 1996], 71–72), and Broughton (Huntingdonshire) in 1345, for which the village was fined 6s. 8d. (BL Additional Roll 39754; I am grateful to Judith M. Bennett for this reference). Hues and cries were reserved for situations outside of the strictly domestic: for example, when Henry, son of Alexander, beat his wife Alice, and Alice raised a hue on him, her hue was deemed unjust by the court of Halesowen (Worcestershire) (*Court Rolls of the Manor of Hales, 1270–1307*, ed. John Amphlett and Sidney Graves Hamilton, Worcestershire Historical Society Publications, vol. 51 [Oxford: Worcestershire Historical Society, 1910], 245).

46. The use of the hue and cry in England dates back to at least the tenth century, and possibly earlier. It was enshrined in Anglo-Saxon law codes and by statutes of the eleventh and thirteenth centuries. For further discussion of the origins of the hue, see Anne Reiber DeWindt and Edwin Brezette DeWindt, *Ramsey: The Lives of an English Fenland Town, 1200–1600* (Washington, D.C.: Catholic University of America Press, forthcoming), chap. 4.

47. Sherri Olson, *A Chronicle of All That Happens: Voices from the Village Court in Medieval England* (Toronto: Pontifical Institute of Mediaeval Studies, 1996), 92–98. One counterexample has been noted by Miriam Müller for the village of Badbury (Wiltshire). Müller notes that hues at Badbury were first recorded in the 1340s. However, it is not clear how many pre-1340 Badbury court records survive ("Social Control and the Hue and Cry in Two Fourteenth-Century Villages," *Journal of Medieval History* 31 [2005]: 29–53).

48. Studies by J. A. Raftis (*Warboys*, 218–20, 224) and Edwin DeWindt (*Land and People in Holywell-cum-Needingworth: Structures of Tenure and Patterns of Social Organization in an East Midlands Village 1252–1457* [Toronto: Pontifical Institute of Mediaeval Studies, 1972], 272–73) confirm the general pattern of the fading of hues. The disappearance of hues in Ramsey is discussed in detail by Anne and Edwin DeWindt in their forthcoming *Ramsey*. Two examples of late hues, both deemed just, were prosecuted in the manors of Battle (Sussex) in 1463 (HEH BA 590) and Melbourne (Derbyshire) in 1472 (HEH HAM 62/13). Neither jurisdiction prosecuted hues regularly by this stage, so presumably there was something exceptional about the circumstances in each case.

49. TNA: PRO SC 2 203/46–64

50. BL, Additional Charters, 16054.

51. Defamation generally came to the attention of church courts in one of two ways: either an individual complained to the court that he/she had been defamed by another, in effect using the church courts to bring a private suit that would clear his/her own name, or an ex officio case against an alleged defamer was presented by the court itself. Ex officio cases, generated by priests, churchwardens and *inquisitores* who often served as jurors in manorial and borough courts, cited specific instances in which one parishioner had defamed another. Particularly by the fifteenth century, they sometimes also charged individuals as "common defamers," a category which certainly overlapped with that of "scold." (See *Lower Ecclesiastical Jurisdiction in Late-Medieval England: The Courts of the Dean and Chapter of Lincoln, 1336–1349, and the Deanery of Wisbech, 1458–1484*, ed. L. R. Poos [Oxford: Oxford University Press, 2001], li, lx, lxii.)

52. Defamation seemed an unlikely matter for the church to take over, and legal historians, especially R. H. Helmholz, have struggled to justify its place within the interstices of ecclesiastical law. As Helmholz has pointed out, canon law normally decreed that members of the laity should not seek redress for secular matters in church courts except in particular circumstances. In the case of defamation, an assault on truth and reputation, one sought to recover good fame, both in the eyes of one's peers and in the eyes of God (*Select Cases on Defamation to 1600*). As Robert Mannyng claimed in the early fourteenth century, a backbiter (roughly equivalent to our modern "backstabber") was responsible for slaying three people before God: himself or herself; the person whose reputation was damaged; and the person to whom he or she told the tale. (*Robert of Brunne's "Handlyng Synne,"* ed. Frederick J. Furnivall, EETS, vol. 119 [London: Kegan Paul, Trench, Trübner, 1901], 55, lines 1523–30, Bodleian 415 manuscript version). Similarly, the sin of *detractio*, or evil backbiting, was said to "steal God's love from man's heart." *Vices and Virtues: Being a Soul's Confession of Its Sins with Reason's Description of the Virtues: A Middle-English Dialogue of about 1200 A.D.*, ed. F. Holthausen, EETS, vol. 89 (London: N. Trübner, 1888), 11.

53. Helmholz, "Introduction," in Helmholz, ed., *Select Cases on Defamation to 1600*, xiv–xv.

54. Defamation cases in sixteenth- and seventeenth-century church courts,

rich in detail, have provided source material for several recent studies. Best among these is Laura Gowing's *Domestic Dangers: Women, Words and Sex in Early Modern London* (Oxford: Clarendon Press, 1996). See also James A. Sharpe, *Defamation and Sexual Slander in Early Modern England: The Church Courts at York*, Borthwick Papers, no. 58 (York: University of York, Borthwick Institute of Historical Research, 1980) and Laura Kay Deal, "Whores and Witches: The Language of Female Misbehavior in Early Modern England, 1560–1650" (Ph.D. diss., University of Colorado at Boulder, 1996). Less recent but still useful is C. A. Haigh's "Slander and the Church Courts in the Sixteenth Century," *Transactions of the Lancashire and Cheshire Antiquarian Society* 78 (1975): 1–13.

55. L. R. Poos, "Sex, Lies, and the Church Courts of Pre-Reformation England," *Journal of Interdisciplinary History* 25 (1995): 585–607, at p. 594.

56. McIntosh, *Controlling Misbehavior*, 168–208.

57. This verse was attributed (doubtless spuriously) to Seneca. It was probably written in Latin in the mid-fourteenth century and translated into English (via French) in the fifteenth century. A version is printed in "Prouerbes of diuerse profetes and of poetes and of our seyntes," in *Minor Poems of the Vernon Manuscript*, part 2, ed. Furnivall, 533, lines 171–76.

58. Hanna, "Pilate's Voice/Shirley's Case," 797.

59. R. I. Moore, "Heresy as Disease," in *The Concept of Heresy in the Middle Ages*, ed. W. Lourdaux and D. Verhelst (The Hague: Martinus Nijhoff, 1976), 1–11.

60. "Think Before You Speak," in *Religious Lyrics of the Fifteenth Century*, ed. Carleton Brown (Oxford: Clarendon Press, 1939), 280–82, lines 41–42.

61. "An Homelie agaynst Contencion and Braulynge," in *Certain Sermons or Homilies (1547) and A Homily against Disobedience and Wilful Rebellion (1570): A Critical Edition*, ed. Ronald B. Bond (Toronto: University of Toronto Press, 1987), 193–94.

62. McIntosh, *Controlling Misbehavior*, 74–78.

63. TNA: PRO DL 30 66/828.

64. Hanna, "Pilate's Voice/Shirley's Case," 798–99. For further discussion of late medieval condemnations of alehouses and drunkenness, see G. R. Owst, *Literature and Pulpit in Medieval England: A Neglected Chapter in the History of English Letters and of the English People*, 2nd ed. (Oxford: B. Blackwell, 1961), 423–49.

65. "Prouerbes of diuerse profetes and of poetes and of our seyntes," in *Minor Poems of the Vernon Manuscript*, ed. Furnivall, 547, lines 381–84.

66. See, for example, regulations of the Guild of St. Edmund, Bishop's Lynn, in *English Gilds*, ed. Smith and Smith, 95, and regulations of the guild based at Watlington in Rosser, "Going to the Fraternity Feast," 441.

67. Christopher Dyer, *Standards of Living in the Later Middle Ages: Social Change in England c. 1200–1520* (Cambridge: Cambridge University Press, 1989), 153–60.

68. William Langland, *Piers Ploughman: A New Translation of the B-text*, trans. A. V. C. Schmidt (Oxford: Oxford University Press, 1992), 73–74.

Chapter 2

1. "The Castle of Perseverance," in *The Macro Plays*, ed. Frederick J. Furnivall and Alfred W. Pollard, EETS, extra series, vol. 91 (London: Kegan Paul, Trench, Trübner, 1904), 156, line 2650.

2. G. L. Apperson, *English Proverbs and Proverbial Phrases: A Historical Dictionary* (London: J. M. Dent and Sons, 1929), 705. See also Michael Roberts, "'Words

they are Women, and Deeds they are Men': Images of Work and Gender in Early Modern England," in *Women and Work in Pre-Industrial England*, ed. Lindsay Charles and Lorna Duffin (London: Croom Helm, 1985), 122–80.

3. 1 Tim. 2.11–12; 5.11–13 Revised Standard Version.

4. One genre not considered here, for example, is that of late medieval satirical poems that purported to claim women's virtue while simultaneously cataloguing their faults; in this genre, women were often "praised" for their silence and humility. See, for instance, poems in *The Early English Carols*, ed. R. L. Greene, 2nd ed. (Oxford: Clarendon Press, 1977), 233–39.

5. For discussion of late medieval English advice literature, see especially Cameron Louis, "Proverbs, Precepts, and Monitory Pieces," in *A Manual of the Writings in Middle English, 1050–1500*, vol. 9, ed. Albert E. Hartung (New Haven: Connecticut Academy of Arts and Sciences, 1975), 2957–3048.

6. *Ancrene Riwle*, 3rd ed., ed. and trans. M. D. Salu (Exeter: University of Exeter Press, 1990), 28–39. The translations quoted here are not my own but those of Salu.

7. "Proverbs of Alfred," in *An Old English Miscellany*, ed. Richard Morris, EETS, vol. 49 (London: N. Trübner, 1872), 118–22, lines 268–84. At least six thirteenth- and fourteenth-century manuscripts containing these proverbs survive. See Louis, "Proverbs, Precepts and Monitory Pieces," 3358–59.

8. For instance, see "Great Cato, or Cato's Distichs," bk. 1, in *The Minor Poems of the Vernon Manuscript (With a Few from the Digby Manuscripts 2 and 86)*, part 2, ed. Frederick J. Furnivall, EETS, vol. 117 (London: Kegan Paul, Trench, Trübner, 1901), 564, lines 141–44.

9. Bartholomaeus Anglicus, *Mediaeval Lore from Bartholomew Anglicus*, ed. Robert Steele (New York: Cooper Square Publishers, 1966), 57. The initial Middle English translation of this text, Bartholomaeus Anglicus's *De Proprietatibus Rerum*, was made in 1397 by John de Trevisa.

10. "Tell Me, Wight in the Broom," in *English Lyrics of the Thirteenth Century*, ed. Carleton Brown (Oxford: Clarendon Press, 1932), 32, lines 5–6; "How the Good Wife Taught Her Daughter" in *The Babees' Book, etc.* [also published under the title of *Early English Meals and Manners*], ed. Frederick J. Furnivall, EETS, vol. 32 (London: N. Trübner, 1868), 36–47, line 41.

11. "The vij. scoles," in *Mittelenglishe Dichtungen aus der Handschrift 432 des Trinity College in Dublin*, ed. Rudolf Brotanek (Halle: M. Niemeyer, 1940), 48–49, lines 4, 23–24, 27. Two other versions of the poem survive, and in one of these (Trinity College Cambridge MS R.4.20) the poet warns sons not to let their lovers' presence prompt them to "flyghte," which in this instance means quarrel.

12. Marjorie Keniston McIntosh, "Finding Language for Misconduct: Jurors in Fifteenth-Century Local Courts," in *Bodies and Disciplines: Intersections of Literature and History in Fifteenth-Century England*, ed. Barbara A. Hanawalt and David Wallace (Minneapolis: University of Minnesota Press, 1996), 87–122 at p. 95.

13. *The Babees' Book, etc.*, ed. Furnivall, 36–47, 48–53. The translation of "How the Good Wife Taught Her Daughter" used here comes primarily from Edith Rickert's edition of *The Babees' Book: Medieval Manners for the Young* (New York: Cooper Square Publishers, 1966), 31–42, with only minimal changes by me; the translation of "How the Wise Man Taught His Son" is my own.

14. G. R. Owst, *Literature and Pulpit in Medieval England: A Neglected Chapter in the History of English Letters and of the English People*, 2nd ed. (Oxford: B. Blackwell, 1961), 44.

15. Owst, *Literature and Pulpit*, 387. Lichfield's sermon was based closely on

the thirteenth-century *Ancrene Wisse.* See *Ancrene Riwle,* ed. Salu, 29. Another version (similarly adapted from the *Ancrene Wisse*) may be found in *Book for a Simple and Devout Woman: A Late Middle English Adaptation of Peraldus's Summa de Vitiis et Virtutibus and Friar Laurent's Somme le Roi, Edited from British Library Mss Harley 6571 and Additional 30944,* ed. F. N. M. Diekstra (Groningen: Egbert Forsten, 1998), 296.

16. "The Nun's Priest's Tale," in Geoffrey Chaucer, *The Riverside Chaucer,* ed. Larry D. Benson, 3rd ed. (Boston: Houghton Mifflin, 1987), 259, lines 3257–58.

17. Owst, *Literature and Pulpit,* 387. For other references to Mary's limited speech see, for instance, *Ancrene Riwle,* ed. Salu, 33–34; John Mirk, *Mirk's Festial: A Collection of Homilies,* ed. Theodor Erbe, EETS, extra series, vol. 96 (London: Kegan Paul, Trench, Trübner, 1892), 230.

18. In early versions of the Tutivillus tale the whole congregation was sometimes guilty of chattering, but whenever individual churchgoers were mentioned, as in most thirteenth- to fifteenth-century versions of the tale, they were always women (Margaret Jennings, *Tutivillus: The Literary Career of the Recording Demon,* Studies in Philology, Texts and Studies, no. 74 [Chapel Hill: University of North Carolina Press, 1977], 27).

19. For a complete list of English examples, see Jennings, *Tutivillus,* appendix 1. Jennings has also discussed Tutivillus's function as a demon who collected the words and phrases that priests skipped over or mumbled when they said mass; texts which give only this exemplum have not been included in my count.

20. "On Chattering in Church," in *Religious Lyrics of the Fifteenth Century,* ed. Carleton Brown (Oxford: Clarendon Press, 1939), 277, lines 1–9, 16–17.

21. In her dissertation "Late Medieval Wall Painting in England: Content and Context (c. 1330–c. 1530)" (Ph.D. diss., Courtauld Institute of Art, University of London, 2002), Miriam Gill identifies fifteen wall paintings, of which twelve are currently visible: Brook (Kent), Wissington (Suffolk), Colton (Norfolk), Little Melton (Norfolk), Peakirk (Northamptonshire), Grundisburgh (Suffolk), Lower Halstow (Kent), Slapton (Northamptonshire), Eaton (Norfolk), Nedging by Naughton (Suffolk), Crostwight (Norfolk), Melbourne (Derbyshire), Wiston (Suffolk), Stokesby (lost), Great Conrad (Suffolk). Misericords representing Tutivillus and the gossiping women survive at Ely Cathedral, Enville (Staffordshire), Gayton (Northamptonshire), New College Chapel in Oxford, Minster-in-Thanet (Kent), and St. Katherine's Hospital of Stepney (London) (see G. L. Remnant, *A Catalogue of Misericords in Great Britain* [Oxford: Clarendon Press, 1969]). An example of Tutivillus on a nave arcade stone carving may be found at Sleaford (Lincolnshire) (see Veronica Sekules, "Women and Art in England in the Thirteenth and Fourteenth Centuries," in *Age of Chivalry: Art in Plantagenet England 1200–1400,* ed. Jonathan Alexander and Paul Binski [London: Royal Academy of Arts, with Weidenfeld and Nicolson, 1987], 41–48, fig. 13.)

22. This window is reproduced in Richard Marks, *Stained Glass in England During the Middle Ages* (Toronto: University of Toronto Press, 1993), 80–81 and in *Age of Chivalry,* ed. Alexander and Binski, 446.

23. Nearly all the wall paintings of Tutivillus, however, are found in the east of England—Norfolk, Suffolk, Northamptonshire, and Kent—which is the area of best wall painting survival.

24. See, for instance, M. D. Anderson, *History and Imagery in British Churches* (London: J. Murray, 1971), 155.

25. David Park, "Wall Painting," in *Age of Chivalry,* ed. Alexander and Binski, 125–30 at p. 125. For further discussion of how to interpret Gregory's instruc-

tions, see Celia Chazelle, "Pictures, Books, and the Illiterate: Pope Gregory's Letters to Serenus of Marseilles," *Word and Image* 6 (1990): 138–53 and Lawrence G. Duggan, "Was Art Really the 'Book of the Illiterate'?" *Word & Image* 5 (1989): 227–51. In his survey of medieval understandings of Gregory's pronouncement, Lawrence G. Duggan has demonstrated that the role of images in religion prompted anxiety throughout the Middle Ages, because the clergy feared that the laity might misinterpret them or stray into idolatry.

26. E. W. Tristram, *English Wall Painting of the Fourteenth Century* (London: Routledge and Paul, 1955), 95.

27. For discussion of medieval parishioners' familiarity with wall paintings and the ways in which paintings were interpreted by their audiences, see C. David Benson, "*Piers Plowman* and Parish Wall Paintings," *Yearbook of Langland Studies* 11 (1997): 1–38. Unlike wall paintings, misericords were located in the choir, which was the responsibility of the rector. Often they were commissioned by wealthy patrons. The misericord series in St. George's Chapel, Windsor, and in Henry VII's Chapel of Westminster Abbey, for example, were both royal commissions (Christa Grössinger, *The World Upside-Down: English Misericords* [London: Harvey Miller, 1997], 34). The citizens of Bourg-en-Bresse, France, funded the choir stalls in the local Collegiate Church, and the contract for the carving of misericords insisted that the artisans "make the seats according to the desire of those paying for them." Hence many of the carvings of people on misericords at Bourg-en-Bresse are thought to be portraits of the donors (Dorothy Kraus and Henry Kraus, *The Hidden World of Misericords* [New York: G. Braziller, 1975], 123, xii). We lack English examples of such direct lay control over the subject matter of misericords, however.

28. The quote comes from the parishioners of Farnworth near Broughton in Amounderness (Lancashire) in 1512. Cited in Eamon Duffy, *The Stripping of the Altars: Traditional Religion in England, c. 1400–c. 1580* (New Haven, Conn.: Yale University Press, 1992), 160.

29. In the parish of Yatton (Somerset) in 1467–68, for example, the churchwardens commissioned two new wall paintings: one of Saint Mary and one of Saint Christopher. The parishioners approved of the painting of Mary, but for some reason they did not like the Saint Christopher, so in 1470 they had it repainted and made their former churchwardens bear the cost: Katherine L. French, *The People of the Parish: Community Life in a Medieval English Diocese* (Philadelphia: University of Pennsylvania Press, 2001), 73. See also pp. 200–201, in which French discusses the relationship between sermons and visual images sponsored and controlled by the parishioners. A similar level of control was exercised by the members of the guild of St. Mary in the parish of St. Cuthbert's in Wells: when, in 1470, the guild sought to sponsor a stone carving behind the altar, they drew up a contract for the carver that specified both the subject of the carving (an image of Jesse) and details on how it should be executed. Even individual sponsors, such as Alice Chester of Bristol who paid for a new roodscreen in 1483, took into account the wishes of "the worshipful of the parish, with others having best understanding and sights in carving" when choosing the subjects for depiction (Duffy, *Stripping of the Altars*, 159–60).

30. M. R. James, "Pictor in Carmine," *Archaeologia* 94 (1951): 141–66.

31. For an interesting and informed discussion on the roles played by the rector, the patrons, and the artisans in the building and decoration of St. Andrew's Church at Heckington (Lincolnshire), see Veronica Sekules, "Beauty and the Beast: Ridicule and Orthodoxy in Architectural Marginalia in Early Fourteenth-Century Lincolnshire," *Art History* 18 (1995): 37–62, especially at p. 39.

32. *Registrum Hamonis Hethe, Diocesis Roffensis AD 1319–52*, ed. Charles Johnson, Canterbury and York Society Publications, vol. 88 (Oxford: Oxford University Press, 1948), 974–75. Can Henry's wife be considered a scold? Perhaps: Andrew John Finch characterizes Henry as describing his wife as a scold ("Sexual Morality and Canon Law: The Evidence of the Rochester Consistory Court," *Journal of Medieval History* 20 [1994]: 261–75, at p. 269). I do not fully agree with his characterization, however. Although there is a narrow line between a scold per se and someone who uses "contumelious words" to oppose her husband, I would nonetheless argue that Henry's wife was not quite a scold according to Henry's description. The Latin words used to describe her behavior ("*verba sua contumeliosa*") are not those typically used in scolding presentments, and there is no suggestion that her behavior is a problem for anyone other than Henry. However, as part of his response to the case, the bishop ordered that Henry's wife desist from scolding, using the term "*rixosa.*" Scolds were sometimes convicted using the term "*rixatrices*," which suggests that the bishop, at least, identified her behavior as scoldlike.

33. For extensive discussion of the various legends, see Anna Jean Mill, "Noah's Wife Again," *PMLA* 56 (1941): 613–26. For an overview of scholarship on Noah's Wife, see Alfred David, "Noah's Wife's Flood," in *The Performance of Middle English Culture: Essays on Chaucer and the Drama in Honor of Martin Stevens*, ed. James J. Paxton, Laurence M. Clopper, and Sylvia Tomasch (Cambridge: D. S. Brewer, 1998), 97–109.

34. Katherine Garvin, "A Note on Noah's Wife," *Modern Language Notes* (1934): 88–90.

35. Adelaide Bennett, "Noah's Recalcitrant Wife in the Ramsey Abbey Psalter," *Source* 2 (1982): 2–5. In addition to the French captions that explain the content of each picture, the hand gestures of Noah's Wife, Noah, and the devil make it clear that they are engaged in conversation. On folio 7r., the devil is shown escaping the ark through a hole in the hull. (See George Warner, *Queen Mary's Psalter: Miniatures and Drawings by an English Artist of the Fourteenth Century, Reproduced from Royal ms. 2 B.VII in the British Museum* [London: Trustees of the British Museum, 1912], 13–15, 57, plates 10, 12.)

36. For general discussion of the plays, see Rosemary Woolf, *The English Mystery Plays* (London: Routledge and Kegan Paul, 1972). I have used the following editions: *The Chester Plays*, part 1, ed. Hermann Deimling, EETS, extra series, vol. 62 (London: Kegan Paul, Trench, Trübner, 1892), 48–63; *York Plays: The Plays Performed by the Crafts or Mysteries of York on the Day of Corpus Christi in the Fourteenth, Fifteenth, and Sixteenth Centuries*, ed. Lucy Toulmin Smith (Oxford: Clarendon Press, 1885), 45–55; *The Wakefield Pageants in the Towneley Cycle*, ed. A. C. Cawley (Manchester: Manchester University Press, 1958), 14–28.

37. The York cycle actually incorporates two Noah plays: the first involves the building of the ark and the second the loading of the ark and the flood. Noah's Wife appears only in the second play.

38. Critics have noted that Noah's Wife served a moral purpose for dramatists by symbolizing the obstinate sinner who must be forced to enter the church. See, for instance, Woolf, *English Mystery Plays*, 139; V. A. Kolve, *The Play Called Corpus Christi* (Stanford, Calif.: Stanford University Press, 1966), 146–51. In the Flood play of the N-Town cycle (or *Ludus Coventriae*), the scene of the building and loading of the ark is omitted, and Noah's Wife does not have the opportunity for rebellion. A similarly docile Noah's Wife appears in the Cornish *Creation* play. The first part of the flood play also survives in a fragment from the Newcas-

tle cycle, in which the devil prompts Noah's Wife to give Noah a magic potion to persuade him to reveal his secrets. Unfortunately, the second half of the play, which very likely involved the loading of the ark (and probable further insubordination on the part of Noah's Wife), is lost. For discussion of the variations and similarities among the flood plays, see Woolf, *English Mystery Plays*, 132–45; Melvin Storm, "Uxor and Alison: Noah's Wife in the Flood Plays and Chaucer's Wife of Bath," *Modern Language Quarterly* 48 (1987): 303–19; J. P. Lewis, *A Study of the Interpretation of Noah and the Flood in Jewish and Christian Literature* (Leiden: Brill, 1978). Other important scholarship includes Sarah Sutherland, "'Not or I see more neede': The Wife of Noah in the Chester, York, and Towneley Cycles," in *Shakespeare and Dramatic Tradition: Essays in Honor of S. F. Johnson*, ed. W. R. Elton and William B. Long (Newark: University of Delaware Press, 1989), 181–93. For discussion of feminist interpretations of the character of Noah's Wife, see Ruth Evans, "Feminist Re-Enactments: Gender and the Towneley *Uxor Noe*," in *A Wyf Ther Was: Essays in Honour of Paule Mertens-Fonck*, ed. Juliette Dor (Liège: Université de Liège, 1992), 141–54.

39. *York Plays*, ed. Smith, 45, line 5.

40. *Wakefield Pageants*, ed. Cawley, 18–19, lines 183–89.

41. Ibid., 19–20, lines 208, 229, 232.

42. *York Plays*, ed. Smith, 49–50, lines 143, 151–52. *Chester Plays*, ed. Deimling, 56, lines 201–8. In the Middle Ages, the noun "gossip" did not necessarily share the negative connotations that it carries today. For discussion of the changing meaning of this term across time, see Patricia Anderson, "Gossips, Ale-wives, Midwives and Witches" (Ph.D. diss., State University of New York at Buffalo, 1992), 22–27.

43. *Chester Plays*, ed. Deimling, 57n.

44. Ibid., 56, lines 205–8.

45. For links between Noah's Wife and the Wife of Bath, see especially Storm, "Uxor and Alison," and Anderson, "Gossips, Ale-wives, Midwives and Witches," 158–62. Indeed, Chaucer directly refers to the tradition of Noah's obstreperous wife in "The Miller's Tale," in which one character recalls the "sorrow of Noah with his fellowship" as he struggled to get his wife aboard the ark (*Riverside Chaucer*, ed. Benson, 73, line 3539).

46. "The Wife of Bath's Prologue," *Riverside Chaucer*, ed. Benson, 110, 113, lines 638, 386.

47. "The Wife of Bath's Tale," *Riverside Chaucer*, ed. Benson, 118, line 980.

48. "The Wife of Bath's Prologue," *Riverside Chaucer*, ed. Benson, 108, lines 227–28.

49. Ibid., 115, lines 775–81.

50. Barbara Gottfried, "Conflict and Relationship, Sovereignty and Survival: Parables of Power in the Wife of Bath's Prologue," *Chaucer Review* 19 (1985): 202–24.

51. "The Wife of Bath's Prologue," in *Riverside Chaucer*, ed. Benson, 114, lines 693–96.

52. Ralph Hanna III, "Jankyn's Book," *Pacific Coast Philology* 21 (1986): 30–36. See also Margaret Hallissy, *Clean Maids, True Wives, Steadfast Widows: Chaucer's Women and Medieval Codes of Conduct* (Westport, Conn.: Greenwood Press, 1993), 173–76, 187–88; Priscilla Martin, *Chaucer's Women: Nuns, Wives, and Amazons* (Iowa City: University of Iowa Press, 1990), 5–13, 210–17. Note that, while the Wife of Bath claims that texts are male centered and hence invalid, she nonetheless cites two texts by women: Trotula (who wrote medical treatises) and Heloise

(a nun most famous for her relationship and subsequent correspondence with the scholar Peter Abelard).

53. The Pardoner interrupts the Wife of Bath in "The Wife of Bath's Prologue," *Riverside Chaucer*, ed. Benson, 107, lines 163–68; the Friar speaks in "The Friar's Prologue," 122, line 1277. On the preaching issue see Susan Signe Morrison, "Don't Ask, Don't Tell: The Wife of Bath and Vernacular Translations," *Exemplaria* 8 (1996): 96–123, and Hallissy, *Clean Maids, True Wives, Steadfast Widows*, 171–73. Margery Kempe faced similar sanctions against female preaching: see, for instance, Ruth Sklar, "Cobham's Daughter: *The Book of Marjory Kempe* and the Power of Heterodox Thinking," *Modern Language Quarterly* 56 (1995): 277–304.

54. For a discussion of interpretations of feminism in the Wife of Bath, see Elaine Tuttle Hansen, "Fearing for Chaucer's Good Name," *Exemplaria* 2 (1990): 23–36. With regard to the Wife of Bath's speech, see also Karma Lochrie, *Covert Operations: The Medieval Uses of Secrecy* (Philadelphia: University of Pennsylvania Press, 1999), 56–60.

55. These poems were first classified as "Ale-Wife poems" by Francis Lee Utley in his index of poems on women (*The Crooked Rib: An Analytical Index to the Argument about Women in English and Scots Literature to the End of the Year 1568* [Columbus: Ohio State University Press, 1944]). Utley's label was taken up by Rossell Hope Robbins ("Poems Dealing with Contemporary Conditions," in *A Manual of the Writings in Middle English*, vol. 5, ed. Albert E. Hartung [New Haven: Connecticut Academy of Arts and Sciences, 1975], 1385–1538), but has recently been challenged by Patricia Anderson. Anderson has pointed out that women in these poems were less often brewsters or ale sellers than they were consumers of ale, and that the poems center more closely around the practice of gossip than around the practice of drinking (Anderson, "Gossips, Ale-wives, Midwives and Witches," 70–71). For a complete listing of poems that fit the category of "gossips' poems," see Anderson, "Gossips, Ale-wives, Midwives and Witches," 188–89.

56. Three versions are printed in *Early English Carols*, ed. Greene, 249–53; quote at p. 249. See also Anderson, "Gossips, Ale-wives, Midwives and Witches," 44–105, 185, and Lochrie, *Covert Operations*, 75–79. For an interesting discussion of contemporary German poems in which women are overheard by a male narrator, see Ann Marie Rasmussen, "Gendered Knowledge and Eavesdropping in the Late-Medieval *Minnerede*," *Speculum* 77 (2002): 1168–94. Note particularly the texts that Rasmussen classifies as "urban," in which women, usually lower-class, break social conventions in their discussions of sex and treat men as objects. As Rasmussen points out, the presence of the male eavesdropper results in an ambiguous effect, in which female conversation is "shadowed" by male anxiety.

57. "The Gospelles of Dystaves," in *The Oxford Book of Late Medieval Verse and Prose*, ed. Douglas Gray (Oxford: Clarendon Press, 1985), 379–80.

58. William Dunbar, *The Poems of William Dunbar*, ed. William MacKay MacKenzie (Edinburgh: Porpoise Press, 1932), 84, 85–97.

59. *Jyl of Breyntford's Testament*, ed. Frederick J. Furnivall (London: Printed for private circulation, 1871), 29–33, lines 5–6.

60. Karen A. Winstead, *Virgin Martyrs: Legends of Sainthood in Late Medieval England* (Ithaca, N.Y.: Cornell University Press, 1997). Winstead has suggested that, during the fifteenth century, hagiographers began to tone down the conflictual and rebellious elements of virgin martyrs' behavior. Yet as late as 1447,

the treatment of women's speech in sources such as Osbern Bokenham's *Legendary* still emphasized the role of speech in martyrs' resistance to authority.

61. Winstead, *Virgin Martyrs,* 64–111; "The Second Nun's Tale," *Riverside Chaucer,* ed. Benson, 268, lines 497, 439.

62. Sheila Delany, *Impolitic Bodies: Poetry, Saints, and Society in Fifteenth-Century England: The Work of Osbern Bokenham* (New York: Oxford University Press, 1998), 89–105. The quote comes from p. 97 and is Delany's translation.

63. Joy Wiltenburg, for instance, has argued that some female readers of sixteenth-century English and German misogynist pamphlets might have interpreted characters of disorderly women as liberating (*Disorderly Women and Female Power in the Street Literature of Early Modern England and Germany* [Charlottesville: University Press of Virginia, 1992]).

64. Lochrie, *Covert Operations,* 57. Theoretical work on gossip has also paid testimony to its empowering qualities. See, for instance, Patricia A. M. Spacks, *Gossip* (New York: Knopf, 1985); J. R. Bergmann, *Discreet Indiscretions: The Social Organization of Gossip* (New York: Aldine de Gruyter, 1993); James C. Scott, *Domination and the Arts of Resistance: Hidden Transcripts* (New Haven, Conn.: Yale University Press, 1990).

65. Anonymous, *A Plaine Description of the Auncient Petigree of Dame Slaunder* (London: H. Middleton for Iohn Hamilton, 1573); William Winstanley, *Poor Robin's True Character of a Scold: or The Shrews Looking-glass* (London: L. C., 1678), 7. For discussion of dramatic representations of the scoldlike character, see Pamela Allen Brown, *Better a Shrew than a Sheep: Women, Drama, and the Culture of Jest in Early Modern England* (Ithaca, N.Y.: Cornell University Press, 2003).

66. Sharon Farmer, "Persuasive Voices: Clerical Images of Medieval Wives," *Speculum* 61 (1986): 517–43.

67. Silvana Vecchio, "The Good Wife," in *Silences of the Middle Ages,* edited by Christiane Klapisch-Zuber, vol. 2 of *The History of Women in the West,* edited by Georges Duby and Michelle Perrot (Cambridge, Mass.: Belknap Press of Harvard University Press, 1992), 105–35, at pp. 115–17.

68. For discussion of the "Planctus Mariæ" in late medieval English poems and passion plays, see George C. Taylor, "The English 'Planctus Mariæ,'" *Modern Philology* 5 (1907): 605–37. Comparable traditions existed on the Continent. For a list of some of the texts and treatises dealing with the theme, see Francis Lee Utley, "Dialogues, Debates, and Catechisms," in *A Manual of the Writings in Middle English,* vol. 3, ed. Albert E. Hartung (New Haven: Connecticut Academy of Arts and Sciences, 1972), 669–745 at p. 685.

69. In *Mittelenglishe Dichtungen aus de Handschrift 432,* ed. Brotanek, 99–102, lines 9–16.

70. For discussion of speech (including scolding) in Puritan New England, see Jane Kamensky, *Governing the Tongue: The Politics of Speech in Early New England* (New York: Oxford University Press, 1997). The Priory Church of St. Peter and St. Paul in Leominster (Herefordshire) houses a ducking stool that was apparently last used in 1808 or 1809 to duck a "very disorderly old woman" who had presumably committed the crime of scolding. Another woman, also probably a scold, was paraded through the town in 1817 but was not ducked because the river was too low (T. N. Brushfield, "On Obsolete Punishments, With Particular Reference to Those of Cheshire. Part II: The Cucking Stool and Allied Punishments," *Journal of the Architectural, Archaeological and Historic Society, for the County, City and Neighbourhood of Chester,* 1st series, 2 [1861], 203–34, at p. 233). One Anne Runcorn was apparently led through the streets of Congleton (Cheshire) in 1824 wearing a scold's bridle "as an example to all scolding women" (Vernon

Mortimer, "The Tongue Can No Man Tame," *Cheshire Life* [March 1975], 72–73. Mortimer does not cite his source for this information). The "gossip" character conducts tours at Old Sturbridge Village, Sturbridge, Massachusetts.

71. Ruth Mazo Karras, *Common Women: Prostitution and Sexuality in Medieval England* (Oxford: Oxford University Press, 1996), passim but esp. 107–11.

Chapter 3

1. TNA: PRO SC 2 156/5. The previous scolding of Agnes by Margaret can be found in SC 2 156/4.

2. TNA: PRO SC 2 156/1.

3. In the Huntingdonshire villages of Upwood and Ellington, as Sherri Olson has shown, they appeared in only 13 and 14 percent respectively of the thousands of appearances noted in the court records (*A Chronicle of All That Happens: Voices from the Village Court in Medieval England* [Toronto: Pontifical Institute of Mediaeval Studies, 1996], 32). In the manors of Brigstock (Northamptonshire), Iver (Buckinghamshire), and Houghton-cum-Wyton (Huntingdonshire), examined by Judith M. Bennett, women accounted for 22, 14, and 14 percent respectively of court appearances. When women did participate directly in courts, they tended to do so less often. Bennett has shown that in the manor of Brigstock, each man appeared an average of 21 times in surviving records. Each woman, by contrast, appeared only 8 times (*Women in the Medieval English Countryside: Gender and Household in Brigstock before the Plague* [New York: Oxford University Press, 1987], 23). In the ecclesiastical visitation of 1397 carried out by John Trefnant, Bishop of Hereford (unpublished typescript from original in Hereford Cathedral Archives, MS 1779), women accounted for 685 (36.8 percent) of 1,863 court appearances (or, more accurately, court summons, since this number includes those summoned to court or cited to the next court who did not appear).

4. Judith M. Bennett, "Public Power and Authority in the Medieval English Countryside," in *Women and Power in the Middle Ages*, ed. Mary Erler and Maryanne Kowaleski (Athens: University of Georgia Press, 1988), 18–36.

5. Women may also have outnumbered men among those accused of gleaning offenses (Bennett, *Women in the Medieval English Countryside*, 39, 41). For discussion of the leyrwite fee, see Bennett, "Writing Fornication: Medieval Leyrwite and Its Historians," *Transactions of the Royal Historical Society* 13 (2003): 131–62.

6. TNA: PRO SC 2 203/57.

7. Olson, *Chronicle of all that Happens*, 95; Miriam Müller, "Social Control and the Hue and Cry in Two Fourteenth-Century Villages," *Journal of Medieval History* 31 (2005): 29–53, at pp. 38–39. Note that this pattern does not hold for Brigstock, where women raised fifteen of twenty-four false hues (Bennett, *Women in the Medieval English Countryside*, 39, 41). A. M. Tonkinson notes that women in the borough and manor of Macclesfield (Cheshire) were responsible for at least thirty-one of fifty-two hues raised between 1349 and 1396 and observes that women were especially likely to be involved with raising false hues, but does not give numbers to support this observation. *Macclesfield in the Later Fourteenth Century: Communities of Town and Forest*, Chetham Society Publications, 3rd series, vol. 42 (Manchester: Chetham Society, 1999), 164.

8. Anne Reiber DeWindt and Edwin Brezette DeWindt, *Ramsey: The Lives of an English Fenland Town, 1200–1600* (Washington, D.C.: Catholic University of

America Press, forthcoming), chap. 4. I am grateful to Anne and Edwin DeWindt for sharing with me a copy of their work on hues and cries.

9. These numbers include instances of "hamsoken," in which people were assaulted in their own homes or had their homes broken into violently.

10. Two of these involved an attack on their husbands' dogs as opposed to their husbands themselves!

11. TNA: PRO SC 2 203/64.

12. Müller, "Social Control and the Hue and Cry," 47.

13. Bennett, "Public Power and Authority," 25–26.

14. DeWindt and DeWindt, *Ramsey*. Working independently of one another and with different sets of data, the DeWindts and I have reached remarkably similar conclusions about changes in hue-raising and their consequences for women's voices under the law in the late Middle Ages.

15. BL Additional Charters 16054, 16065a.

16. *Court Rolls of the Borough of Colchester*, vol. 1, ed. and trans. Isaac Herbert Jeayes and W. Gurney Benham (Colchester: s.n., 1921), 88. In fact, Jeayes and Benham translate the Latin here as "litigious person": see n. 28 below for discussion of how this term might be translated.

17. TNA: PRO CHES 19/3.

18. TNA: PRO DL 30 67/842; DL 30 67/844. In the 1392 court roll, Christina is listed as having raised the hue justly on Agnes Badyngham, who had struck Christina. Nonetheless, Christina was fined 1d. for the hue, suggesting that the court found her culpable, at least to some extent.

19. *Bridgwater Borough Archives*, vol. 2, ed. Thomas Bruce Dilks, Somerset Record Society Publications, vol. 53 (London: Somerset Record Society, 1938), 3, 15, 49, 52, 104; *Records of the Borough of Nottingham*, vol. 1, ed. W. H. Stevenson (London: B. Quaritch, 1882), 294–95, 304–5, 308–9; *The Court Rolls of Ramsey, Hepmangrove and Bury, 1268–1600*, ed. Edwin Brezette DeWindt (Toronto: Pontifical Institute of Mediaeval Studies, 1990), 539, 615, 618, 652, 701. Because no court series is complete, these figures are minimum numbers: in other words, more scolds might have been false hue-raisers and vice versa.

20. R. H. Helmholz, Introduction to *Select Cases on Defamation to 1600*, ed. R. H. Helmholz, Seldon Society Publications, vol. 101 (London: Seldon Society, 1985).

21. *Court Rolls of the Manor of Ingoldmells in the County of Lincoln*, ed. W. O. Massingberd (London: Spottiswoode, 1902), 21–22.

22. *Registrum Hamonis Hethe, Diocesis Roffensis AD 1319–52*, ed. Charles Johnson, Canterbury and York Society Publications, vol. 49 (Oxford: Oxford University Press, 1948).

23. *Ecclesiastical Cause Papers at York: The Court of York 1301–1399*, ed. David M. Smith, Borthwick Texts and Calendars, vol. 15 (York: University of York, Borthwick Institute of Historical Research, 1988).

24. "Visitation of Parishes by John Trefnant, Bishop of Hereford, 1397" (unpublished typescript from original in Hereford Cathedral Archives MS 1779).

25. L. R. Poos, "Sex, Lies, and the Church Courts of Pre-Reformation England," *Journal of Interdisciplinary History* 25 (1995): 585–607.

26. *The Register of John Chandler, Dean of Salisbury 1404–1417*, ed. T. C. B. Timmins, Wiltshire Record Society Publications, vol. 39 (Devizes: Wiltshire Record Society, 1984). Note that a further five men were reported as having defamed the vicar (two individually, plus one group of three). Defamations of the clergy

are slightly different than defamations of nonclergy, since priests had the ability to report crimes to the court directly, rather than via the *inquisitores.*

27. Laura Gowing, *Domestic Dangers: Women, Words and Sex in Early Modern London* (Oxford: Clarendon Press, 1996).

28. It is not always easy to decide whether or not someone should be adjudged a scold when dealing with a court record written in Latin. It is harder still when the record has been translated back into English. In their volume of Colchester borough records, Jeayes and Benham list Alice Wyger as a "common litigious person" in the court records for February 24, 1311 (*Court Rolls of the Borough of Colchester,* vol. 1, ed. Jeayes and Benham, 24). If the word that they are translating is "*litigatrix,*" then probably Alice does qualify as a scold, since later courts are fairly clear that "*litigators*" and "*litigatrices*" are indeed Latin versions of "scold." Sixteen other women appear in the courts of Colchester in 1311–12 also charged as "litigious persons." On the other hand, I do not regard Hugh de Stowe, charged in Colchester the previous year for "having constantly made use of litigious and opprobrious language against several persons in the market of Colchester" as a scold. Hugh's case, which seems to have involved slander about the quality of others' merchandise, seems more akin to defamation (*Court Rolls of the Borough of Colchester,* vol. 1, ed. Jeayes and Benham, 13). This is, however, a hard call to make and illustrates the evolving awareness of scolding as a crime. For three other preplague scolds, see *The Court Rolls of the Manor of Wakefield from October 1338 to September 1340,* ed. K. M. Troup, Wakefield Court Rolls Series of the Yorkshire Archaeological Society, vol. 12 (Leeds: Yorkshire Archaeological Society, 1999), 78, 222. For Welsh scolds in the town of Ruthin and lordship of Dyffryn Clwyd in the 1340s and 1350s, see TNA: PRO SC 2 217/11–218/3. I am grateful to Maryanne Kowaleski for pointing these out to me.

29. Without a complete series of courts, it is impossible to be sure that one has ever found the truly *earliest* presentment, even within a single jurisdiction, because of the irregular frequency of scolding prosecutions. Half a dozen scolds might be presented each year for a year or two, but then scolding might disappear from the records for a few years, almost as if the offense had dropped temporarily from the court's radar. While sampling multiple jurisdictions over particular years can help turn up scolds, therefore, it is a blunt measure: one can never be sure that no scolds were prosecuted in previous or subsequent courts. To try to find scold-prosecuting jurisdictions, I sampled more than four hundred court sessions from twenty-three to forty-nine jurisdictions for three years: 1344, 1359, and 1369. I also read all surviving fourteenth-century court records for courts that I knew to have prosecuted scolds by the late fourteenth or early fifteenth centuries. These included Bradford (Yorkshire), Methwold (Norfolk), Chedzoy (Somerset), Halton (Cheshire), Widnes (Lancashire), and Congleton (Cheshire). In addition, I looked at surviving court records for Pleshey (Essex) and its associated jurisdictions from 1352 onward, and for Clare (Suffolk) from 1345 onward.

30. TNA: PRO DL 30 63/801, m. 22r.

31. In fact, they were described in the first presentment as "*communes and notorii obiurgatrices et ——atrices,*" but the first part of the last word is illegible. TNA: PRO DL 30 1957/129.

32. Agnes Bastholpt may well be the same Agnes de Baksholt presented in 1355. Medieval spellings of surnames were by no means standardized. TNA: PRO DL 30 1957/129.

33. Or the masculine forms of these: "*maledictores,*" "*obiurgatores,*" or "*litigatores.*"

34. TNA: PRO DL 30 1/21. In other fourteenth-century courts, scolds were described as "*garulatrices*" (or "*garulatores*"), a word which stems from the Latin for "gossip," and is related to the modern adjective "garrulous." Ecclesiastical courts often presented scolds as "*communes diffamatrices*" (or "*diffamatores*"), or "common defamers," reflecting the church's jurisdiction over matters of defamation. Another frequent ecclesiastical court term was "*suscitatrices* [or *suscitatores*] *dissensiones*," or "sowers of dissension."

35. Wolveston: "Injunctum est omnibus mulieribus istius villæ quod nulla earum litigant dedicant al. in verbis vel factis, sub pœna de qualibet vice xij d., et eciam quod nullus homo trahat cultellum vel levat [*sic*] baculum sub pœna xl d. et si percusciant [*sic*] di. marc." East Merrington: "Ordinatum est tam ex assensu domini quam omnium ten. villarum infra dominium suum, quod nullus commorans in eisdem extrahat cultellum vel levet baculum pro male faciendo, sub pœna xl d. Et eciam illi qui percussit [*sic*] aliquem cum baculo, cultello, vel gladio solvat domino di. marc. Et eciam quod mulieres compescant linguas suas, no maledicendo seu litigando, sub pœna xij d. solvend. per illam qui [*sic*] in deffectu reperitur." *Halmota Prioratus Dunelmensis: Containing Extracts from the Halmote Court or Manor Rolls of the Prior and Convent of Durham 1296–1384*, ed. W. H. D. Longstaffe and John Booth, Surtees Society Publications, vol. 82 (Durham: Surtees Society Publications, 1886), 154, 153. Wives were also specifically warned to restrain their tongues at Hesilden in 1375 (132), at Billingham in 1378 (144), and in other portions of the court rolls not printed by Longstaffe and Booth (see comments at xxvii–xxviii and 154, n. 1).

36. *The Court Rolls of Yeadon 1361–1476: With the Early Rentals and Accounts of Esholt Priory, Charters, Deeds and Associated Material to 1500 A.D., Dissolution Rentals and Accounts*, ed. G. R. Price (Skipton: Maple-Bowes Publishers, 1984), 81, 99. Price does not supply Latin of original.

37. *Monumenta Juridica: The Black Book of the Admiralty*, vol. 2, *Appendix*, ed. Travers Twiss, Rolls Series, vol. 55 (London: Longman, 1873), 165; John Wodderspoon, *Memorials of the Ancient Town of Ipswich in the County of Suffolk* (Ipswich: Pawsey, 1850), 266–67. For discussion of the dating of the Ipswich Custumal, see *Ipswich Borough Archives 1255–1835: A Catalogue*, ed. David Allen, Suffolk Records Society Publications, vol. 43 (Woodbridge: Boydell Press, 2000), xx, xxii–xxiv, xxviii, 413–15 (I am grateful to Maryanne Kowaleski for this citation); *Liber Albus: The White Book of the City of London*, ed. and trans. H. T. Riley (London: R. Griffin, 1861), 394–96: "Of the Penalties inflicted upon Courtesans, Bawds, [and] Priests taken in Adultery."

38. *Liber Albus*, ed. Riley, 287.

39. "Item concordatum fuit de objurgatricibus quod per eas multa mala in civitate per tales oriuntur . . ." Hereford Ordinances, cap. 97 in *Borough Customs*, vol. 1, ed. Mary Bateson, Seldon Society Publications, vol. 18 (London: B. Quaritch, 1904), 79–80.

40. Cited in Marjorie Keniston McIntosh, *Controlling Misbehavior in England, 1370–1600* (Cambridge: Cambridge University Press, 1998), 63–64.

41. There are exceptions to this rule, however: ordinances of the mayor and his brethren from Leicester in 1467 specify punishments for "all manner [of] scolds that are dwelling within this town, man or woman" (*Records of the Borough of Leicester*, vol. 2, *1327–1509*, ed. Mary Bateson [London: C. J. Clay and Sons, 1901], 291).

42. Karen Jones and Michael Zell, "Bad Conversation? Gender and Social Control in a Kentish Borough, c. 1450–c. 1570," *Continuity and Change* 13

(1998): 11–31; Marjorie Keniston McIntosh, "Finding Language for Misconduct: Jurors in Fifteenth-Century Local Courts," in *Bodies and Disciplines: Intersections of Literature and History in Fifteenth-Century England*, ed. Barbara A. Hanawalt and David Wallace (Minneapolis: University of Minnesota Press, 1996), 87–122; McIntosh, *Controlling Misbehavior*, 59.

43. *A Series of Precedents and Proceedings in Criminal Cases, Extending from the Year 1475 to 1640*, ed. William Hale Hale (London: F. & J. Rivington, 1847), 94.

44. Ibid., 77.

45. For an exception to this rule see the case of Thomas Smyth, presented to the Consistory Court of the Diocese of London in 1513 as a "*communis diffamator vicinorum et scolda*" (*Select Cases on Defamation*, ed. Helmholz, 23). The word "*scolda*," an attempt to 'Latinize' the English word "scold," could easily have been made into the masculine "*scoldus*"—the fact that it was not suggests the reflexively female association of the word "scold."

46. Galfridus Anglicanus, *Promptorium Parvulorum: The First English-Latin Dictionary*, ed. A. L. Mayhew, EETS, extra series, vol. 102 (London: Kegan Paul, Trench, Trübner, 1908), 402.

47. One manuscript of the *Catholicon Anglicum* dictionary, a microfilm of which is in the possession of the editors of the *Middle English Dictionary*, gives this definition (*The Middle English Dictionary*, ed. Hans Kurath et al. [Ann Arbor: University of Michigan Press, 1956–present), part S.2]).

Chapter 4

1. Vern L. Bullough, "On Being Male in the Middle Ages," in *Medieval Masculinities: Regarding Men in the Middle Ages*, ed. Clare A. Lees (Minneapolis: University of Minnesota Press, 1994), 31–46.

2. "Against Venomous Tongues," in John Skelton, *The Complete Poems of John Skelton, Laureate*, 4th ed., ed. Philip Henderson (London: J. M. Dent, 1959), 245–49, lines 73–76.

3. "A Homelie Against Contencion and Braullynge," in *Certain Sermons or Homilies (1547) and A Homily against Disobedience and Wilful Rebellion (1570): A Critical Edition*, ed. Ronald B. Bond (Toronto: University of Toronto Press, 1987), 195.

4. Patricia Parker, "On the Tongue: Cross Gendering, Effeminacy, and the Art of Words," *Style* 23 (1989): 445–65.

5. "Poem on the Evil Times of Edward II," in *The Political Songs of England: From the Reign of John to That of Edward II*, ed. Thomas Wright, Camden Society Publications, vol. 6 (London: Camden Society, 1839), 323–45, lines 259–60.

6. For discussion of late medieval satirical and complaint literature on the subject of knights, see G. R. Owst, *Literature and Pulpit in Medieval England: A Neglected Chapter in the History of English Letters and of the English People*, 2nd ed. (Oxford: B. Blackwell, 1961), 331–38.

7. As John Peter has discussed, the clergy faced attack in late medieval literature far more often than any other profession (*Complaint and Satire in Early English Literature* [Oxford: Clarendon Press, 1956], 80–84).

8. Both quotes are from synodal sermons preached at York in 1372 and 1373, quoted by Owst, *Literature and Pulpit*, 274. For Owst's general discussion of attacks on the clergy, see 222–86.

9. "A Song Against the Friars," in *Reliquiæ Antiquæ: Scraps from Ancient Manuscripts, Illustrating Chiefly Early English Literature and the English Language*, vol. 2,

ed. Thomas Wright and James Orchard Halliwell-Phillips (London: J. R. Smith, 1845), 247, lines 12–13.

10. R. N. Swanson, "Angels Incarnate: Clergy and Masculinity from Gregorian Reform to Reformation," in *Masculinity in Medieval Europe*, ed. D. M. Hadley (London: Longman, 1999), 160–77.

11. "The Wife of Bath's Tale," in Geoffrey Chaucer, *The Riverside Chaucer*, 3rd ed., ed. Larry D. Benson (Boston: Houghton Mifflin, 1987), 118, line 980.

12. "Visitation of Parishes by John Trefnant, Bishop of Hereford, 1397," (unpublished typescript of original in Hereford Cathedral Archives MS 1779); *The Register of John Chandler, Dean of Salisbury 1404–1417*, ed. T. C. B. Timmins, Wiltshire Record Society Publications, vol. 39 (Devizes: Wiltshire Record Society, 1984), 25; *The Register of John Morton, Archbishop of Canterbury 1486–1500*, vol. 3, *Norwich Sede Vacante, 1499*, ed. Christopher Harper-Bill, Canterbury and York Society Publications, vol. 89 (Woodbridge: Boydell Press, 2000), 201–02. In most cases, priests were able to find the requisite number of compurgators who would attest to their innocence, but the very necessity of appearing in front of one's bishop on such a charge must have proven humiliating.

13. *Calendar of Plea and Memoranda Rolls Preserved among the Archives of the Corporation of the City of London at the Guild-hall*, vol. 4, *1413–37*, ed. A. H. Thomas (Cambridge: Cambridge University Press, 1943), 127.

14. Robert Mannyng, *Robert of Brunne's "Handlyng Synne,"* ed. Frederick J. Furnivall, EETS, vol. 119 (London: Kegan Paul, Trench, Trübner, 1901), 126, lines 3655–74.

15. See, for example, *The Register of John Waltham, Bishop of Salisbury 1388–1395*, ed. T. C. B. Timmins, Canterbury and York Society Publications, vol. 80 (Woodbridge: Boydell Press, 1994), 122–23, 127; *Register of John Chandler*, ed. Timmins, 25, 48, 74, 85–86, 93–94.

16. *Register of John Chandler*, ed. Timmins, 85–86.

17. Ibid., 14.

18. *Kentish Visitations of Archbishop William Warham and His Deputies, 1511–12*, ed. K. L. Wood-Legh, Kent Records, vol. 24 (Maidstone: Kent Archaeological Society, 1984), 180.

19. I owe this latter suggestion to Kit French.

20. *Lower Ecclesiastical Jurisdiction in Late-Medieval England: The Courts of the Dean and Chapter of Lincoln, 1336–1349, and the Deanery of Wisbech, 1458–1484*, ed. L. R. Poos (Oxford: Oxford University Press, 2001), 275, 318, 360, 388, 466.

21. See Barbara D. Palmer, "An Iconography for Swearers: The Almondsbury Passion Poem," *Early Drama, Art, and Music Review* 12 (1989): 9–16. For discussion of connections between representations of Christ's broken body and the "Sunday Christ" theme (which warned people to abstain from labor on holy days), see Pallas Athene Reiss, "The Sunday Christ: Sabbatarianism in English Medieval Wall Painting" (Ph.D. diss., University of Chicago, 1995), vol. 1, 176–79.

22. Charges of such blasphemy did occasionally appear in ecclesiastical courts, but were rare: John Wulrerd of Walberswick, for example, was charged in 1499 as a "common blasphemer by the body of Christ and His other limbs." John admitted the charge and was ordered to carry a candle worth 4d. to the altar on the following Sunday and offer it to the honor of the body of Christ. *Register of John Morton*, ed. Harper-Bill, 184.

23. This story, reproduced in Owst, *Literature and Pulpit*, 423–24, originally appeared in Brother Whitford of Sion's *Werke for Housholders* (1533).

24. Owst, *Literature and Pulpit*, 424.

25. Ibid., 416.

26. For discussion of the appearance of male and female characters in exempla, see Ruth Mazo Karras's analysis of the thirteen hundred exempla collected by John of Bromyard around the mid-fourteenth century: "Gendered Sin and Misogyny in John of Bromyard's 'Summa Predicantium,'" *Traditio* 47 (1992): 233–57. For an exemplum involving a slanderous nun, see John Mirk, *Mirk's Festial: A Collection of Homilies*, ed. Theodor Erbe, EETS, extra series, vol. 96 (London: Kegan Paul, Trench, Trübner, 1892), 96–97.

27. Mirk, *Mirk's Festial*, 113–4. A similar story appears in Robert Mannyng, *Robert of Brunne's "Handlyng Synne,"* part 2, 25–28, lines 9261–314, Bodl. 415 manuscript version. See also Owst, *Literature and Pulpit*, 424–25.

28. "A Lamentation of Our Lady on Swearing," in *Mittelenglishe Dichtungen aus der Handschrift 432 des Trinity College in Dublin*, ed. Rudolf Brotanek (Halle: M. Niemeyer, 1940), 99–102, line 10.

29. For a discussion of this window, see Christopher Woodforde, *The Norwich School of Glass-Painting in the Fifteenth Century* (New York: Oxford University Press, 1950), chap. 8: "The 'Blasphemy' Window at Heydon."

30. The other two men, seated below Christ and his mother, are playing some kind of board game, and one strikes the other on the head with his sword. The relationship of these last two men to the scene is unclear, except that poems and exempla often represented dice players or other game players as habitual swearers and sometimes coupled warnings against swearing with warnings against gaming.

31. On the left hand side of the Corby wall painting is a naked woman seated on a red-horned beast, holding an unidentifiable object in her left hand and uttering something recorded on a scroll. Christopher Woodforde has suggested that she might represent lust, but her absence from exempla, poems, and other artistic representations concerning cursing, plus her peripheral placement in the wall painting, might indicate that she was included as something of a space-filler rather than as an integral part of the scene. Alternately, she might represent a tapster. For a representation of the Corby wall painting, see Conway Library photograph negative # 176/3 (16) at the Courtauld Institute, London. It has been suggested that a third wall painting, now lost, also represented the theme of Christ and the swearers. The wall painting, at Walsham-le-Willows church in Suffolk, was photographed before it was destroyed, and a copy is reproduced in Woodforde, *Norwich School*, facing p. 186.

32. "The Wife of Bath's Prologue," *Riverside Chaucer*, ed. Benson, 108, lines 227–28. Note also that John Wycliffe argued for a female-associated meaning of the word "blasphemy" when he suggested that it was derived from the words "*blas*" and "*femina*," meaning a foolish and harmful woman (David Lawton, *Blasphemy* [Philadelphia: University of Pennsylvania Press, 1993], 105). For one mention of women swearing oaths, see *A Selection of Latin Stories from Manuscripts of the Thirteenth and Fourteenth Centuries*, ed. Thomas Wright, Percy Society Publications, vol. 8 (London: Percy Society, 1842), 61–62.

33. Michael Roberts, "'Words they are Women, and Deeds they are Men': Images of Work and Gender in Early Modern England," in *Women and Work in Pre-Industrial England*, ed. Lindsay Charles and Lorna Duffin (London: Croom Helm, 1985), 122–80 at p. 161, n. 1. See also William George Smith and F. P. Wilson, *Oxford Dictionary of English Proverbs*, 3rd ed. (Oxford: Oxford University Press, 1970), 175. The Latin proverb "Where there is a breast, there is a swelling;

facts are masculine, words feminine" began Erasmus's 1525 treatise "On the Tongue." (Parker, "On the Tongue," esp. 460, n. 6.)

34. *Select Cases on Defamation to 1600*, ed. R. H. Helmholz, Seldon Society Publications, vol. 101 (London: Seldon Society, 1985), 33. Richard might have retorted that Geoffrey's "wind" had tangible consequences indeed. Allegedly, Geoffrey told others that Richard had assaulted another man, drawing blood, and Richard was indicted at the sheriff's tourn and fined 40d.

35. Linguists and theorists have recently considered distinctions between speech that is mere "wind" and speech that performs some action by its very utterance. J. L. Austin's work on performative speech (*How to Do Things with Words*, 2nd ed. [Cambridge, Mass.: Harvard University Press, 1975]), in which he identified particular words and phrases as ones that performed actions by their very utterance (for example, spoken in the right circumstances, "I thee wed" performs the action of marrying someone) has inspired work on "performance theory." Recent scholars have sought to extend the notion of performance to a wide variety of social categories. Best-known to historians of women, perhaps, is Judith Butler's work on the performance of gender, in which she argues that gender identity is constituted by performances or expressions of gender (*Gender Trouble: Feminism and the Subversion of Identity* [New York: Routledge, 1990]). Butler's more recent book, *Excitable Speech: A Politics of the Performative* (New York: Routledge, 1997), considers the violence that can be performed through hate speech and negative labels. For an example of a medievalist's application of Austin's speech-act theory, see Lester K. Little, *Benedictine Maledictions: Liturgical Cursing in Romanesque France* (Ithaca, N.Y.: Cornell University Press, 1993).

36. In Brigstock (Northamptonshire), women were charged with 17 percent of 175 assaults, threatened assaults, and hamsokens (housebreakings) between 1287 and 1348 (Judith M. Bennett, *Women in the Medieval English Countryside: Gender and Household in Brigstock before the Plague* [New York: Oxford University Press, 1987], 39. In the manor court of Wakefield, they accounted for 11 percent of 632 assaults. They were also charged with 7 percent of 2,696 homicides among gaol delivery rolls from Norfolk, Yorkshire, and Northamptonshire between 1300 and 1348 (Barbara Hanawalt, "The Female Felon in Fourteenth-Century England," *Viator* 5 [1974]: 253–68, at pp. 258, 268).

37. HEH BA 546–648.

38. *Records of the Borough of Leicester*, vol. 2, *1327–1509*, ed. Mary Bateson (London: C. J. Clay and Sons, 1901), 183.

39. Sherri Olson notes that before the plague women in Upwood and Ellington tended to be cited for contempt of officials whereas men were more likely to be cited for rebellion against officials (*A Chronicle of All That Happens: Voices from the Village Court in Medieval England* [Toronto: Pontifical Institute of Mediaeval Studies, 1996], 112).

40. *The Court Rolls of the Manor of Wakefield from September 1348 to September 1350*, ed. Helen M. Jewell, Wakefield Court Rolls Series of the Yorkshire Archaeological Society, 2nd series, vol. 2 (Leeds: Yorkshire Archaeological Society, 1981), 82, 92, 104, 126, 133, 139.

41. Olson, *Chronicle of All That Happens*, 217.

42. Karen Jones and Michael Zell, "Bad Conversation? Gender and Social Control in a Kentish Borough, c. 1450–c. 1570," *Continuity and Change* 13 (1998): 11–31.

43. Maryanne Kowaleski, "Gossip, Gender, and the Economy: The Origins of Scolding Indictments in Medieval England," forthcoming.

44. The sample of twenty men that I am using here consists of five men from Middlewich (TNA: PRO SC 2 156/2–7), three from London (*Calendar of Pleas and Memoranda Rolls*, vol. 4, *1413–47*, ed. Thomas), five from Nottingham (*Records of the Borough of Nottingham*, vol. 2, ed. W. H. Stevenson [London: B. Quaritch, 1883]), one from Bridgwater (*Bridgwater Borough Archives*, vol. 2., ed. Thomas Bruce Dilks, Somerset Record Society Publications, vol. 53 [London: Somerset Record Society, 1938]), two from Colchester (*Court Rolls of the Borough of Colchester*, vol. 3, ed. and trans. Isaac Herbert Jeayes and W. Gurney Benham [Colchester: s.n., 1941]), two from East Merrington (*Halmota Prioratus Dunelmensis: Containing Extracts from the Halmote Court or Manor Rolls of the Prior and Convent of Durham 1296–1384*, ed. W. H. D. Longstaffe and John Booth, Surtees Society Publications, vol. 82 [Durham: Surtees Society Publications, 1886]), one from Chedzoy (TNA: PRO SC 2 198/19), and one from Battle (HEH BA 610).

45. TNA: PRO SC 2 156/6, m. 8v.

46. TNA: PRO CHES 25/12, m. 10r.

47. *Calendar of Pleas and Memoranda Rolls*, vol. 4, *1413–47*, ed. Thomas, 127; *Bridgwater Borough Archives*, vol. 2., ed. Dilks; TNA: PRO CHES 25/12 mm. 5r.–10r.

48. Ruth Mazo Karras, *Common Women: Prostitution and Sexuality in Medieval England* (Oxford: Oxford University Press, 1996), 139.

49. "The Clerk's Prologue," *Riverside Chaucer*, ed. Benson, 137, lines 2–4; Priscilla Martin, *Chaucer's Women: Nuns, Wives, and Amazons* (Iowa City: University of Iowa Press, 1990), 222–24.

50. *Book for a Simple and Devout Woman: A Late Middle English Adaptation of Peraldus's Summa de Vitiis et Virtutibus and Friar Laurent's Somme le Roi, Edited from British Library Mss Harley 6571 and Additional 30944*, ed. F. N. M. Diekstra (Groningen: Egbert Forsten, 1998), 298.

Chapter 5

1. The prosecutions of Middlewich scolds on July 23, 1426 are recorded in TNA: PRO SC 2 156/5, m. 11r. In each case, it was alleged that scolds "*obiurgata fuit*" their targets. Four of the ten were said to have "*dispersonauit*" (defamed) their targets, or family members of their targets, too. No civil suits were brought, however. In addition to the scolding cases, the Middlewich borough court did conduct routine business, although it heard no other cases, civil or criminal. The routine business consisted of the granting of one essoin (an excuse for nonattendance for one of the parties in a civil suit) and the collection of local taxes and brewing fees.

2. A. M. Tonkinson, *Macclesfield in the Later Fourteenth Century: Communities of Town and Forest*, Chetham Society Publications, 3rd series (Manchester: Chetham Society, 1999), 52.

3. Martin Ingram, in particular, has argued that scolds were often "mentally disturbed," "dismal negotiators of social relationships," or "temperamentally inclined to confrontation rather than compromise" ("'Scolding Women Cucked or Washed': A Crisis in Gender Relations in Early Modern England?" in *Women, Crime and the Courts*, ed. Jenny Kermode and Garthine Walker [London: University College of London Press, 1994], 48–80, at p. 72).

4. Galfridus Anglicanus, *Promptorium Parvulorum: The First English-Latin Dictionary*, ed. A. L. Mayhew, EETS, extra series, vol. 102 (London: Kegan Paul, Trench, Trübner, 1908), 402.

5. Jean Palsgrave, *L'éclaircissement de la langue française,* ed. F. Génin (Paris: Imprimerie Nationale, 1852), 706.

6. See, for example, John Kitchin, *Jurisdictions: Or, The Lawful Authority of Courts Leet, Courts Baron, Court of Marshalseys, Court of Pypowder and Ancient Demesne, etc,* 5th ed. (London: Henry Twyford and Samuel Herrick, 1675), 20; William Hawkins, *A Treatise of the Pleas of the Crown* (London: Elizabeth Nutt, 1716), 197–200.

7. William Sheppard, *A Grand Abridgement of the Common and Statute Law of England* (London, 1675), as quoted in John Webster Spargo, *Juridical Folklore in England Illustrated by the Cucking-Stool* (Durham, N.C.: Duke University Press, 1944), 121–22. Giles Jacob, the eighteenth-century compiler of an authoritative law dictionary, echoed Sheppard in defining scolds as "troublesome and angry women who, by their brawling and wrangling among their neighbours, break the public peace, increase discord, and become a public nuisance to the neighbourhood." *The Law-Dictionary,* 1st American ed. (New York and Philadelphia: I. Riley and P. Byrne, 1811), 29. See also William Blackstone, *Commentaries on the Laws of England,* 4 vols., from the last London edition (Boston: T.B. Wait and Sons, 1818), bk. 4, ch. 13, 166–68.

8. TNA: PRO DL 30 4/54, mm. 4r, 13v. Note that scolds in Congleton were sometimes recorded in the Halton way, using the Latin word for "scold" as a verb. Both Halton and Congleton were part of the Duchy of Lancaster and were administered by the same court steward, so jurisdictional differences cannot alone account for the difference in the format of presentation.

9. TNA: PRO CHES 19/4.

10. *Materials for the History of the Town and Parish of Wellington in the County of Somerset,* Part 2, *Manorial Court Rolls 1277–1908,* ed. Arthur L. Humphreys (London: s.n., 1910), 156, 191. Humphreys does not indicate the Latin words that he translates as "common scolds."

11. TNA: PRO SC 2 156/5.

12. TNA: PRO SC 2 156/5. It is possible that 6d. of this fine was due to the fact that she failed to attend court when first summoned. Still, 10d. was a high fine for scolds in Middlewich.

13. TNA: PRO DL 30 1/22–5/70; SC 2 155/84.

14. Arguments between members of a household or a family were very seldom described as scolding. One exception can be seen when John, son of Richard de Grymesdiche of More (Cheshire), was fined 2d. in 1358 for calling his sister Margery a whore. It is not clear, however, where the argument took place, nor even if John and Margery were still living under the same roof (TNA: PRO DL 30 1/21). Similarly, I have found one instance in a Halton court of 1424 in which a servant was fined for scolding her master's wife, but it is unclear if the servant was living in the same household as her master and perhaps curious that her master's wife was not described as her mistress (TNA: PRO DL 30 4/56, 2r.). These cases of scolding among people with close kin or servant-master relationships are, however, very much the exception to the rule.

15. TNA: PRO CHES 19/3; *Kentish Visitations of Archbishop William Warham and His Deputies, 1511–12,* ed. K. L. Wood-Legh, Kent Records, vol. 24 (Maidstone: Kent Archaeological Society, 1984), 187.

16. For a similar instance from a Cheshire sheriff's tourn from the hundred of Edesbury in which a woman allegedly called a man a "thief and son of a thief," see TNA: PRO CHES 19/3, m. 32r.

17. The Latin word recorded is "*genus*" which can mean race or family or

kind. It is unclear what Agnes meant here. It may be relevant that Margery was a prominent brewster, baker, and seller of foodstuffs, and such occupations were frequently suspected and maligned in the fourteenth and fifteenth centuries (see Judith M. Bennett, *Ale, Beer, and Brewsters in England: Women's Work in a Changing World 1300–1600* [New York: Oxford University Press, 1996], 122–44).

18. See, for instance, TNA: PRO CHES 19/3, m. 33r. (sheriff's tourn for the hundred of Wirral); TNA: PRO DL 30 5/61, m. 4r. (Halton halmote court).

19. L. R. Poos, "Sex, Lies, and the Church Courts of Pre-Reformation England," *Journal of Interdisciplinary History* 25 (1995): 585–607, at p. 591.

20. Ruth Mazo Karras, *Common Women: Prostitution and Sexuality in Medieval England* (Oxford: Oxford University Press, 1996).

21. Poos, "Sex, Lies, and the Church Courts," 591. For Cecilia de Aston, see the sheriff's tourn from the hundred of Wirral: TNA: PRO CHES 19/3, m. 33r.

22. Marjorie Keniston McIntosh, *Controlling Misbehavior in England, 1370–1600* (Cambridge: Cambridge University Press, 1998), 57, 174–76, 239.

23. Maryanne Kowaleski, "Gossip, Gender, and the Economy: The Origins of Scolding Indictments in Medieval England," forthcoming.

24. *Court Rolls of the Borough of Colchester*, vol. 3, ed. and trans. Isaac Herbert Jeayes and W. Gurney Benham (Colchester: s.n., 1941), 163; *Records of the Borough of Nottingham*, vol. 2, ed. W. H. Stevenson (London: B. Quaritch, 1883), 107.

25. Kowaleski, "Gossip, Gender, and the Economy."

26. *Extracts from Records in the Possession of the Municipal Corporation of the Borough of Portsmouth and from Other Documents Relating Thereto*, ed. Richard J. Murrell and Robert East (Portsmouth: H. Lewis, 1884), 82; *Liber Albus: The White Book of the City of London*, ed. and trans. H. T. Riley (London: R. Griffin, 1861), 394–96; *English Gilds: The Original Ordinances of More than One Hundred Early English Gilds*, ed. Joshua Toulmin Smith and Lucy Toulmin Smith, EETS, vol. 40 (London: N. Trübner, 1870), 34–35; *Reprint of the Barnstaple Records*, vol. 1, ed. J. R. Chanter and Thomas Wainwright (Barnstaple: A. E. Barnes, 1900), 174.

27. *A Transcript of the Court Rolls of Yeadon 1361–1476: With the Early Rentals and Accounts of Esholt Priory, Charters, Deeds and Associated Material to 1500 A.D., Dissolution Rentals and Accounts*, ed. G. R. Price (Skipton: Maple-Bowes Publishers, 1984), 81, 99; *Halmota Prioratus Dunelmensis: Containing Extracts from the Halmote Court or Manor Rolls of the Prior and Convent of Durham 1296–1384*, ed. W. H. D. Longstaffe and John Booth, Surtees Society Publications, vol. 82 (Durham: Surtees Society Publications, 1886), xxvii–xxviii, 132, 144, 153–54.

28. *The Oath Book; or, Red Parchment Book of Colchester*, ed. W. Gurney Benham (Colchester: "Essex County Standard" Office, 1907), 4, 223.

29. TNA: PRO SC 2 156/4–5. I suspect that Thomas and William Batesson may have been brothers or cousins because their careers were roughly contemporary and they supported each other in pledging. I have no direct evidence of their kinship, however. Information about Thomas and William has been drawn from court rolls, account rolls, and other miscellaneous sources as outlined in the introduction. For a similar case of a sensitive official, see Kowaleski, "Gossip, Gender, and the Economy."

30. One of these men, Richard Burgess, brought a scolding accusation himself in 1423, when he and his daughter were allegedly scolded: TNA: PRO SC 2 156/4.

31. Variation in personal influence is perhaps also discernible in the outcomes of these cases: in all four cases in which Thomas was said to have been scolded, the alleged scold was found guilty, whereas William's alleged abusers

were found guilty in only two of the six cases. I have combined here the numbers of civil cases and cases brought by the bailiffs. Elsewhere, civil cases are not counted as scolding prosecutions unless explicitly stated.

32. TNA: PRO DL 30 3/43–3/47. No scolds had been recorded at Widnes since 1399. Scolds were not presented at Widnes halmotes in 1410. One was presented (by the bailiff) in a fee court, but this was in January 1410 and William de Stanley was not appointed until May.

33. TNA: PRO DL 30 1/22–5/70; SC 2 155/84. Fee courts were held in the manor of Halton every two weeks, incorporating business from the small communities of Runcorn and More, each of which lay less than three miles distant. Scolds were normally presented, however, at halmote courts, held three times a year. The smaller manor of Widnes, located across the river Mersey only a couple of miles from Halton, held fee courts every three weeks, and halmotes three times a year. Congleton, on the other hand, was a borough, located twenty-four miles to the southeast. Among the Duchy of Lancaster records, three Congleton courts per year survive, although it seems possible that more regular courts (lacking surviving records) were also held.

34. The earliest surviving court roll from Halton and Widnes dates to 1347 and contains no scolds (TNA: PRO DL 30 1/20). By the time of the next surviving roll, however, in 1357, juries in all three jurisdictions knew about the concept of scolding and were prosecuting both women and the occasional man as scolds.

Chapter 6

1. "Visitation of Parishes by John Trefnant, Bishop of Hereford, 1397" (unpublished typescript from original in Hereford Cathedral Archives MS 1779), 36.1.8, 36.1.21, 36.1.22, 36.1.24.

2. SARS DD/L P 17/3; DD/L P 11/4.

3. For Henry le Vernon's prosecution, see TNA: PRO SC 2 156/6. Other information about Henry has been compiled from records of borough courts, sheriff's tourns, eyre courts, account rolls, and land deeds. For one example of him being listed as a "yomon," see TNA: PRO CHES 25/12, m. 11r.

4. P. J. P. Goldberg, *Women, Work, and Life-Cycle in a Medieval Economy: Women in York and Yorkshire c. 1300–1520* (Oxford: Clarendon Press, 1992); Judith M. Bennett and Amy Froide, "A Singular Past," in *Singlewomen in the European Past, 1250–1800*, ed. Judith M. Bennett and Amy Froide (Philadelphia: University of Pennsylvania Press, 1998), 1–37; Maryanne Kowaleski, "Singlewomen in Medieval and Early Modern Europe: The Demographic Perspective," in *Singlewomen in the European Past*, ed. Bennett and Froide, 38–81.

5. Martin Ingram, " 'Scolding Women Cucked or Washed': A Crisis in Gender Relations in Early Modern England?" in *Women, Crime and the Courts*, ed, Jenny Kermode and Garthine Walker (London: University College of London Press, 1994), 48–80, at p. 65; Linda Lees, " 'Lewd and Dissolute Women': Women and Crime in Seventeenth Century Nottinghamshire," *Transactions of the Thoroton Society of Nottinghamshire* 105 (2001): 111–21, at p. 112.

6. David E. Underdown, "The Taming of the Scold: The Enforcement of Patriarchal Authority in Early Modern England," in *Order and Disorder in Early Modern England*, ed. A. Fletcher and J. Stevenson (Cambridge: Cambridge University Press, 1985), 116–36, at p. 120.

7. Robert Mannyng, *Robert of Brunne's "Handlyng Synne,"* ed. Frederick J. Fur-

nivall, EETS, vol. 119 (London: Kegan Paul, Trench, Trübner, 1901), 56–57, lines 1585–86, Bodl. 415 manuscript version; John Mirk, *Mirk's Festial: A Collection of Homilies*, ed. Theodor Erbe, EETS, extra series, vol. 96 (London: Kegan Paul, Trench, Trübner, 1892), 96–97.

8. Mirk, *Mirk's Festial*, 229–30.

9. "A Noble Tretys of Maydenhode," BL Arundel 286, ff. 134v.–148r.; "Tretis of Mayndenhod," Cambridge University Library Ii.6.39, mm. 71v.–74v.

10. *The Early English Carols*, ed. R. L. Greene, 2nd ed. (Oxford: Clarendon Press, 1977), 235, lines 3–6. Note that Audeley recycled and adapted these lines in a poem on the Virgin Mary: "In word, in will, in deed, in thought, / Her maidenhood befouled she not" (*Early English Carols*, ed. Greene, 234, lines 5–6.)

11. Maryanne Kowaleski, "Gossip, Gender, and the Economy: The Origins of Scolding Indictments in Medieval England," forthcoming.

12. John Lydgate, *The Minor Poems of John Lydgate*, Part 2, *Secular Poems*, ed. H. N. MacCracken, EETS, vol. 119 (Oxford: Oxford University Press, 1934), 433–38, especially lines 23, 79, 86; "The Clerk's Tale," in Geoffrey Chaucer, *The Riverside Chaucer*, 3rd ed., ed. Larry D. Benson (Boston: Houghton Mifflin, 1987), 152, lines 1183–84.

13. Lydgate, *Minor Poems of John Lydgate*, Part 2, 433, preface. For photographs of the wall paintings at Puy-de-Dôme, see R. S. Loomis, *A Mirror of Chaucer's World* (Princeton, N.J.: Princeton University Press, 1965), nos. 161–62. For discussion of the theme, with copies and translations of some French versions of the tales, see Steven M. Taylor, "Monsters of Misogyny: The Medieval French 'Dit de Chincheface' and 'Dit de Bigorne,'" *Allegorica* 5 (1980): 98–124.

14. M. D. Anderson, *History and Imagery in British Churches* (London: J. Murray, 1971), 154; Christa Grössinger, *The World Upside-Down: English Misericords* (London: Harvey Miller, 1997), 88.

15. See, for instance, the case of Henry Cok of Trottiscliffe in 1347 who justified his abandonment of his wife on the grounds of her "contumelious words" (*Registrum Hamonis Hethe, Diocesis Roffensis AD 1319–52*, ed. Charles Johnson, Canterbury and York Society Publications, vol. 49 [Oxford: Oxford University Press, 1948], 974–75).

16. TNA: PRO SC 2 156/6. Similarly, Annabel Gregory found that witchcraft accusations in early seventeenth-century Rye (Sussex) served as a way to perpetuate local feuds and tensions ("Witchcraft, Politics and 'Good Neighbourhood' in Early Seventeenth-Century Rye," *Past and Present* 133 [1991]: 31–66).

17. See, for example, Caroline M. Barron, "The 'Golden Age' of Women in Medieval London," *Reading Medieval Studies* 15 (1989): 33–58; Maryanne Kowaleski and Judith M. Bennett, "Crafts, Gilds and Women in the Middle Ages: Fifty Years after Marian K. Dale," in *Sisters and Workers in the Middle Ages*, ed. Judith M. Bennett et al. (Chicago: University of Chicago Press, 1989), 11–38; Barbara A. Hanawalt, "The Widow's Mite: Provisions for Medieval London Widows," in *Upon My Husband's Death: Widows in the Literature and Histories of Medieval Europe*, ed. Louise Mirrer (Ann Arbor: University of Michigan Press, 1992), 21–45; Caroline M. Barron, "Introduction: The Widow's World in Later Medieval London," in *Medieval London Widows, 1300–1500*, ed. Caroline M. Barron and Anne F. Sutton (London: Hambledon Press, 1994), pp. xiii–xxxiv.

18. See, for example, A. D. J. Macfarlane, *Witchcraft in Tudor and Stuart England: A Regional and Comparative Study* (London: Routledge & K. Paul, 1970); Keith Thomas, *Religion and the Decline of Magic* (New York: Scribner, 1971).

19. Aelred of Rievaulx, *The Works of Aelred of Rievaulx*, vol. 1 (Spencer, Mass.:

Cistercian Publications, 1971), 46; *Ancrene Riwle*, ed. and trans. M. D. Salu (Exeter: University of Exeter Press), 39.

20. William Dunbar, *The Poems of William Dunbar*, ed. William MacKay MacKenzie (Edinburgh: Porpoise Press, 1932), 85–97.

21. See Francis Lee Utley, *The Crooked Rib: An Analytical Index to the Argument about Women in English and Scots Literature to the End of the Year 1568* (Columbus: Ohio State University Press, 1944); Patricia Anderson, "Gossips, Ale-wives, Midwives and Witches" (Ph.D. diss., State University of New York at Buffalo, 1992).

22. "The Gospelles of Dystaves," in *The Oxford Book of Late Medieval Verse and Prose*, ed. Douglas Gray (Oxford: Clarendon Press, 1985), 379–80.

23. Susan Karant-Nunn has noted that several sixteenth-century German funerary monuments of widows depict them with their clothing pulled up to cover their mouths. Karant-Nunn has interpreted this motif as a symbolic representation of *mundtod* ("deadmouth"), the legal principle by which medieval German widows were denied a legal voice or identity but were instead covered by the legal personalities of one of their male relatives (*The Reformation of Ritual: An Interpretation of Early Modern Germany* [London: Routledge, 1997], 40).

24. On another Winchester misericord, the gagged woman again appears on the left. The center of the misericord depicts a small horned demon, while on the right is a serious-looking man who seems to be wearing a crown. Two further gagged female heads appear in the carved wooden choir stalls of Winchester Cathedral. A similar cluster of caricatures can be found carved in stone in the pulpit canopies at Southwell Minster (Nottinghamshire), among them a gagged woman. Another gagged woman is nestled into the west wall of the passage to the chapter house. This time, she is depicted from the waist upward, with her arms folded in front of her, as if resigned to her fate. A third representation of a gagged female head supports one of the vaulting shafts within the chapter house itself. The woman's features are carved in detail, and her top lip extends beyond the gorget, as if she has her mouth open. Other gagged female heads survive in parish churches at, for instance, East Retford (Nottinghamshire), Oundle (Northamptonshire), Claypole (Lincolnshire), Heydour (Lincolnshire), and Patrington (Yorkshire), varying in style from crude to elaborate. I found these examples by searching photographs held by the Conway Library, Courtauld Institute, London.

25. Underdown, "Taming of the Scold," 120; Ingram, "'Scolding Women Cucked or Washed,'" 65; Karen Jones and Michael Zell, "Bad Conversation? Gender and Social Control in a Kentish Borough, c. 1450–c. 1570," *Continuity and Change* 13 (1998): 11–31, at p. 18; Kowaleski, "Gossip, Gender, and the Economy."

26. TNA: PRO SC 2 156/3, m. 4r.

27. TNA: PRO CHES 25/11, m. 20v.

28. Underdown, "Taming of the Scold," 120.

29. Ingram, "'Scolding Women Cucked or Washed,'" 65; Jones and Zell, "Bad Conversation?" 19–23, 25, 28–29.

30. Kowaleski, "Gossip, Gender, and the Economy."

31. I have been able to find names of 799 people who lived in or around Middlewich in the first half of the fifteenth century, but I have only been able to find secure socioeconomic data for 458 of these. The main sources I used were a complete series of ministers' accounts from 1400 to 1450 (which list chamberlains, bailiffs, seneschals, and sometimes details of salthouse ownership) (TNA: PRO SC 6 791/1–797/8), rentals, land deeds, and marriage contracts in the

Cheshire Record Office (Cheshire Record Office DSS 3991 Drawer 2/2, DVE 1/K/28–32, 1/M3/61–82, M4/1–17, 1/R/1–10) and those copied by a seventeenth-century antiquarian and subsequently printed (*A Middlewich Chartulary*, part 1, ed. Joan Varley, Chetham Society Publications, new series, vol. 105 [Manchester: Chetham Society and the Liverpool School of Local History and Records, 1941]; *A Middlewich Chartulary*, part 2, ed. Joan Varley and James Tait, Chetham Society Publications, new series, vol. 108 [Manchester: Chetham Society and the Liverpool School of Local History and Records, 1944]), Middlewich borough courts (TNA: PRO SC 2 156/1–7), Cheshire eyre courts (TNA: PRO CHES 17/7–8, 25/9), Cheshire sheriffs' tourns (TNA: PRO CHES 19/3–5), Cheshire county court indictment rolls (TNA: PRO CHES 25/10–14), and lists of rectors and borough officers from George Ormerod, *History of the County Palatine and City of Chester*, vol. 3 (London: G. Routledge, 1882), 173–86. In line with contemporary sources such as sumptuary laws and treatises that discuss social precedence, I assigned wives the same social status as their husbands (see, for instance, the sumptuary law of 1390 and John Russell's *Boke of Nurture* described by S. H. Rigby, *English Society in the Later Middle Ages: Class, Status and Gender* [Basingstoke: Macmillan Press, 1995], 192). I did not, however, assume that daughters occupied the same social status as their fathers. Some women in my database were lifelong single women, and their socioeconomic status was likely lower than that of their parents. Members of the local elite included wealthier merchants, artisans who had been particularly successful in their trade and/or occupied higher status trades such as goldsmithing, yeomen who owned significant amounts of land, and those who were linked with the gentry, even if they could not quite claim gentle status for themselves. The minimum qualification for members of this group was the holding of the office of chamberlain or seneschal and/or appearance on eyre or county court juries and/or ownership of multiple pieces of land. Men in this category frequently acted as pledges for others and witnessed land deeds, but I did not use either pledging or witnessing as criteria for inclusion. The burgess category consists primarily of artisans and salt boilers who never achieved the status of local elite yet were of higher status than laborers. In many places, such individuals were eligible to be admitted as "freemen," or "burgesses" and for ease of reference here I have referred to this category as "burgesses" even though both terms were used interchangeably in the town. The minimum qualification for "burgess" classification in Middlewich, in my reckoning, was payment of fees for salt boiling, butchery, stall rental, or baking, or service as bailiff (in Middlewich called "catchpoll"), governor of salt boiling, or borough court juror. People also qualified if they were described in county courts as "yeomen," that is, individuals from the area around Middlewich who possessed sufficient land for them to make a good living. They were also included if they employed servants or acted as attorneys for individuals of any of the "judger towns" (small local settlements that sent representatives to Middlewich's burgess courts) and were not already a member of the local elite. Laborers and the transient poor are even harder to identify in surviving records because they are, by definition, absent from land deeds and lists of officers. Some can be identified, however, from account rolls, from occasions when they were in trouble in county courts, and from fees paid for performing certain low-status occupations such as carting clay or serving as a tranter. In addition to these three main categories of local elite, burgesses, and laborers and the poor, the database also included twenty-four men identified as members of the clergy and thirty-one individuals who were part of the "county elite" of barons, knights, esquires, gentlemen, and gentlewomen. Although few of the latter lived in the immediate vicinity of Middlewich, they were often involved with the transfer of property and trade in the town.

32. Because there are some gaps in Middlewich's courts, the length of residence of Middlewich scolds has been counted as a minimum number. That is to say, if all court records survived, it is possible (indeed, likely) that more individuals could be traced from earlier courts and that the numbers appearing for the first time would be lower. To ascertain family relationships, I have relied here on stated marital or parental links (in which people were specifically identified as wives or daughters), not on mere surname linkage.

33. *Records of the Borough of Nottingham*, vol. 2, ed. W. H. Stevenson (London: B. Quaritch, 1883), 241.

34. A. M. Tonkinson, *Macclesfield in the Later Fourteenth Century: Communities of Town and Forest*, Chetham Society Publications, 3rd series, vol. 42 (Manchester: Chetham Society, 1999), 168.

35. Ibid., 165.

36. TNA: PRO SC 2 156/4; *Kentish Visitations of Archbishop William Warham and his Deputies, 1511–12*, ed. K. L. Wood-Legh, Kent Records, vol. 24 (Maidstone: Kent Archaeological Society, 1984), 279.

37. Kowaleski, "Gossip, Gender, and the Economy."

38. TNA: PRO SC 2 156/4, 156/5.

39. SARS DD/L P 12/2.

40. Kowaleski, "Gossip, Gender, and the Economy."

41. Ruth Mazo Karras, *Common Women: Prostitution and Sexuality in Medieval England* (Oxford: Oxford University Press, 1996), 138–39; Ruth Mazo Karras, "The Regulation of Brothels in Later Medieval England," in *Sisters and Workers in the Middle Ages*, ed. Judith M. Bennett et al. (Chicago: University of Chicago Press, 1989), 100–134, at pp. 131, 134.

42. TNA: PRO CHES 19/3.

43. *Court Rolls of the Borough of Colchester*, vol. 3, ed. and trans. Isaac Herbert Jeayes and W. Gurney Benham (Colchester: s.n., 1941), 31; HEH BA 620.

Conclusion

1. Maryanne Kowaleski suggests that the thewe, cucking stool, and ducking stool were in fact distinct from one another, but I am not as certain. See Maryanne Kowaleski, "Gossip, Gender, and the Economy: The Origins of Scolding Indictments in Medieval England," forthcoming.

2. *Bridgwater Borough Archives*, vol. 2, ed. Thomas Bruce Dilks, Somerset Record Society Publications, vol. 53 (London: Somerset Record Society, 1938), 49, 52, 197; *Memorials of London and London Life in the Thirteenth, Fourteenth, and Fifteenth Centuries: Being a Series of Extracts, Local, Social, and Political, from the Early Archives of the City of London, A.D. 1276–1419*, ed. H. T. Riley (London: Longmans, Green, 1868), 319, 526; *Court Rolls of the Borough of Colchester*, vol. 1, ed. and trans. Isaac Herbert Jeayes and W. Gurney Benham (Colchester: s.n., 1921), 123.

3. *The Court Rolls of the Lordship of Ruthin or Dyffryn-Clwydd of the Reign of Edward the First*, ed. Richard Arthur Roberts, Cymmrodorion Record Series, vol. 2 (London: s.n., 1893), 15.

4. *Monumenta Juridica: The Black Book of the Admiralty*, vol. 2, *Appendix*, ed. Travers Twiss, Rolls Series, vol. 55 (London: Longman, 1873), 165; John Wodder-

spoon, *Memorials of the Ancient Town of Ipswich in the County of Suffolk* (Ipswich: Pawsey, 1850), 266–67. An illustration of a woman seated on what may be a cucking stool appears in the margins of a thirteenth-century manuscript (the Rutland Psalter, BL Additional Manuscript 62925). She holds a distaff and spindle, but looks more frightened than obstreperous, so she is more likely to represent an alewife or baker than a scold. See Lillian Randall, *Images in the Margins of Gothic Manuscripts* (Berkeley and Los Angeles: University of California Press, 1966), plate 731.

5. P. H. Reaney, *The Place-Names of Essex*, English Place Name Society Publications, vol. 12 (Cambridge: Cambridge University Press, 1935), 537; J. McN. Dodgson, *The Place-Names of Cheshire*, part 1, English Place Name Society Publications, vol. 44 (London: Cambridge University Press, 1970), 115. Fields were also sometimes named for cucking stools: see examples in Dunham Massey, Altrincham, Allostock, and Nether Peover (all in Cheshire) in J. McN. Dodgson, *The Place-Names of Cheshire*, part 2, English Place Name Society Publications, vol. 45 (London: Cambridge University Press, 1967–68), 9, 22, 219, 221.

6. *Memorials of London and London Life*, ed. Riley.

7. Cited in Marjorie Keniston McIntosh, *Controlling Misbehavior in England, 1370–1600* (Cambridge: Cambridge University Press, 1998), 63–64.

8. Examples may be seen at Ripon and at Beverley Minster (Yorkshire). In the Beverley example, the supporting carving on the left-hand side depicts a man raising a beam, as if to lower a cucking stool into the water. By the 1450s, if not sooner, Beverley possessed a cucking stool (town accounts list payments to men for cleaning out the cucking stool pit), but rituals surrounding its use have not been recorded (George Poulson, *Beverlac; Or, The Antiquities and History of the Town of Beverley*, vol. 1 [London: G. Scaum, 1829], 221).

9. *Records of the Borough of Leicester*, vol. 2, *1327–1509*, ed. Mary Bateson (London: C. J. Clay and Sons, 1901), 291.

10. "The Othe ffor the Meire and Clerke of the Merket and Charge," Liber Custumarum of Northampton, in *The Records of the Borough of Northampton*, vol. 1, ed. Christopher A. Markham (London: E. Stock, 1898), 373.

11. For discussion of cucking stools, see T. N. Brushfield, "On Obsolete Punishments, With Particular Reference to Those of Cheshire. Part II: The Cucking Stool and Allied Punishments," *Journal of the Architectural, Archaeological and Historic Society, for the County, City and Neighbourhood of Chester*, 1st series, 2 (1861): 203–34, and John Webster Spargo, *Juridical Folklore in England Illustrated by the Cucking-Stool* (Durham, N.C.: Duke University Press, 1944). For hypothetical cucking stools in Middlewich, see C. Frederick Lawrence, "Random Notes on Bygone Cheshire, With Special Reference to Middlewich," *Cheshire Notes and Queries* 2 (1897): 19–26, at p. 20 and A. F. Earl, *Middlewich 900–1900* (Chester: Ravenscroft, 1990), 32–33.

12. TNA: PRO SC 2 156/5, m. 11r.

13. SARS DD/L P 12/4; *Court Rolls of the Manor of Tottenham*, vol. 7, *23 Hen VIII–1 Edw VI*, ed. Ian George Murray (London: London Borough of Haringey, Libraries, Museum and Arts Service, 1975), 51.

14. For discussion of scolds' bridles see Brushfield, "On Obsolete Punishments," and Lynda E. Boose, "Scolding Brides and Bridling Scolds: Taming the Woman's Unruly Member," *Shakespeare Quarterly* 42 (1991): 179–213.

15. Olaudah Equiano, *The Life of Olaudah Equiano, or Gustavus Vassa the African*, ed. Paul Edwards (Harlow: Longman, 1989), 29.

16. *Lower Ecclesiastical Jurisdiction in Late-Medieval England: The Courts of the*

Dean and Chapter of Lincoln, 1336–1349, and the Deanery of Wisbech, 1458–1484, ed. L. R. Poos (Oxford: Oxford University Press, 2001), xlvii–xlviii.

17. Ibid., 312. Also see L. R. Poos, "Sex, Lies, and the Church Courts of Pre-Reformation England," *Journal of Interdisciplinary History* 25 (1995): 585–607, at p. 591 n. 10 for discussion of the term "fyssenag."

18. See, for example, *The Register of John Morton, Archbishop of Canterbury 1486–1500*, vol. 3, *Norwich Sede Vacante, 1499*, ed. Christopher Harper-Bill, Canterbury and York Society Publications, vol. 89 (Woodbridge: Boydell Press, 2000), 228–29; *The Courts of the Archdeaconry of Buckingham 1483–1523*, ed. Elizabeth M. Elvey, Buckinghamshire Record Society, vol. 19 (Aylesbury: Buckinghamshire Record Society, 1975), 313.

19. The bishop's order was translated using the term "*rixosa*," and scolds were sometimes described as "*rixatrices*." *Registrum Hamonis Hethe, Diocesis Roffensis AD 1319–52*, vol. 2, ed. Charles Johnson, Canterbury and York Society Publications, vol. 49 (Oxford: Oxford University Press, 1948), 973–74.

20. This theme is embedded in much of Foucault's work, but he focuses on it particularly in his discussion of the "repressive hypothesis" in *The History of Sexuality: An Introduction*, vol. 1 (New York: Vintage Books, 1990), 17–49.

21. For discussion of the concept of "patriarchal bargains," see Deniz Kandiyoti, "Bargaining with Patriarchy," *Gender and Society* 2 (1988): 274–90.

22. Natalie Zemon Davis, "Women on Top," in *Society and Culture in Early Modern France* (Stanford, Calif.: Stanford University Press, 1975), 124–51; Joy Wiltenburg, *Disorderly Women and Female Power in the Street Literature of Early Modern England and Germany* (Charlottesville: University Press of Virginia, 1992).

23. Jane Kamensky, *Governing the Tongue: The Politics of Speech in Early New England* (New York: Oxford University Press, 1997).

24. Terri L. Snyder, *Brabbling Women: Disorderly Speech and the Law in Early Virginia* (Ithaca, N.Y.: Cornell University Press, 2003).

25. Another woman, also probably a scold, was paraded through Leominster in 1817 but was not ducked because the river was too low (Brushfield, "On Obsolete Punishments," 233). For Congleton, see Vernon Mortimer, "The Tongue Can No Man Tame," *Cheshire Life* (March 1975), 72–73. Mortimer does not cite his source for the 1824 punishment of Anne Runcorn with the scold's bridle. For Beverley, see Poulson, *Beverlac*, 221.

Bibliography

Manuscript Sources

CAMBRIDGE, CAMBRIDGE UNIVERSITY LIBRARY

Ii.6.39: Collection of theological tracts, fourteenth century: "Tretis of Maynden-hod." mm. 71v.-74v.

CHESTER, CHESHIRE RECORD OFFICE

DSS 3991 Drawer 2/2: Deeds in the Shockley Collection relating to Middlewich
DVE 1/K/28–32: Deeds from Kinderton
DVE 1/M3/61–82: Deeds from Middlewich
DVE 1/M4/1–17: Deeds from Middlewich
DVE 1/R/1–10: Rentals from Kinderton, Middlewich, and elsewhere
DVE 1/W/2: Will of Hugh Venables of Kinderton, 1449

LINCOLN, LINCOLNSHIRE ARCHIVES

CM 1/3–1/42: Court rolls of Crowle; consulted on microfilm

LONDON, BRITISH LIBRARY

Arundel 286: Collection of religious and moral treatises and letters: "A Noble Tretys of Maydenhode." mm. 134v.-148r.
Additional Roll 39754: Court rolls of Broughton (Huntingdonshire)
Additional Charters 15947–16102: Court rolls of Chedzoy (Somerset)

LONDON, THE NATIONAL ARCHIVES: PUBLIC RECORD OFFICE

Courts of the Palatinate of Chester

CHES 17/7–8, 25/9: Eyre courts
CHES 19/3–5: Sheriffs' tourns
CHES 25/10–14: County court indictments

Manorial and Borough Courts

DL 30 1/20–5/70: Halton, Widnes, Congleton, Runcorn, and More (Cheshire and Lancashire)
DL 30 32/293–94, 300, 306: Duffield (Derbyshire)

DL 30 44/502, 506–7, 514: Wirkworth (Derbyshire)
DL 30 63/801–2, 64/809–69/853: Pleshey, High Easter, Waltham, Mashbury, Chishall, Sawston, and Hoddesdon (Essex)
DL 30 86/1177, 1186, 87/1192: Sutton (Lincolnshire)
DL 30 104/1471–1480: Methwold (Norfolk)
DL 30 128/1922: Scalby (Yorkshire)
DL 30 129/1957: Bradford (Yorkshire)
DL 30 229/8: Newcastle-under-Lyme (Staffordshire)
SC 2 153/69: Bright Waltham (Berkshire)
SC 2 154/77–78: Woolstone (Berkshire)
SC 2 155/49–51: Bottisham (Cambridgeshire)
SC 2 155/56: Ditton Valence (Cambridgeshire)
SC 2 155/83: Frodsham (Cheshire)
SC 2 155/84: Halton (Cheshire)
SC 2 156/1–7: Middlewich (Cheshire)
SC 2 156/10–11: Northwich (Cheshire)
SC 2 156/13: Shotwick (Cheshire)
SC 2 169/26, 30: Fordington (Dorset)
SC 2 171/26: Newhall in Boreham (Essex)
SC 2 171/46, 49: Claret (Essex)
SC 2 172/10: Foxearth (Essex)
SC 2 173/24: Matching (Essex)
SC 2 173/54: Rickling (Essex)
SC 2 173/73: Stambourne (Essex)
SC 2 178/95: St. Ives (Huntingdonshire)
SC 2 180/13–14, 18, 21: Boxley (Kent)
SC 2 181/33: Horton (Kent)
SC 2 198/19: Chedzoy (Somerset)
SC 2 198/75: Milverton, etc. (Somerset)
SC 2 200/4: Odcombe (Somerset)
SC 2 201/51: Totton (Southamptonshire)
SC 2 203/27, 30: Chilton (Suffolk)
SC 2 203/45–70: Clare (Suffolk)
SC 2 203/105: Raydon (Suffolk)
SC 2 203/115, 204/4: Sudbury (Suffolk)
SC 2 205/24: Walworth (Surrey)
SC 2 207/20: Chellesmore (Warwickshire)
SC 2 211/113: Rockeley (Yorkshire)

Ministers' Accounts:

SC 6 791/1–797/8: Chester City, Drakelow and Rudheath, Middlewich, Delamere Forest, Chester Castle, Shotwick, Overmersh, etc.

San Marino, California, H. E. Huntington Library

BA 546–655: Court rolls of Battle (Sussex)
HAM 62/13–14: Court rolls of Melbourne (Derbyshire)

Taunton, Somerset Archive and Record Service

DDL 9/5, 10/2–3, 11/2, 12/1–4, 13/1: Court rolls of Dunster
DDL 10/5: Rental from Dunster

DDL 11/4: Rental from Dunster and Carhampton
DDL 17/3: Court rolls of Carhampton Barton
DDL 26/6, 26/8: Court rolls of Minehead
DDL 31/3: Court rolls of Carhampton Hundred

Published Primary Sources

Aelred of Rievaulx. *The Works of Aelred of Rievaulx.* Vol. 1. Spencer, Mass.: Cistercian Publications, 1971.

Allen, David, ed. *Ipswich Borough Archives 1255–1835: A Catalogue.* Suffolk Records Society Publications, vol. 43. Woodbridge: Boydell Press, 2000.

Amphlett, John, and Sidney Graves Hamilton, eds. *Court Rolls of the Manor of Hales, 1270–1307.* Worcestershire Historical Society Publications, vol. 51. Oxford: Worcestershire Historical Society, 1910.

Anglicanus, Galfridus. *Promptorium Parvulorum: The First English-Latin Dictionary.* Edited by A. L. Mayhew. EETS, extra series, vol. 102. London: Kegan Paul, Trench, Trübner, 1908.

Anglicus, Bartholomaeus. *Mediaeval Lore from Bartholomew Anglicus.* Edited by Robert Steele. New York: Cooper Square Publishers, 1966.

Anonymous. *A Plaine Description of the Auncient Petigree of Dame Slaunder.* London: H. Middleton for Iohn Hamilton, 1573.

Baildon, William Paley, ed. *Court Rolls of the Manor of Wakefield.* Vol. 1, *1274–1297.* Yorkshire Archaeological Society Records Series, vol. 29. Leeds: Yorkshire Archaeological Society, 1900.

———, ed. *Court Rolls of the Manor of Wakefield.* Vol. 2, *1297–1309.* Yorkshire Archaeological Society Records Series, vol. 36. Leeds: Yorkshire Archaeological Society, 1906.

Bateson, Mary, ed. *Borough Customs.* Vol. 1. Seldon Society Publications, vol. 18. London: B. Quaritch, 1904.

———, ed. *Records of the Borough of Leicester.* Vol. 2, *1327–1509.* London: C. J. Clay and Sons, 1901.

Benham, W. Gurney, ed. *The Oath Book; or, Red Parchment Book of Colchester.* Colchester: "Essex County Standard" Office, 1907.

Bond, Ronald B., ed. *Certain Sermons or Homilies (1547) and A Homily against Disobedience and Wilful Rebellion (1570): A Critical Edition.* Toronto: University of Toronto Press, 1987.

Brotanek, Rudolf, ed. *Mittelenglische Dichtungen aus der Handschrift 432 des Trinity College in Dublin.* Halle: M. Niemeyer, 1940.

Brown, Carleton, ed. *English Lyrics of the Thirteenth Century.* Oxford: Clarendon Press, 1932.

———, ed. *Religious Lyrics of the Fifteenth Century.* Oxford: Clarendon Press, 1939.

Capgrave, John. *The Chronicle of England by John Capgrave.* Edited by Francis Charles Hingeston. Rolls Series, vol. 1. London: Longman, Brown, Green, Longmans and Roberts, 1858.

Cawley, A. C., ed. *The Wakefield Pageants in the Towneley Cycle.* Manchester: Manchester University Press, 1958.

Chambers, R. W., and Marjorie Daunt, eds., *A Book of London English 1384–1425.* Oxford: Clarendon Press, 1931.

Chanter, J. R., and Thomas Wainwright, eds. *Reprint of the Barnstaple Records.* 2 vols. Barnstaple: A. E. Barnes, 1900.

Chaucer, Geoffrey. *The Riverside Chaucer.* Edited by Larry D. Benson. 3rd ed. Boston: Houghton Mifflin Co., 1987.

Deimling, Hermann, ed. *The Chester Plays.* Part 1, EETS, extra series, vol. 62. London: Kegan Paul, Trench, Trübner, 1892.

DeWindt, Edwin Brezette, ed. *The Court Rolls of Ramsey, Hepmangrove and Bury, 1268–1600.* Toronto: Pontifical Institute of Mediaeval Studies, 1990.

———, ed. *A Slice of Life: Selected Documents of Medieval English Peasant Experience.* Kalamazoo: Medieval Institute Publications, 1996.

Diekstra, F. N. M., ed., *Book for a Simple and Devout Woman: A Late Middle English Adaptation of Peraldus's Summa de Vitiis et Virtutibus and Friar Laurent's Somme le Roi, Edited from British Library Mss Harley 6571 and Additional 30944.* Groningen: Egbert Forsten, 1998.

Dilks, Thomas Bruce, ed. *Bridgwater Borough Archives.* Vols. 1–3. Somerset Record Society Publications, vols. 48, 53, 58. London: Somerset Record Society, 1933–43.

Dobson, R. B., ed. *The Peasants' Revolt of 1381.* London: Macmillan, 1970.

Dodgson, J. McN. *The Place-Names of Cheshire.* Parts 1–2. English Place Name Society Publications, vols. 44–45. London: Cambridge University Press, 1967–70.

Dunbar, William. *The Poems of William Dunbar.* Edited by William MacKay MacKenzie. Edinburgh: Porpoise Press, 1932.

Elvey, Elizabeth M., ed. *The Courts of the Archdeaconry of Buckingham 1483–1523.* Buckinghamshire Record Society Series, vol. 19. Aylesbury: Buckinghamshire Record Society, 1975.

Equiano, Olaudah. *The Life of Olaudah Equiano, or Gustavus Vassa the African.* Edited by Paul Edwards. Harlow: Longman, 1989.

Fenton, F. W., ed. *Court Rolls of the Manor of Tottenham.* Vol. 6, *2 Hen VIII-22 Hen VIII.* Tottenham: Tottenham Public Libraries, 1960.

Furnivall, Frederick J., ed. *The Babees' Book, etc.* [also published under the title of *Early English Meals and Manners*]. EETS, vol. 32. London: N. Trübner, 1868.

———, ed. *Jyl of Breyntford's Testament.* London: Printed for private circulation, 1871.

———, ed. *The Minor Poems of the Vernon Manuscript (With a Few from the Digby Manuscripts 2 and 86).* Part 2. EETS, vol. 117. London: Kegan Paul, Trench, Trübner, 1901.

Furnivall, Frederick J., and Alfred W. Pollard, eds. *The Macro Plays.* EETS, extra series, vol. 91. London: Kegan Paul, Trench, Trübner, 1904.

Gower, John. *The Major Latin Works of John Gower: The Voice of One Crying, and the Tripartite Chronicle.* Edited by Eric W. Stockton. Seattle: University of Washington Press, 1962.

Gray, Douglas, ed. *The Oxford Book of Late Medieval Verse and Prose.* Oxford: Clarendon Press, 1985.

Greene, R. L., ed. *The Early English Carols.* 2nd ed. Oxford: Clarendon Press, 1977.

Habberjam, Moira, Mary O'Regan, and Brian Hale, eds. *The Court Rolls of the Manor of Wakefield from October 1350 to September 1352.* Wakefield Court Rolls Series of the Yorkshire Archaeological Society, vol. 6. Leeds: Yorkshire Archaeological Society, 1987.

Hale, William Hale, ed. *A Series of Precedents and Proceedings in Criminal Cases, Extending from the Year 1475 to 1640.* London: F. & J. Rivington, 1847.

Harper-Bill, Christopher, ed. *The Register of John Morton, Archbishop of Canterbury 1486–1500.* Vol. 3, *Norwich Sede Vacante, 1499.* Canterbury and York Society Publications, vol. 89. Woodbridge: Boydell Press, 2000.

Harvey, P. D. A., ed. *Manorial Records of Cuxham, Oxfordshire, c. 1200–1359.* Oxfordshire Record Society Series, vol. 50. London: H. M. Stationery Office, 1976.

Hawkins, William. *A Treatise of the Pleas of the Crown.* London: Elizabeth Nutt, 1716.

Hector, L. C., and Barbara Harvey, eds. *The Westminster Chronicle, 1381–1394.* Oxford: Clarendon Press, 1966.

Helmholz, R. H., ed. *Select Cases on Defamation to 1600.* Seldon Society Publications, vol. 101. London: Seldon Society, 1985.

Herrtage, Sidney J. H., ed. *Catholicon Anglicum: An English-Latin Wordbook, Dated 1483.* EETS, vol. 75. London: N. Trübner, 1881.

Holthausen, Ferdinand, ed. *Vices and Virtues: Being a Soul's Confession of Its Sins with Reason's Description of the Virtues: A Middle-English Dialogue of about 1200 A.D.* EETS, vol. 89. London: N. Trübner & Co., 1888.

Horrox, Rosemary, ed. *The Black Death.* Manchester: Manchester University Press, 1994.

Humphreys, Arthur L., ed. *Materials for the History of the Town and Parish of Wellington in the County of Somerset.* Part 2, *Manorial Court Rolls 1277–1908.* London: s.n., 1910.

Jacob, Giles. *The Law-Dictionary.* 1st American ed. New York and Philadelphia: I. Riley and P. Byrne, 1811.

Jeayes, Isaac Herbert and W. Gurney Benham, ed. and trans., *Court Rolls of the Borough of Colchester.* Vols. 1–3. Colchester: s.n., 1921–41.

Jewell, Helen M., ed. *The Court Rolls of the Manor of Wakefield from September 1348 to September 1350.* Wakefield Court Rolls Series of the Yorkshire Archaeological Society, 2nd series, vol. 2. Leeds: Yorkshire Archaeological Society, 1981.

Johnson, Charles, ed. *Registrum Hamonis Hethe, Diocesis Roffensis AD 1319–52.* Canterbury and York Society Publications, vol. 49. Oxford: Oxford University Press, 1948.

Kitchin, John. *Jurisdictions: Or, The Lawful Authority of Courts Leet, Courts Baron, Court of Marshalseys, Court of Pypowder and Ancient Demesne, etc.* 5th ed. London: Henry Twyford and Samuel Herrick, 1675.

Langland, William. *Piers Ploughman: A New Translation of the B-text.* Translated by A. V. C. Schmidt. Oxford: Oxford University Press, 1992.

Leach, Arthur F., ed. *Beverley Town Documents.* Seldon Society Publications, vol. 14. London: B. Quaritch, 1900.

Lister, John, ed. *Court Rolls of the Manor of Wakefield.* Vol. 3, *1313–1316 and 1286.* Yorkshire Archaeological Society Records Series, vol. 57. Leeds: Yorkshire Archaeological Society, 1917.

———, ed. *Court Rolls of the Manor of Wakefield,* Vol. 4, *1315–1317.* Yorkshire Archaeological Society Records Series, vol. 78. Leeds: Yorkshire Archaeological Society, 1930.

Longstaffe, W. H. D., and John Booth, eds. *Halmota Prioratus Dunelmensis: Containing Extracts from the Halmote Court or Manor Rolls of the Prior and Convent of Durham 1296–1384.* Surtees Society Publications, vol. 82. Durham: Surtees Society Publications, 1886.

Lydgate, John. *The Minor Poems of John Lydgate.* Part 2, *Secular Poems.* Edited by H. N. MacCracken. EETS, vol. 192. Oxford: Oxford University Press, 1934.

Mannyng, Robert. *Robert of Brunne's "Handlyng Synne."* Edited by Frederick J. Furnivall. EETS, vol. 119. London: Kegan Paul, Trench, Trübner, 1901.

Markham, Christopher A., ed. *The Records of the Borough of Northampton.* Vol. 1. London: E. Stock, 1898.

Massingberd, W. O., ed. *Court Rolls of the Manor of Ingoldmells in the County of Lincoln.* London: Spottiswoode, 1902.

Mirk, John. *Mirk's Festial: A Collection of Homilies.* Edited by Theodor Erbe. EETS, extra series, vol. 96. London: Kegan Paul, Trench, Trübner, 1892.

Morris, Richard, ed. *An Old English Miscellany.* EETS, vol. 49. London: N. Trübner, 1872.

Murray, Ian George, ed. *Court Rolls of the Manor of Tottenham.* Vol. 7, *23 Hen VIII-1 Edw VI.* London: London Borough of Haringey, Libraries, Museum and Arts Service, 1975.

Murrell, Richard J. and Robert East, eds. *Extracts from Records in the Possession of the Municipal Corporation of the Borough of Portsmouth and from Other Documents Relating Thereto.* Portsmouth: H. Lewis, 1884.

Palsgrave, Jean. *L'éclaircissement de la langue française.* Edited by F. Génin. Paris: Imprimerie Nationale, 1852.

Poos, L. R., ed. *Lower Ecclesiastical Jurisdiction in Late-Medieval England: The Courts of the Dean and Chapter of Lincoln, 1336–1349, and the Deanery of Wisbech, 1458–1484.* Oxford: Oxford University Press, 2001.

Price, G. R., ed. *A Transcript of the Court Rolls of Yeadon, 1361–1476: With the Early Rentals and Accounts of Esholt Priory, Charters, Deeds and Associated Material to 1500 A.D., Dissolution Rentals and Accounts.* Skipton: Maple-Bowes Publishers, 1984.

Reaney, P. H. *The Place-Names of Essex.* English Place Name Society Publications, vol. 12. Cambridge: Cambridge University Press, 1935.

Rickert, Edith. *The Babees' Book: Medieval Manners for the Young.* New York: Cooper Square Publishers, 1966.

Riley, H. T., ed. and trans. *Liber Albus: The White Book of the City of London.* London: R. Griffin, 1861.

———, ed. and trans. *Memorials of London and London Life in the Thirteenth, Fourteenth, and Fifteenth Centuries: Being a Series of Extracts, Local, Social, and Political, from the Early Archives of the City of London, A.D. 1276–1419.* London: Longmans, Green, 1868.

Roberts, Richard Arthur, ed. *The Court Rolls of the Lordship of Ruthin or Dyffryn-Clwydd of the Reign of Edward the First.* Cymmrodorion Record Series, vol. 2. London: s.n., 1893.

Salu, M. D., ed. and trans. *Ancrene Riwle.* 3rd ed. Exeter: University of Exeter Press, 1990.

Skelton, John. *The Complete Poems of John Skelton, Laureate.* Edited by Philip Henderson. 4th ed. London: J. M. Dent, 1959.

Smith, David. M., ed. *Ecclesiastical Cause Papers at York: The Court of York 1301–1399.* Borthwick Texts and Calendars, vol. 15. York: University of York, Borthwick Institute of Historical Research, 1988.

Smith, Joshua Toulmin, and Lucy Toulmin Smith, eds. *English Gilds: The Original Ordinances of More than One Hundred Early English Gilds.* EETS, vol. 40. London: N. Trübner, 1870.

Smith, Lucy Toulmin, ed. *York Plays: The Plays Performed by the Crafts or Mysteries of York on the Day of Corpus Christi in the Fourteenth, Fifteenth, and Sixteenth Centuries.* Oxford: Clarendon Press, 1885.

Statutes of the Realm: Printed by Command of His Majesty King George the Third . . . from Original Records and Authentic Manuscripts. 11 vols. Reprint of 1810–28 ed. London: Dawsons, 1963.

Stevenson, W. H., ed. *Records of the Borough of Nottingham.* Vols. 1–3. London: B. Quaritch, 1882–85.

Thomas, A. H., ed. *Calendar of Plea and Memoranda Rolls Preserved among the Archives of the Corporation of the City of London at the Guild-hall.* Vol. 4, *1413–37.* Cambridge: Cambridge University Press, 1943.

Thompson, A. Hamilton, ed. *Visitations in the Diocese of Lincoln, 1517–1531.* Vol. 1. Lincoln Record Society Publications, vol. 33. Hereford: Lincoln Record Society, 1940.

Timmins, T. C. B., ed. *The Register of John Chandler, Dean of Salisbury 1404–1417.* Wiltshire Record Society Publications, vol. 39. Devizes: Wiltshire Record Society, 1984.

———, ed. *The Register of John Waltham, Bishop of Salisbury 1388–1395.* Canterbury and York Society Publications, vol. 80. Woodbridge: Boydell Press, 1994.

Troup, K. M., ed. *The Court Rolls of the Manor of Wakefield from October 1338 to September 1340.* Wakefield Court Rolls Series of the Yorkshire Archaeological Society, vol. 12. Leeds: Yorkshire Archaeological Society, 1999.

Twiss, Travers, ed. *Monumenta Juridica: The Black Book of the Admiralty.* Vol. 2, *Appendix.* Rolls Series, vol. 55. London: Longman, 1873.

Varley, Joan, ed. *A Middlewich Chartulary.* Part 1. Chetham Society Publications, new series, vol. 105. Manchester: Chetham Society and the Liverpool School of Local History and Records, 1941.

Varley, Joan, and James Tait, eds. *A Middlewich Chartulary.* Part 2. Chetham Society Publications, new series, vol. 108. Manchester: Chetham Society and the Liverpool School of Local History and Records, 1944.

Walker, J. W., ed. *Court Rolls of the Manor of Wakefield.* Vol. 5, *1322–1331.* Yorkshire Archaeological Society Records Series vol. 109. Leeds: Yorkshire Archaeological Society, 1944.

Walker, Sue Sheridan, ed. *The Court Rolls of the Manor of Wakefield from October 1331 to September 1333.* Wakefield Court Rolls Series of the Yorkshire Archaeological Society, vol. 3. Leeds: Yorkshire Archaeological Society, 1982.

Walsingham, Thomas. *Historia Anglicana.* Vol. 2, *A.D. 1381–1422.* Edited by H. T. Riley. Rolls Series, vol. 28, part 1. London: Longman, Green, Longman, Roberts & Green, 1864.

Winstanley, William. *Poor Robin's True Character of a Scold: Or The Shrews Looking-Glass.* London: L. C., 1678.

Wood-Legh, K. L., ed. *Kentish Visitations of Archbishop William Warham and his Deputies, 1511–12.* Kent Records, vol. 24. Maidstone: Kent Archaeological Society, 1984.

Wright, Thomas, ed. *The Political Songs of England: From the Reign of John to That of Edward II.* Camden Society Publications, vol. 6. London: Camden Society, 1839.

———, ed. *A Selection of Latin Stories from Manuscripts of the Thirteenth and Fourteenth Centuries.* Percy Society Publications, vol. 8. London: Percy Society, 1842.

Wright, Thomas, and James Orchard Halliwell-Phillips, eds. *Reliquiæ Antiquæ: Scraps from Ancient Manuscripts, Illustrating Chiefly Early English Literature and the English Language,* 2 vols. London: J. R. Smith, 1845.

Unpublished Primary Sources

Dale, M. K., ed. and trans. "Court Rolls of Tamworth." Unpublished typescript, 1959.

"Visitation of Parishes by John Trefnant, Bishop of Hereford, 1397." Unpublished typescript from original in Hereford Cathedral Archives MS 1779.

Secondary Sources

Alexander, Jonathan, and Paul Binski, eds. *Age of Chivalry: Art in Plantagenet England 1200–1400.* London: Royal Academy of Arts, with Weidenfeld and Nicolson, 1987.

Anderson, M. D. *History and Imagery in British Churches.* London: J. Murray, 1971.

Anderson, Patricia. "Gossips, Ale-wives, Midwives and Witches." Ph.D. diss., State University of New York at Buffalo, 1992.

Andrews, William. "Punishing Scolding Women." In *Bygone Cheshire,* edited by William Andrews. Chester: Phillipson and Golder, 1895.

Apperson, G. L. *English Proverbs and Proverbial Phrases: A Historical Dictionary.* London: J. M. Dent and Sons, 1929.

Aston, Margaret. "Corpus Christi and Corpus Regni: Heresy and the Peasants' Revolt." *Past and Present* 143 (1994): 3–48.

Austin, J. L. *How to Do Things with Words.* 2nd ed. Cambridge, Mass.: Harvard University Press, 1975.

Bailey, Mark. *The English Manor, c. 1200–c. 1500.* Manchester: Manchester University Press, 2002.

Baker, J. H. Introduction to *The Reports of Sir John Spelman.* Vol. 2. Seldon Society Publications, vol. 94. London: Seldon Society, 1978.

Bardsley, Sandy. "Debate—Women's Work Reconsidered: Gender and Wage Differentiation in Late Medieval England—Reply." *Past and Present* 173 (2001): 199–202.

———. "Women's Work Reconsidered: Gender and Wage Differentiation in Late Medieval England." *Past and Present* 165 (1999): 3–29.

Barron, Caroline M. "The 'Golden Age' of Women in Medieval London." *Reading Medieval Studies* 15 (1989): 33–58.

———. "Introduction: The Widow's World in Later Medieval London." In *Medieval London Widows, 1300–1500,* edited by Caroline M. Barron and Anne F. Sutton. London: Hambledon Press, 1994.

Beaumont, William. *A History of the Castle of Halton and the Priory or Abbey of Norton.* Warrington: P. Pearse, 1873.

Beckerman, John S. "The Articles of Presentment of a Court Leet and Court Baron, in English, c. 1400." *Bulletin of the Institute of Historical Research* 48 (1974): 230–34.

Bellamy, J. G. *The Law of Treason in England in the Later Middle Ages.* Cambridge: Cambridge University Press, 1970.

Bennett, Adelaide. "Noah's Recalcitrant Wife in the Ramsey Abbey Psalter." *Source* 2 (1982): 2–5.

Bennett, H. S. *Life on the English Manor: A Study of Peasant Conditions 1150–1400.* Cambridge: Cambridge University Press, 1937.

Bennett, Judith M. *Ale, Beer, and Brewsters in England: Women's Work in a Changing World, 1300–1600.* New York: Oxford University Press, 1996.

———. "Confronting Continuity." *Journal of Women's History* 9 (1997): 73–94.

———. "Public Power and Authority in the Medieval English Countryside." In *Women and Power in the Middle Ages,* edited by Mary Erler and Maryanne Kowaleski. Athens: University of Georgia Press, 1988.

———. *Women in the Medieval English Countryside: Gender and Household in Brigstock before the Plague.* New York: Oxford University Press, 1987.

———. "Writing Fornication: Medieval Leyrwite and Its Historians." *Transactions of the Royal Historical Society* 13 (2003): 131–62.

Bennett, Judith M., and Amy Froide. "A Singular Past." In *Singlewomen in the*

European Past, 1250–1800, edited by Judith M. Bennett and Amy Froide. Philadelphia: University of Pennsylvania Press, 1998.

Benson, C. David. "*Piers Plowman* and Parish Wall Paintings." *Yearbook of Langland Studies* 11 (1997): 1–38.

Bergmann, J. R. *Discreet Indiscretions: The Social Organization of Gossip*. New York: Aldine de Gruyter, 1993.

Beveridge, Lord William Henry. "Westminster Wages in the Manorial Era." *Economic History Review*, 2nd series, 8 (1955–56): 18–35.

Blackstone, William. *Commentaries on the Laws of England*. 4 vols. From the last London edition. Boston: T. B. Wait and Sons, 1818.

Block, Elaine C. "Half Angel—Half Beast: Images of Women on Misericords." *Reinardus* 5 (1992): 17–34.

Boose, Lynda E. "Scolding Brides and Bridling Scolds: Taming the Woman's Unruly Member." *Shakespeare Quarterly* 42 (1991): 179–213.

Borlase, William. *The Natural History of Cornwall*. Oxford: Printed for private circulation, 1758.

Bourdieu, Pierre. *Language and Symbolic Power*. Cambridge, Mass.: Harvard University Press, 1991.

Bridbury, A. R. *England and the Salt Trade in the Later Middle Ages*. Oxford: Clarendon Press, 1955.

Brown, Pamela Allen. *Better a Shrew than a Sheep: Women, Drama, and the Culture of Jest in Early Modern England*. Ithaca, N.Y.: Cornell University Press, 2003.

Brushfield, T. N. "On Obsolete Punishments, With Particular Reference to Those of Cheshire. Part II: The Cucking Stool and Allied Punishments." *Journal of the Architectural, Archaeological and Historic Society, for the County, City and Neighbourhood of Chester*, 1st series, 2 (1861): 203–34.

Bullough, Vern L. "On Being Male in the Middle Ages." In *Medieval Masculinities: Regarding Men in the Middle Ages*, edited by Clare A. Lees. Minneapolis: University of Minnesota Press, 1994.

Butler, Judith. *Excitable Speech: A Politics of the Performative*. New York: Routledge, 1997.

———. *Gender Trouble: Feminism and the Subversion of Identity*. New York: Routledge, 1990.

Capp, Bernard. *When Gossips Meet: Women, Family, and Neighbourhood in Early Modern England*. Oxford: Oxford University Press, 2003.

Chazelle, Celia. "Pictures, Books, and the Illiterate: Pope Gregory's Letters to Serenus of Marseilles." *Word and Image* 6 (1990): 138–53.

Clayton, Dorothy J. *The Administration of the County Palatine of Chester 1442–1485*. Chetham Society Publications, 3rd series, vol. 35. Manchester: Chetham Society, 1990.

Coleman, Janet. *Medieval Readers and Writers, 1350–1400*. New York: Columbia University Press, 1981.

Craun, Edwin D. *Lies, Slander, and Obscenity in Medieval English Literature: Pastoral Rhetoric and the Deviant Speaker*. Cambridge: Cambridge University Press, 1997.

———, ed. *The Hands of the Tongue: Essays on Deviant Speech*. Kalamazoo, Mich.: Medieval Institute Publications, forthcoming.

Crump, W. B. "Saltways from the Cheshire Wiches." *Transactions of the Lancashire and Cheshire Antiquarian Society* 54 (1940): 84–142.

David, Alfred. "Noah's Wife's Flood." In *The Performance of Middle English Culture: Essays on Chaucer and the Drama in Honor of Martin Stevens*, edited by James J. Paxton, Laurence M. Clopper, and Sylvia Tomasch. Cambridge: D. S. Brewer, 1998.

Davis, Natalie Zemon. "Women on Top." In *Society and Culture in Early Modern France.* Stanford, Calif.: Stanford University Press, 1975.

Deal, Laura Kay. "Whores and Witches: The Language of Female Misbehavior in Early Modern England, 1560–1650." Ph.D. diss., University of Colorado at Boulder, 1996.

Delany, Sheila. *Impolitic Bodies: Poetry, Saints, and Society in Fifteenth-Century England: The Work of Osbern Bokenham.* New York: Oxford University Press, 1998.

DeWindt, Anne Reiber. "Local Government in a Small Town: A Medieval Leet Jury and Its Constituents." *Albion* 23 (1991): 627–54.

DeWindt, Anne Reiber, and Edwin Brezette DeWindt. *Ramsey: The Lives of an English Fenland Town, 1200–1600.* Washington, D.C.: Catholic University of America Press, forthcoming.

DeWindt, Edwin. *Land and People in Holywell-cum-Needingworth: Structures of Tenure and Patterns of Social Organization in an East Midlands Village 1252–1457.* Toronto: Pontifical Institute of Mediaeval Studies, 1972.

Dignan, Patricia Grace. "Hellmouth and Villains: The Role of the Uncontrolled Mouth in Four Middle English Mystery Cycles." Ph.D. diss., University of Cincinnati, 1994.

Duffy, Eamon. *The Stripping of the Altars: Traditional Religion in England, c. 1400-c. 1580.* New Haven, Conn.: Yale University Press, 1992.

Duggan, Lawrence G. "Was Art Really the 'Book of the Illiterate'?" *Word & Image* 5 (1989): 227–51.

Dyer, Christopher. *Everyday Life in Medieval England.* 2nd ed. London: Hambledon and London, 2000.

———. *Standards of Living in the Later Middle Ages: Social Change in England c. 1200–1520.* Cambridge: Cambridge University Press, 1989.

Earl, A. F. *Middlewich 900–1900.* Chester: Ravenscroft, 1990.

Evans, Ruth. "Feminist Re-Enactments: Gender and the Towneley *Uxor Noe.*" In *A Wyf Ther Was: Essays in Honour of Paule Mertens-Fonck,* edited by Juliette Dor. Liège: Université de Liège, 1992.

Faith, Rosamond. "The 'Great Rumour' of 1377 and Peasant Ideology." In *The English Rising of 1381,* edited by R. H. Hilton and T. H. Aston. Cambridge: Cambridge University Press, 1984.

Farmer, David. "Prices and Wages, 1350–1500." In *The Agrarian History of England and Wales.* Vol. 3, *1348–1500,* edited by Edward Miller. Cambridge: Cambridge University Press, 1991.

Farmer, Sharon. "Persuasive Voices: Clerical Images of Medieval Wives." *Speculum* 61 (1986): 517–43.

Fenster, Thelma, and Daniel Lord Smail, eds. *Fama: The Politics of Talk and Reputation in Medieval Europe.* Ithaca, N.Y.: Cornell University Press, 2003.

Ferster, Judith. *Fictions of Advice: The Literature and Politics of Counsel in Late Medieval England.* Philadelphia: University of Pennsylvania Press, 1996.

Finch, Andrew John. "Sexual Morality and Canon Law: The Evidence of the Rochester Consistory Court." *Journal of Medieval History* 20 (1994): 261–75.

Foucault, Michel. *The Archaeology of Knowledge.* London: Tavistock Publications, 1972.

———. *The History of Sexuality: An Introduction.* Vol. 1. New York: Vintage Books, 1990.

French, Katherine L. *The People of the Parish: Community Life in a Medieval English Diocese.* Philadelphia: University of Pennsylvania Press, 2001.

Garvin, Katherine. "A Note on Noah's Wife." *Modern Language Notes* 49 (1934): 88–90.

Gill, Miriam. "Female Piety and Impiety: Selected Images of Women and Their Reception in Wall Paintings in England after 1300." In *Gender and Holiness: Men, Women and Saints in Late Medieval Europe*, edited by Samantha J. E. Riches and Sarah Salih. London: Routledge, 2002.

Gill, Miriam. "From 'Urban Myth' to Monumental Image: English Warning to Swearers." In *The Hands of the Tongue: Essays on Deviant Speech*, edited by Edwin D. Craun. Kalamazoo, Mich.: Medieval Institute Publications, forthcoming.

Gill, Miriam Clare. "Late Medieval Wall Painting in England: Content and Context (c. 1330–c. 1530)." Ph.D. diss., Courtauld Institute of Art, University of London, 2002.

Gill, Miriam. "Preaching and Image: Sermons and Wall Paintings in Later Medieval England." In *Medieval Monastic Education*, edited by George Ferzoco and Carolyn Muessig. London: Continuum, 2000.

Godsall-Myers, Jean E., ed. *Speaking in the Medieval World.* Leiden: Brill, 2003.

Goldberg, P. J. P. *Women, Work, and Life-Cycle in a Medieval Economy: Women in York and Yorkshire c. 1300–1520.* Oxford: Clarendon Press, 1992.

Goody, Jack. *The Interface Between the Written and the Oral.* Cambridge: Cambridge University Press, 1987.

Gottfried, Barbara. "Conflict and Relationship, Sovereignty and Survival: Parables of Power in the Wife of Bath's Prologue." *Chaucer Review* 19 (1985): 202–24.

Gowing, Laura. *Domestic Dangers: Women, Words and Sex in Early Modern London.* Oxford: Clarendon Press, 1996.

Gregory, Annabel. "Witchcraft, Politics and 'Good Neighbourhood' in Early Seventeenth-Century Rye." *Past and Present* 133 (1991): 31–66.

Gross, Kenneth. *Shakespeare's Noise.* Chicago: University of Chicago Press, 2001.

Grössinger, Christa. *The World Upside-Down: English Misericords.* London: Harvey Miller, 1997.

Haigh, C. A. "Slander and the Church Courts in the Sixteenth Century." *Transactions of the Lancashire and Cheshire Antiquarian Society* 78 (1975): 1–13.

Hallissy, Margaret. *Clean Maids, True Wives, Steadfast Widows: Chaucer's Women and Medieval Codes of Conduct.* Westport, Conn.: Greenwood Press, 1993.

Hanawalt, Barbara A. "The Female Felon in Fourteenth-Century England." *Viator* 5 (1974): 253–68.

———. "Good Governance in the Medieval and Early Modern Context." *Journal of British Studies* 37 (1998): 246–57.

———. "Peasant Women's Contribution to the Home Economy in Late Medieval England." In *Women and Work in Preindustrial Europe*, edited by Barbara A. Hanawalt. Bloomington: Indiana University Press, 1986.

———. "The Widow's Mite: Provisions for Medieval London Widows." In *Upon My Husband's Death: Widows in the Literature and Histories of Medieval Europe*, edited by Louise Mirrer. Ann Arbor: University of Michigan Press, 1992.

Hanna, Ralph, III. "Jankyn's Book." *Pacific Coast Philology* 21 (1986): 30–36.

———. "Pilate's Voice/Shirley's Case." *South Atlantic Quarterly* 91 (1992): 793–812.

Hansen, Elaine Tuttle. "Fearing for Chaucer's Good Name." *Exemplaria* 2 (1990): 23–36.

Hatcher, John. "Debate—Women's Work Reconsidered: Gender and Wage Differentiation in Late Medieval England." *Past and Present* 173 (2001): 191–98.

Hearnshaw, F. J. C. *Leet Jurisdiction in England: Especially as Illustrated by the Records of the Court Leet of Southampton.* Southampton: Cox & Sharland, 1908.

Helmholz, R. H. "Crime, Compurgation and the Courts of the Medieval Church." *Law and History Review* 1 (1983): 1–26.

Hewitt, H. J. *Mediaeval Cheshire: An Economic and Social History of Cheshire in the Reigns of the Three Edwards.* Chetham Society Publications, new series, vol. 88. Manchester: Chetham Society, 1929.

Hilton, R. H. *Bond Men Made Free: Medieval Peasant Movements and the English Uprising of 1381.* London: Temple Smith, 1973.

———. *The English Peasantry in the Later Middle Ages: The Ford Lectures for 1973 and Related Studies.* Oxford: Clarendon Press, 1975.

Hindle, Steve. "The Shaming of Margaret Knowsley: Gossip, Gender and the Experience of Authority in Early Modern England." *Continuity and Change* 9 (1994): 391–419.

Hogan, M. Patricia. "The Slight to Honor: Slander and Wrongful Prosecution in Five English Medieval Villages." *Studies in Medieval and Renaissance History* 12 (1991): 3–42.

Holdsworth, W. S. *A History of English Law.* Vol. 2. 3rd ed. London: Methuen, 1922.

Ingram, Martin. "'Scolding Women Cucked or Washed': A Crisis in Gender Relations in Early Modern England?" In *Women, Crime and the Courts,* edited by Jenny Kermode and Garthine Walker. London: University College of London Press, 1994.

James, M. R. "Pictor in Carmine." *Archaeologia* 94 (1951): 141–66.

James, W. R. "Lollards and Images: The Defense of Religious Art in Later Medieval England." *Journal of the History of Ideas* 34 (1973): 27–50.

Jennings, Margaret. *Tutivillus: The Literary Career of the Recording Demon.* Studies in Philology, Texts and Studies, no. 74. Chapel Hill: University of North Carolina Press, 1977.

Jones, Karen, and Michael Zell. "Bad Conversation? Gender and Social Control in a Kentish Borough, c. 1450-c. 1570." *Continuity and Change* 13 (1998): 11–31.

Kamensky, Jane. *Governing the Tongue: The Politics of Speech in Early New England.* New York: Oxford University Press, 1997.

Kandiyoti, Deniz. "Bargaining with Patriarchy." *Gender and Society* 2 (1988): 274–90.

Karant-Nunn, Susan. *The Reformation of Ritual: An Interpretation of Early Modern Germany.* London: Routledge, 1997.

Karras, Ruth Mazo. *Common Women: Prostitution and Sexuality in Medieval England.* Oxford: Oxford University Press, 1996.

———. "Gendered Sin and Misogyny in John of Bromyard's 'Summa Predicantium.'" *Traditio* 47 (1992): 233–57.

———. "The Regulation of Brothels in Later Medieval England." In *Sisters and Workers in the Middle Ages,* edited by Judith M. Bennett et al. Chicago: University of Chicago Press, 1989.

Kolve, V. A. *The Play Called Corpus Christi.* Stanford, Calif.: Stanford University Press, 1966.

Kowaleski, Maryanne. "Gossip, Gender, and the Economy: The Origins of Scolding Indictments in Medieval England." forthcoming.

———. "Singlewomen in Medieval and Early Modern Europe: The Demographic Perspective." In *Singlewomen in the European Past, 1250–1800,* edited by Judith M. Bennett and Amy Froide. Philadelphia: University of Pennsylvania Press, 1998.

Kowaleski, Maryanne, and Judith M. Bennett, "Crafts, Gilds and Women in the Middle Ages: Fifty Years after Marian K. Dale." In *Sisters and Workers in the Middle Ages,* edited by Judith M. Bennett et al. Chicago: University of Chicago Press, 1989.

Kraus, Dorothy, and Henry Kraus. *The Hidden World of Misericords.* New York: G. Braziller, 1975.

Kurath, Hans, et al., eds. *The Middle English Dictionary.* Ann Arbor: University of Michigan Press, 1956-present.

Laughton, Jane. "Women in Court: Some Evidence from Fifteenth-Century Chester." In *England in the Fifteenth Century: Proceedings of the 1992 Harlaxton Symposium,* edited by Nicholas Rogers. Stamford: P. Watkins, 1994.

Lawrence, C. Frederick. "Random Notes on Bygone Cheshire, With Special Reference to Middlewich." *Cheshire Notes and Queries* 2 (1897): 19–26.

Lawton, David. *Blasphemy.* Philadelphia: University of Pennsylvania Press, 1993.

Lees, Linda. "'Lewd and Dissolute Women': Women and Crime in Seventeenth Century Nottinghamshire." *Transactions of the Thoroton Society of Nottinghamshire* 105 (2001): 111–21.

Lewis, J. P. *A Study of the Interpretation of Noah and the Flood in Jewish and Christian Literature.* Leiden: Brill, 1978.

Lindorfer, Bettina. "*Peccatum Linguae* and the Punishment of Speech Violations in the Middle Ages and Early Modern Times." In *Speaking in the Medieval World,* edited by Jean E. Godsall-Myers. Leiden: Brill, 2003.

Little, Lester K. *Benedictine Maledictions: Liturgical Cursing in Romanesque France.* Ithaca, N.Y.: Cornell University Press, 1993.

Lochrie, Karma. *Covert Operations: The Medieval Uses of Secrecy.* Philadelphia: University of Pennsylvania Press, 1999.

Loomis, R. S. *A Mirror of Chaucer's World.* Princeton, N.J.: Princeton University Press, 1965.

Louis, Cameron. "Proverbs, Precepts, and Monitory Pieces." In *A Manual of the Writings in Middle English, 1050–1500,* vol. 9, edited by Albert E. Hartung. New Haven: Connecticut Academy of Arts and Sciences, 1992.

Lyte, H. C. Maxwell. *A History of Dunster and of the Families of Mohun and Luttrell.* London: St. Catherine's Press, 1909.

Macfarlane, A. D. J. *Witchcraft in Tudor and Stuart England: A Regional and Comparative Study.* London: Routledge & K. Paul, 1970.

Marks, Richard. *Stained Glass in England During the Middle Ages.* Toronto: University of Toronto Press, 1993.

Martin, Priscilla. *Chaucer's Women: Nuns, Wives, and Amazons.* Iowa City: University of Iowa Press, 1990.

McIntosh, Marjorie Keniston. *Controlling Misbehavior in England, 1370–1600.* Cambridge: Cambridge University Press, 1998.

———. "Finding Language for Misconduct: Jurors in Fifteenth-Century Local Courts." In *Bodies and Disciplines: Intersections of Literature and History in Fifteenth-Century England,* edited by Barbara A. Hanawalt and David Wallace. Minneapolis: University of Minnesota Press, 1996.

McSheffrey, Shannon. "Jurors, Respectable Masculinity, and Christian Morality: A Comment on Marjorie McIntosh's *Controlling Masculinity.*" *Journal of British Studies* 37 (1998): 269–78.

Mill, Anna Jean. "Noah's Wife Again." *PMLA* 56 (1941): 613–26.

Moore, R. I. "Heresy as Disease." In *The Concept of Heresy in the Middle Ages,* edited by W. Lourdaux and D. Verhelst. The Hague: Martinus Nijhoff, 1976.

Morrison, Susan Signe. "Don't Ask, Don't Tell: The Wife of Bath and Vernacular Translations." *Exemplaria* 8 (1996): 96–123.

Mortimer, Vernon. "The Tongue Can No Man Tame." *Cheshire Life*, March 1975, 72–73.

Müller, Miriam. "Social Control and the Hue and Cry in Two Fourteenth-Century Villages." *Journal of Medieval History* 31 (2005): 29–53.

Musson, Anthony. *Public Order and Law Enforcement: The Local Administration of Criminal Justice in England, 1294–1350.* Woodbridge: Boydell Press, 1996.

Musson, Anthony, and W. M. Ormrod. *The Evolution of English Justice: Law, Politics and Society in the Fourteenth Century.* Basingstoke: Macmillan Press, 1999.

Olson, Sherri. *A Chronicle of All That Happens: Voices from the Village Court in Medieval England.* Toronto: Pontifical Institute of Mediaeval Studies, 1996.

Ong, Walter. *Orality and Literacy: The Technologizing of the Word.* London: Methuen, 1982.

Ormerod, George. *The History of the County Palatine and City of Chester.* 3 vols. 2nd ed. London: G. Routledge, 1882.

Owen, D. Huw. "Wales and the Marches." In *The Agrarian History of England and Wales.* Vol. 3, *1348–1500*, edited by Edward Miller. Cambridge: Cambridge University Press, 1991.

Owst, G. R. *Literature and Pulpit in Medieval England: A Neglected Chapter in the History of English Letters and of the English People.* 2nd ed. Oxford: B. Blackwell, 1961.

Palmer, Barbara D. "An Iconography for Swearers: The Almondsbury Passion Poem." *Early Drama, Art, and Music Review* 12 (1989): 9–16.

Palmer, Robert. *The County Courts of Medieval England, 1150–1350.* Princeton, N.J.: Princeton University Press, 1982.

Park, David. "Wall Painting." In *Age of Chivalry: Art in Plantagenet England 1200–1400*, edited by Jonathan Alexander and Paul Binski. London: Royal Academy of Arts, with Weidenfeld and Nicolson, 1987.

Parker, Patricia. "On the Tongue: Cross Gendering, Effeminacy, and the Art of Words." *Style* 23 (1989): 445–65.

Penn, Simon A. C. "Female Wage-Earners in Late Fourteenth-Century England." *Agricultural History Review* 35 (1987): 1–14.

Peter, John D. *Complaint and Satire in Early English Literature.* Oxford: Clarendon Press, 1956.

Poos, L. R. "Sex, Lies, and the Church Courts of Pre-Reformation England." *Journal of Interdisciplinary History* 25 (1995): 585–607.

Poulson, George. *Beverlac; Or, The Antiquities and History of the Town of Beverley.* Vol. 1. London: G. Scaum, 1829.

Raftis, J. A. *Warboys: Two Hundred Years in the Life of an English Mediaeval Village.* Toronto: Pontifical Institute of Mediaeval Studies, 1974.

Randall, Lillian. *Images in the Margins of Gothic Manuscripts.* Berkeley and Los Angeles: University of California Press, 1966.

Rasmussen, Ann Marie. "Gendered Knowledge and Eavesdropping in the Late-Medieval *Minnerede.*" *Speculum* 77 (2002): 1168–94.

Reiss, Pallas Athene. "The Sunday Christ: Sabbatarianism in English Medieval Wall Painting." Ph.D. diss., University of Chicago, 1995.

Remnant, G. L. *A Catalogue of Misericords in Great Britain.* Oxford: Clarendon Press, 1969.

Riddy, Felicity. "Mother Knows Best: Reading Social Change in a Courtesy Text." *Speculum* 71 (1996): 66–86.

Rigby, S. H. *English Society in the Later Middle Ages: Class, Status and Gender.* Basingstoke: Macmillan, 1995.
Roberts, Michael. "'Words they are Women, and Deeds they are Men': Images of Work and Gender in Early Modern England." In *Women and Work in Pre-Industrial England,* edited by Lindsay Charles and Lorna Duffin. London: Croom Helm, 1985.
Robbins, Rossell Hope. "Poems Dealing with Contemporary Conditions." In *A Manual of the Writings in Middle English, 1050–1500,* vol. 5, edited by Albert E. Hartung. New Haven: Connecticut Academy of Arts and Sciences, 1975.
Rogers, James E. Thorold. *A History of Agriculture and Prices in England.* Vol. 1, *1259–1400.* Oxford: Clarendon Press, 1866.
———. *Six Centuries of Work and Wages: The History of English Labour.* 7th ed. New York: Swan Sonnenschein, 1903.
Rosser, Gervase. "Going to the Fraternity Feast: Commensality and Social Relations in Late Medieval England." *Journal of British Studies* 33 (1994): 430–46.
Schofield, P. R. "Peasants and the Manor Court: Gossip and Litigation in a Suffolk Village at the Close of the Thirteenth Century." *Past and Present* 159 (1998): 3–42.
Scott, James C. *Domination and the Arts of Resistance: Hidden Transcripts.* New Haven, Conn.: Yale University Press, 1990.
Sekules, Veronica. "Beauty and the Beast: Ridicule and Orthodoxy in Architectural Marginalia in Early Fourteenth-Century Lincolnshire." *Art History* 18 (1995): 37–62.
———. "Women and Art in England in the Thirteenth and Fourteenth Centuries." In *Age of Chivalry: Art in Plantagenet England 1200–1400,* edited by Jonathan Alexander and Paul Binski. London: Royal Academy of Arts, with Weidenfeld and Nicolson, 1987.
Sharpe, James A. *Defamation and Sexual Slander in Early Modern England: The Church Courts at York,* Borthwick Papers, no. 58. York: University of York, Borthwick Institute of Historical Research, 1980.
Sheingorn, Pamela. "'Who can open the doors of his face?': The Iconography of Hell Mouth." In *The Iconography of Hell,* edited by Clifford Davidson and Thomas H. Seilor. Kalamazoo, Mich.: Medieval Institute Publications, 1992.
Sheneman, Paul. "The Tongue as a Sword: Psalms 56 and 63 and the Pardoner." *Chaucer Review* 27 (1993): 396–400.
Sklar, Ruth. "Cobham's Daughter: *The Book of Marjory Kempe* and the Power of Heterodox Thinking." *Modern Language Quarterly* 56 (1995): 277–304.
Smith, Richard. "Human Resources." In *The Countryside of Medieval England,* edited by Grenville Astill and Annie Grant. Oxford: B. Blackwell, 1988.
Smith, William George, and F. P. Wilson. *Oxford Dictionary of English Proverbs.* 3rd ed. Oxford: Oxford University Press, 1970.
Snyder, Terri L. *Brabbling Women: Disorderly Speech and the Law in Early Virginia.* Ithaca, N.Y.: Cornell University Press, 2003.
Spacks, Patricia A. M. *Gossip.* New York: Knopf, 1985.
Spargo, John Webster. *Juridical Folklore in England Illustrated by the Cucking-Stool.* Durham, N.C.: Duke University Press, 1944.
Stock, Brian. *The Implications of Literacy: Written Language and Models of Interpretation in the Eleventh and Twelfth Centuries.* Princeton, N.J.: Princeton University Press, 1983.
Storm, Melvin. "Uxor and Alison: Noah's Wife in the Flood Plays and Chaucer's Wife of Bath." *Modern Language Quarterly* 48 (1987): 303–19.

Strohm, Paul. *Hochon's Arrow: The Social Imagination of Fourteenth-Century Texts.* Princeton, N.J.: Princeton University Press, 1992.

Sutherland, Sarah. " 'Not or I see more neede': The Wife of Noah in the Chester, York, and Towneley Cycles." In *Shakespeare and Dramatic Tradition: Essays in Honor of S. F. Johnson,* edited by W. R. Elton and William B. Long. Newark: University of Delaware Press, 1989.

Swanson, R. N. "Angels Incarnate: Clergy and Masculinity from Gregorian Reform to Reformation." In *Masculinity in Medieval Europe,* edited by D. M. Hadley. London: Longman, 1999.

Sylvester, Dorothy, and Geoffrey Nuty. *The Historical Atlas of Cheshire.* Chester: Cheshire Community Council, 1958.

Taylor, George C. "The English 'Planctus Mariæ.' " *Modern Philology* 5 (1907): 605–37.

Taylor, Steven M. "Monsters of Misogyny: The Medieval French 'Dit de Chincheface' and 'Dit de Bigorne.' " *Allegorica* 5 (1980): 98–124.

Thomas, Keith. *Religion and the Decline of Magic.* New York: Scribner, 1971.

Tonkinson, A. M. *Macclesfield in the Later Fourteenth Century: Communities of Town and Forest.* Chetham Society Publications, 3rd series, vol. 42. Manchester: Chetham Society, 1999.

Tristram, E. W. *English Wall Painting of the Fourteenth Century.* London: Routledge and Paul, 1955.

Underdown, David E. "The Taming of the Scold: The Enforcement of Patriarchal Authority in Early Modern England." In *Order and Disorder in Early Modern England,* edited by A. Fletcher and J. Stevenson. Cambridge: Cambridge University Press, 1985.

Utley, Francis Lee. *The Crooked Rib: An Analytical Index to the Argument about Women in English and Scots Literature to the End of the Year 1568.* Columbus: Ohio State University Press, 1944.

———. "Dialogues, Debates, and Catechisms." In *A Manual of the Writings in Middle English, 1050–1500,* vol. 3, edited by Albert E. Hartung. New Haven: Connecticut Academy of Arts and Sciences, 1972.

Vecchio, Silvana. "The Good Wife." In *Silences of the Middle Ages,* edited by Christiane Klapisch-Zuber. Vol. 2 of *The History of Women in the West,* edited by Georges Duby and Michelle Perrot. Cambridge, Mass.: Belknap Press of Harvard University Press, 1992.

Warner, George. *Queen Mary's Psalter: Miniatures and Drawings by an English Artist of the Fourteenth Century, Reproduced from Royal ms. 2 B.VII in the British Museum.* London: Trustees of the British Museum, 1912.

Wickham, Chris. "Gossip and Resistance among the Medieval Peasantry." *Past and Present* 160 (1998): 3–24.

Wiltenburg, Joy. *Disorderly Women and Female Power in the Street Literature of Early Modern England and Germany.* Charlottesville: University Press of Virginia, 1992.

Winstead, Karen A. *Virgin Martyrs: Legends of Sainthood in Late Medieval England.* Ithaca, N.Y.: Cornell University Press, 1997.

Wodderspoon, John. *Memorials of the Ancient Town of Ipswich in the County of Suffolk.* Ipswich: Pawsey, 1850.

Woodforde, Christopher. "A Medieval Campaign Against Blasphemy." *Downside Review* 55 (1937): 1–6.

———. *The Norwich School of Glass-Painting in the Fifteenth Century.* New York: Oxford University Press, 1950.

Woolf, Rosemary. *The English Mystery Plays.* London: Routledge and Kegan Paul, 1972.

Index

Acknowledgments

I have been fortunate to have had fabulous support at every stage of this project. For help and feedback in its early stages, I am grateful to Erin Lang Bonin, Stan Chojnacki, Laine Doggett, Jennifer Halloran, Barbara Harris, Cynthia Herrup, Suzanne Kissel, John McGowan, Julie Mell, Catherine Peyroux, Tim Spaulding, Miranda Wilson, and Hilary Wyss. For references, ideas, and good advice, I especially thank Judith Bennett, David Benson, Edwin Craun, Anne DeWindt, Edwin DeWindt, Katherine French, Miriam Gill, Jenny Kermode, Maryanne Kowaleski, Marjorie McIntosh, Shannon McSheffrey, Derek Neal, Larry Poos, Jim Skalnik, Paul Strohm, and Chris Whittick. Jim Tyler and John Black have helped me with Latin and Middle English translations respectively (although any remaining errors are very much my own). Rachel Colancecco, in her capacity as Moravian College History Department research assistant, did a great job of tracking down line numbers for Middle English verse, and the Interlibrary Loan staffs at Moravian College and Emory & Henry College were both helpful and persistent in finding obscure texts.

I am grateful to Patrick St. John for the map and the illustration of the Tutivillus wall painting. Christa Grössinger kindly intervened to reduce copyright fees for the photograph of the Tutivillus misericord. Parts of Chapters 1 and 3 have been published as "Sin, Speech, and Scolding in Late Medieval England" in *Fama: The Politics of Talk and Reputation in Medieval Europe*, edited by Thelma Fenster and Daniel Lord Smail, copyright © 2003 by Cornell University. They are used here by permission of the publisher, Cornell University Press. The image of the Tutivillus misericord is © G.ten, University of Manchester, United Kingdom, and the image of the wall painting of cursing men is © Conway Library, Courtauld Institute of Art, London.

I owe sincere thanks to the staffs of the Bodleian Library, British Library, Cambridge University Library, Cheshire Record Office, Conway Library of the Courtauld Institute of Art, Henry E. Huntington Library, Public Record Office, and Somerset Archive and Record Service. I am also grateful for financial support from the Department of History, University Center for International Studies, and Royster Society of Fellows of the University of North Carolina at Chapel Hill, to the Woodrow Wilson Foundation, the British Federation of Women Graduates, the National Endowment for the Humanities, the W. M. Keck Foundation, the American Historical Association, and Moravian College.

To those who have read all or parts of the manuscript, I am especially grateful. In particular, I thank Judith Bennett, Katherine French, Ruth Karras, Maryanne Kowaleski, Jerry Singerman, and the two anonymous reviewers at the University of Pennsylvania Press who helped me immeasurably.

Among all this wonderful support, I must acknowledge three people who have helped me most of all: Dianne Bardsley, my mother, who taught me to read and write and has not stopped encouraging and supporting me since; Judith Bennett, my former advisor, who has continued to read and advise wisely long since her official role ended; and Marianne Cutler, my partner, who has been hearing about this project for a decade now yet has always been willing to talk through and offer suggestions on the latest incarnation. I thank you.